Queen Victoria
After Albert

Queen Victoria After Albert

Her Life and Loves

Ilana D. Miller

First published in Great Britain in 2023 by
Pen & Sword History
An imprint of
Pen & Sword Books Ltd
Yorkshire – Philadelphia

Copyright © Ilana D. Miller 2023

ISBN 978 1 39909 971 4

The right of Ilana D. Miller to be identified as Author of this work has been asserted by her in accordance with the Copyright, Designs and Patents Act 1988.

A CIP catalogue record for this book is available from the British Library.

All rights reserved. No part of this book may be reproduced or transmitted in any form or by any means, electronic or mechanical including photocopying, recording or by any information storage and retrieval system, without permission from the Publisher in writing.

Typeset by Mac Style
Printed in the UK by CPI Group (UK) Ltd, Croydon, CR0 4YY.

Pen & Sword Books Limited incorporates the imprints of Atlas, Archaeology, Aviation, Discovery, Family History, Fiction, History, Maritime, Military, Military Classics, Politics, Select, Transport, True Crime, Air World, Frontline Publishing, Leo Cooper, Remember When, Seaforth Publishing, The Praetorian Press, Wharncliffe Local History, Wharncliffe Transport, Wharncliffe True Crime, White Owl and After the Battle.

For a complete list of Pen & Sword titles please contact

PEN & SWORD BOOKS LIMITED
47 Church Street, Barnsley, South Yorkshire, S70 2AS, England
E-mail: enquiries@pen-and-sword.co.uk
Website: www.pen-and-sword.co.uk

Or

PEN AND SWORD BOOKS
1950 Lawrence Rd, Havertown, PA 19083, USA
E-mail: Uspen-and-sword@casematepublishers.com
Website: www.penandswordbooks.com

Contents

Acknowledgements		vii
List of Personages and their Relationship to Queen Victoria		ix
Introduction		xvii

Part I: Beginnings		1
Chapter 1	The Race for an Heir	3
Chapter 2	'I beheld Albert….'	17
Chapter 3	'…only the husband….'	30

Part II: Widowhood		45
Introduction		47
Chapter 4	'My dreadful & overwhelming calamity….'	48
Chapter 5	'…we, authors, ma'am….'	64
Chapter 6	Family Matters	79
Chapter 7	'…we, authors, ma'am' redux	93
Chapter 8	'…the queen's stallion….'	105
Chapter 9	Beatrice's Lohengrin	124

Part III: Jubilee		139
Chapter 10	'…this never-to-be-forgotten day….'	141
Chapter 11	'Mother of Europe'	153

Chapter 12	The *Munshi* and other Trials	171
Chapter 13	'Our Hearts Thy Throne'	185
Chapter 14	'…a long, full and beautiful life.'	202

Afterword   208
Notes   210
Bibliography   221
Index   226

Acknowledgements

I would like to acknowledge the following institutions and people:

Her Majesty Queen Elizabeth II for her gracious permission to print quotes from the Royal Archives and specifically from the digitised *Queen Victoria's Journals*.

Arturo Beéche for his help and kindly giving permission to use his map and the wonderful photographs, all from the Eurohistory Archive.

Julie Crocker from the Royal Archives at Windsor for all her assistance.

Stephen Stephanou for working long and hard on the family trees.

Katrina Warne for her advice, reading, corrections, and most especially her excellent eye for detail. However, any errors are mine and mine alone.

Jeremy Whitt, Head of Collection Development and Assessment, Pepperdine University Libraries for making sure I had access to *Queen Victoria's Journals* online.

John Van der Kiste for his kind permission to use his books as sources as well as his excellent advice. Greg King for his help and prompt answers to myriad questions and excellent suggestions.

Jane Tippett for her always exceptional ideas.

Liz Freedman, Tom Heller, Georgia Taylor Michelson and Mike Michelson, and Erika Miller for being 'gentle readers'.

Sarah-Beth Watkins, Laura Hirst, and Claire Hopkins for their help shepherding this work to completion and all their helpful comments and answers to all of my questions.

Sheri de Borchgrave for her cheerleading and encouragement

My wonderful family.

Also, in memory of my parents, my dear friend Soozi Parker Levin who has always been a great inspiration to me, and Bella 'the dog'.

And, lastly, Tom, my husband, for his support and constant reassurance.

List of Personages and their Relationship to Queen Victoria

Adolphus Frederick, Duke of Cambridge, George III's seventh son, Queen Victoria's uncle, father of Princess Mary Adelaide of Cambridge. Queen Victoria's cousin.

Albert, Prince of Saxe-Coburg and Gotha, Prince Consort. Married to Queen Victoria.

Albert Victor, Prince of Great Britain and Ireland, Duke of Clarence and Avondale (Eddy). Eldest son of Bertie and Alix, brother of George, Maud, Victoria, and Louise. Queen Victoria's grandson.

Alexander III, Tsar of Russia.

Alexander, Prince of Battenberg (Sandro). Prince of Bulgaria, Prince Louis of Battenberg's brother, and Princess Victoria of Prussia's (Moretta) erstwhile suitor.

Alexandra, Queen of Great Britain and Ireland, Empress of India (Alix). Married to Bertie. Queen Victoria's daughter-in-law.

Alexandra, Tsarina of Russia (Alicky, Alix). Queen Victoria's Hessian granddaughter.

Alfred, Prince of Great Britain and Ireland (Affie). Queen Victoria's second son, Duke of Edinburgh. Married to Marie Alexandrovna, Grand Duchess of Russia.

Alice, Princess of Great Britain and Ireland, Grand Duchess of Hesse and by Rhine. Queen Victoria's second daughter.

Alice, Princess of Albany, Countess of Athlone, Leopold's daughter. Queen Victoria's granddaughter.

Arthur, Duke of Connaught. Queen Victoria's third son. Married to Louise of Prussia (Louischen), parents of Margaret and Patricia of Connaught.

Augusta Viktoria, Empress of Germany (Dona). Princess of Schleswig-Holstein-Sonderburg-Augustenburg. Married to Kaiser Wilhelm II (Willy).

Beatrice, Princess of Great Britain and Ireland. Queen Victoria's youngest daughter. Married to Prince Henry (Liko) of Battenberg.

Charlotte, Princess of Prussia (Charley). Vicky's eldest daughter, married to Bernhard of Saxe-Meiningen. Queen Victoria's granddaughter.

Constantine I, King of Greece. Son of George I, King of Greece, married Queen Victoria's granddaughter, Sophie of Prussia. Vicky's daughter.

Edward, Duke of Kent, George III's fourth son. Queen Victoria's father.

Edward VII, King of Great Britain and Ireland, Emperor of India (Bertie). Queen Victoria's eldest son.

Elisabeth, Princess of Hesse and by Rhine (Ella). Married to Grand Duke Serge of Russia. Queen Victoria's granddaughter.

Ernst Augustus, Duke of Cumberland and King of Hanover, George III's fifth son. Queen Victoria's uncle.

Ernst Ludwig, Grand Duke of Hesse and by Rhine (Ernie). Married to Princess Victoria Melita of Edinburgh (Ducky), then to Eleonore of Solms-Hohensolm-Lich. Queen Victoria's grandson.

Franz Joseph, Prince of Battenberg (FranzJos), youngest of the Battenberg brothers.

Frederick William, Emperor of Germany (Fritz). Married to Vicky, Queen Victoria's son-in-law.

George III, King of Great Britain and Ireland. Queen Victoria's grandfather.

George IV, King of Great Britain and Ireland, George III's eldest son. Queen Victoria's uncle.

List of Personages and their Relationship to Queen Victoria   xi

George V, King of Great Britain and Ireland, Emperor of India (Georgie). Married to Victoria Mary of Teck (May). Queen Victoria's grandson.

Heinrich, Prince of Prussia (Henry). Second son of Vicky and Fritz brother of Willy. Queen Victoria's grandson.

Helena, Princess of England (Lenchen). Queen Victoria's third daughter. Married to Prince Christian of Schleswig-Holstein, mother of Helena Victoria and Marie Louise.

Henry, Prince of Battenberg (Liko). Married to Beatrice, brother of Louis. Queen Victoria's son-in-law.

Irène, Princess of Hesse and by Rhine. Married to Prince Heinrich of Prussia. Queen Victoria's granddaughter.

Leopold, Prince of Great Britain and Ireland, Duke of Albany (Leopold). Queen Victoria's fourth son, husband of Helena of Waldeck and Pyrmont.

Louis, Prince of Battenberg. Brother of Sandro, Liko, Franzjos. Married to Victoria Battenberg. Queen Victoria's executor.

Louise, Princess of Battenberg, later Lady Louise Mountbatten and then Queen of Sweden. Married to Gustaf VI Adolf, King of Sweden. Queen Victoria's great-granddaughter.

Louise, Princess of Great Britain and Ireland, Marchioness of Lorne, Duchess of Argyll. Queen Victoria's fourth daughter. Married to the Marquess of Lorne, later the Duke of Argyll

Ludwig IV, Grand Duke of Hesse and by Rhine. Married to Alice. Queen Victoria's son-in-law.

Marie, Princess of Great Britain and Ireland, Marie Alexandrovna, Grand Duchess of Russia. Married to Affie, Queen Victoria's second son.

Marie, Queen of Romania (Missy), daughter of Affie and Marie of Edinburgh. Queen Victoria's granddaughter.

Nicholas II, Tsar of Russia (Nicky). Married to Alix of Hesse. Queen Victoria's granddaughter.

Serge, Grand Duke of Russia. Married to Ella of Hesse. Queen Victoria's granddaughter.

Victoire of Saxe-Coburg-Saalfeld, Duchess of Kent. Queen Victoria's mother.

Victoria, Princess Royal of Great Britain and Ireland, Empress of Germany (Vicky). Queen Victoria's eldest daughter

Victoria, Princess of Hesse and by Rhine, later Princess Louis Battenberg, Marchioness of Milford Haven and finally Dowager Marchioness. Queen Victoria's granddaughter.

Victoria, Princess of Prussia (Moretta), Vicky's second daughter. Engaged to Sandro, ultimately married Adolph of Schaumberg-Lippe. Queen Victoria's granddaughter.

Victoria Melita, (Ducky), daughter of Affie and Marie. Married first to Ernie, then to Grand Duke Kyrill of Russia, her first cousin. Queen Victoria's granddaughter.

Wilhelm II, Emperor of Germany (Willy). Son of Vicky and Fritz. Queen Victoria's grandson.

William IV, King of Great Britain and Ireland, George III's third son. Queen Victoria's uncle.

The Race for the Throne

```
                          George III                    m.      Charlotte of Mecklenburg-Strelitz
                          King of Great Britain & Hanover               (1744-1818)
                          (1738-1820)
```

Charlotte Princess of Brunswick-Wolfenbuttel (1764-1821) m. George IV King of Great Britain & Hanover (1762-1830)	William IV King of Great Britain & Hanover (1765-1837) m. Adelaide of Saxe-Meiningen (1792-1843)	Edward Duke of Kent (1767-1820) m. Victoire of Saxe-Coburg-Saalfeld (1786-1861)	Ernest Augustus Duke of Cumberland then King of Hanover (1771-1851) m. Frederica of Mecklenburg-Strelitz (1778-1841)

Charlotte, Princess of Wales (1796-1817) m. Leopold of Saxe-Coburg & Gotha (1790-1865) later King Leopold I of the Belgians

Victoria Queen of Great Britain (1819-1901) m. Albert of Saxe-Coburg-Gotha (1819-1861)

George V King of Hanover (1819-1866) m. Marie of Saxe-Altenburg (1818-1907)

Descendants include the British Royal House

Descendants include the British Royal House

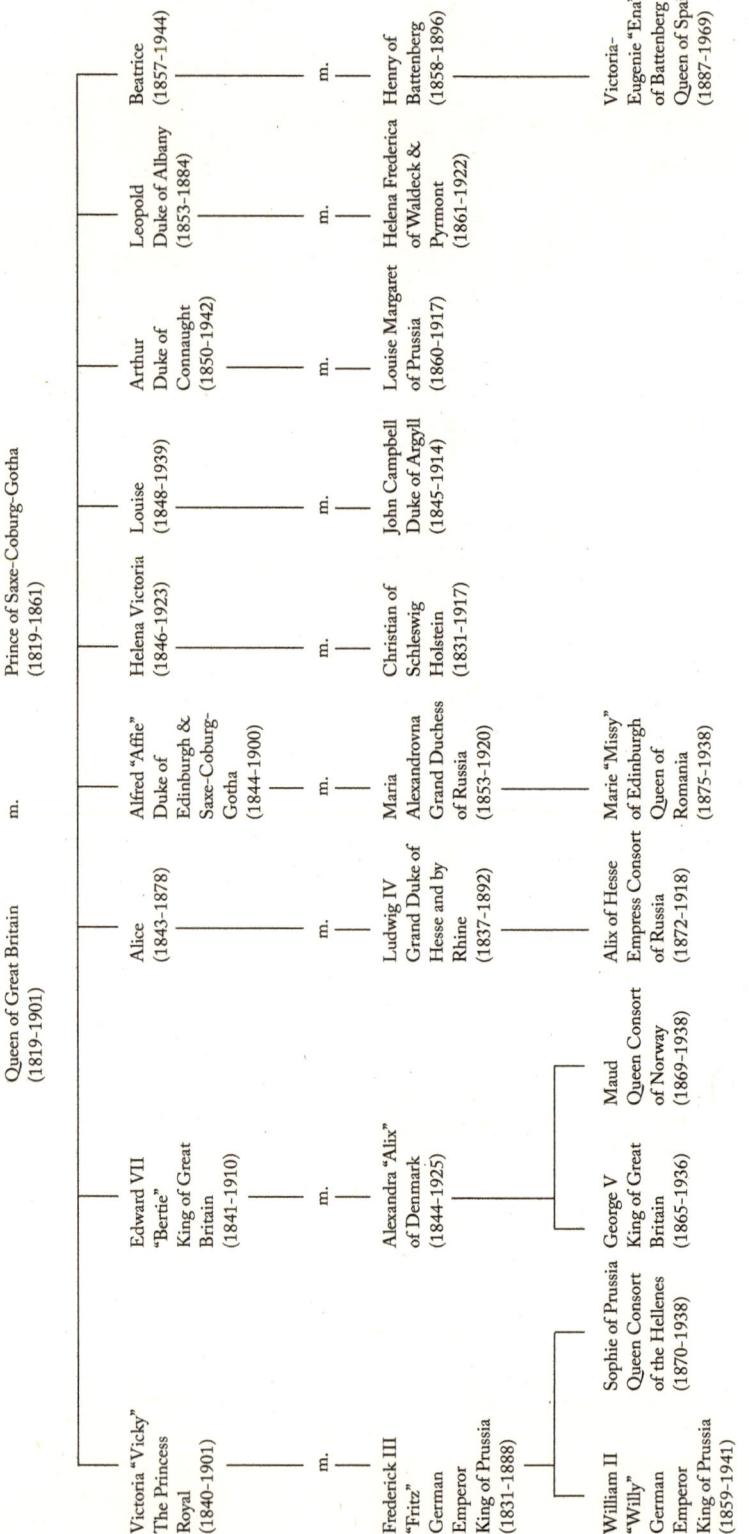
The Children and Reigning Grandchildren of Queen Victoria of Great Britain and Prince Albert of Saxe-Coburg-Gotha

Queen Victoria's Sons' Children

Victoria Queen of Great Britain (1819-1901)	m.	Albert of Saxe-Coburg-Gotha (1819-1861)

Edward VII King of Great Britain (1841-1910) m. Alexandra of Denmark (1844-1925)

- Albert Victor, Duke of Clarence & Avondale (1864-1892)
- George V, King of Great Britain (1865-1936) m. Mary of Teck (1867-1953)
- Louise, Princess Royal (1867-1931) m. Alexander Duff, 1st Duke of Fife (1849-1912)
- Victoria (1868-1935)
- Maud (1869-1938) m. Haakon VII, King of Norway (1872-1957)

Alfred, Duke of Edinburgh, Duke of Saxe-Coburg-Gotha (1944-1900) m. Maria Alexandrovna, Grand Duchess of Russia (1853-1920)

- Alfred (1874-1899)
- Marie (1875-1938) m. Ferdinand I, King of Romania (1865-1927)
- Victoria Melita (1876-1936) m. (1) Ernest Louis, Grand Duke of Hesse & by Rhine (1868-1937) (2) Grand Duke Kyril Vladimirovich (1868-1938)
- Alexandra (1878-1942) m. Ernest II of Hohenlohe-Langenburg (1863-1950)
- Beatrice (1884-1966) m. Alfonso d'Orleans y Borbon Infante of Spain, Duke of Galliera (1886-1975)

Arthur, Duke of Connaught (1850-1942) m. Margaret Louise of Prussia (1860-1917)

- Margaret (1882-1920) m. Gustav VI, King of Sweden (1882-1973)
- Arthur Prince (1883-1938) m. Alexandra, Duchess of Fife (1891-1959)
- Patricia (1886-1974) m. Hon. Alexander Ramsay (1881-1972)

Leopold, Duke of Albany (1853-1884) m. Helen of Waldeck & Pyrmont (1861-1922)

- Alice (1883-1981) m. Alexander, Earl of Athlone (1874-1957)
- Charles Edward, Duke of Albany then Duke of Saxe-Coburg-Gotha (1884-1954) m. Victoria Adelaide of Schleswig-Holstein (1885-1970)

Queen Victoria's Daughters' Children

Victoria Queen of Great Britain (1819-1901)	m.	Albert of Saxe-Coburg- Gotha (1819-1861)			
Victoria Princess Royal (1840-1901)	m.	Frederick III German Emperor King of Prussia (1831-1888)	William II German Emperor King of Prussia (1859-1941)	m.	Augusta Victoria of Schleswig-Holstein- Sonderburg- Augustenburg (1858-1921)
			Charlotte of Prussia (1860-1919)	m.	Bernhard of Saxe-Meiningen (1851-1928)
			Henry of Prussia (1862-1929)	m.	Irène of Hesse (1866-1953)
			Victoria of Prussia (1866-1929)	m.	Adolf of Schaumburg-Lippe (1859-1910) secondly Alexander Zoubkoff (1900-1936)
			Sophie of Prussia (1870-1932)	m.	Constantine I King of the Hellenes (1869-1923)
			Margaret of Prussia (1872-1954)	m.	Frederick Charles Landgrave of Hesse-Cassel (1868-1932)
Alice (1843-1878)	m.	Louis IV Grand Duke of Hesse & by Rhine (1837-1899)	Victoria of Hesse (1863-1950)	m.	Louis of Battenberg (1854-1921)
			Elisabeth Princess of Hesse (1864-1918)	m.	Grand Duke Serge Alexandrovich (1857-1905)
			Irène of Hesse (1866-1953)	m.	Henry of Prussia (1862-1929)
			Ernest Louis Grand Duke of Hesse & by Rhine (1868-1937)	m.	(1) Victoria Melita of Edinburgh and Saxe- Coburg-Gotha (1876-1936) divorced (2) Eleonore of Solms- Hohensolms-Lich (1871-1937).
			Alix of Hesse (1872-1918)	m.	Nicholas II Emperor of Russia (1868-1918)
Helena (1846-1923)	m.	Christian of Schleswig-Holstein (1831-1917)	Christian Victor of Schleswig-Holstein (1867-1900)		
			Albert of Schleswig-Holstein (1869-1931)		
			Helena Victoria of Schleswig-Holstein (1870-1948)		
			Marie Louise of Schleswig-Holstein (1872-1956)	m.	Aribert of Anhalt (1866-1933)
Beatrice (1857-1944)	m.	Henry of Battenberg (1858-1896)	Alexander, Marquess of Carisbrooke (1886-1960)	m.	Lady Irene Denison (1890-1956)
			Victoria Eugenie of Battenberg (1887-1969)	m.	Alfonso XIII King of Spain (1886-1941)
			Leopold of Battenberg later Lord Leopold Mountbatten (1889-1922)		
			Maurice of Battenberg (1891-1914)		

Introduction

Whether the queen caused the period, or the period creates the queen, she fitted her time perfectly.[1]

During the second part of her reign, she ruled Britain at the peak of its imperial power. She was the iconic 'Widow of Windsor', the symbol of it all – Queen-Empress Victoria R.I. This diminutive and rather rotund figure became the bright sun around whom so many of the great events, marvels and accomplishments, as well the tragedies, of the age revolved.

Although so much is known about her, she remains a figure of fascination. This book is not meant to serve as an exhaustive biography of the queen, nor a political one, but to provide a light-hearted more intimate view. For the reader, my aim is to spark an interest in the subject; to highlight this intriguing woman and to inspire a wish to delve more deeply into the wealth of biographies, letters and over seventy years' worth of personal journals that are available.

As the title suggests, this work is about the queen's widowhood, the second forty years of her long life. Most people know something about her youth and marriage from films and television, but not as much about what is a major part of her life. If they do know anything, they picture the tiny woman in widow's weeds, posing in her little bonnets, gazing mournfully at a photograph or a bust of Prince Albert; always attended by a daughter, granddaughter or two, a Scottish ghillie or an Indian servant.

Contrary to this rather superficial perception, the forty years Queen Victoria lived without Albert, the Prince Consort, were by no means barren years. They were not without happiness, love and even light romance. Though the second half of her life seemed to be a time of constant mourning, it was also the most important and eventful period of her life. Victoria emerges as a person who is fully realised not just as a daughter and wife, but as an independent woman who became one of the longest reigning monarchs in European history.

Victoria was also the mother and grandmother of a group she called 'the royal mob', who sat on or near thrones in the major powers of Europe and the world at that time. This book will introduce Victoria, her large and extended family and household to an audience who has not yet explored the rich history of this nineteenth-century queen. The reader will discover that in Victoria's life there exists a much deeper history than had previously been thought possible – one which extends far beyond the queen as merely a symbol of the period's middle-class morality. Finally, I hope they will discover the splendour and excitement of Queen Victoria's reign, as well as the drama of her private life.

An observation by one of her recent biographers says a great deal. A.N. Wilson wrote that what makes Victoria so intriguing is 'she compels us to concentrate upon *her* instead of her deeds … Her life was … that of the inner woman, of whom – from the letters and the journals – we have so vivid a sense.'[2] That is clearly the portrait we get of her. Her intimate life is laid bare in her copious writings – a woman in extraordinary circumstances that is nevertheless relatable, fallible, annoying, and ultimately surprisingly endearing.

Part I

Beginnings

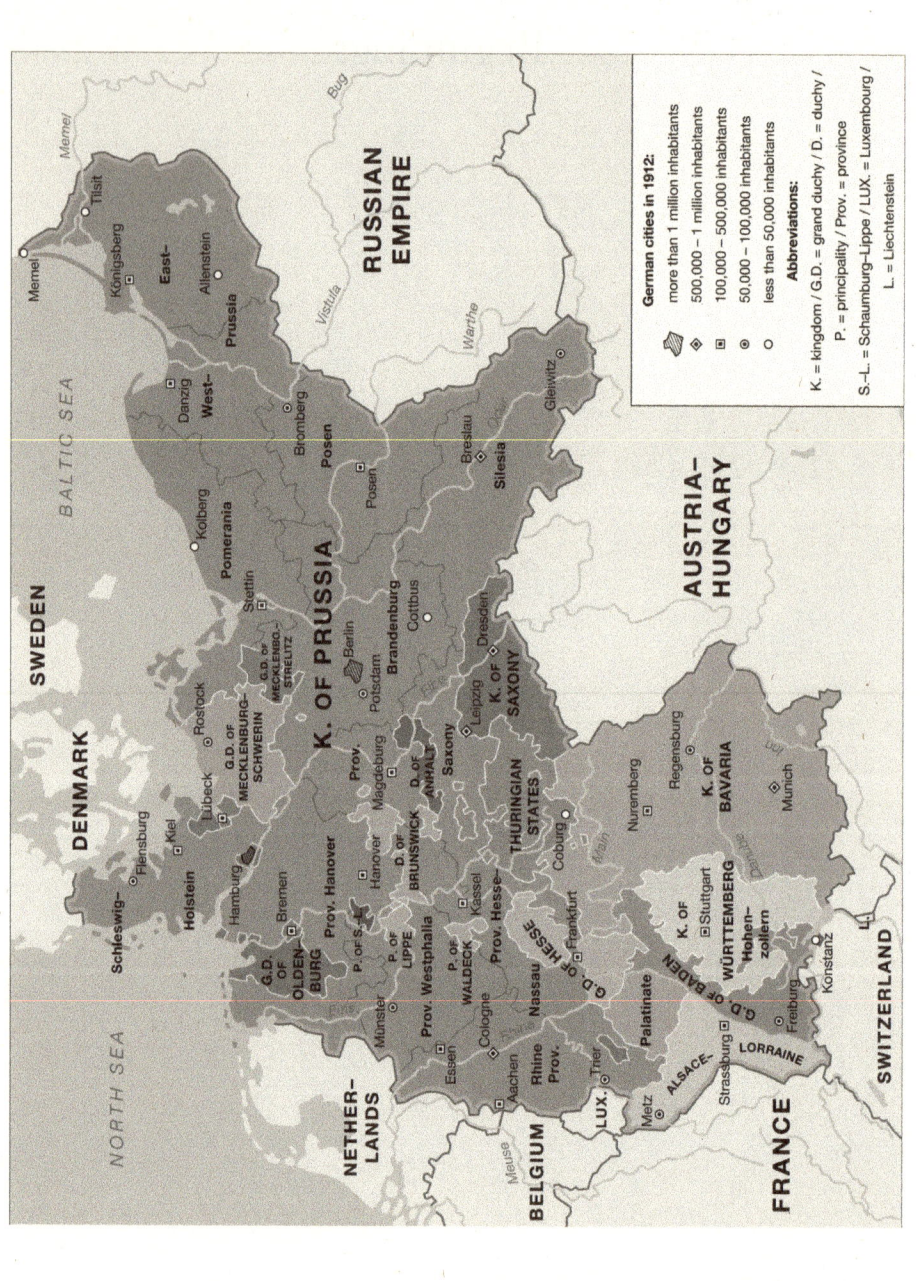

Chapter One

The Race for an Heir

Victoria should never have come to the throne. It was a confluence of events that, if fictional, would have been derided as unlikely. However, to understand what happened, we must put the disparate threads together and go back just a bit.

With his six wives, King Henry VIII managed to have only three surviving children. Edward VI, who ruled England from 1547–1553 and died before his sixteenth birthday. Next in line was Henry's eldest daughter, Mary. Though King Henry had separated completely from Rome, Mary most certainly did not. She was a staunch Roman Catholic like her mother, Catherine of Aragon, and during her five-year reign, she attempted to bring Roman Catholicism back to England. She reigned as Mary I, though by the time she left this mortal coil, she was called 'Bloody Mary' for her persecution of Protestants. After a thankfully short rule, her sister Elizabeth succeeded her in 1558. The persecution of Protestants had seemingly ended. Elizabeth I, the so-called 'Virgin Queen', produced no heirs and so the English throne was inherited by James Stuart or James VI of Scotland, a great-grandson of Henry's sister Margaret Tudor.

King James VI of Scotland became King James I of England. He was a Presbyterian, so all seemed right in the world. The succession was secured as the Stuarts provided seven monarchs until we get to Victoria's closer antecedents (apart from Cromwell's rule as Lord Protector – which came between James' son, Charles I and Charles's son Charles II). As there were no Stuart heirs, in 1701, Parliament passed the Act of Settlement that expressly forbade a Catholic from coming to the throne. So, the choice was then limited when the last Stuart monarch died – the sad Queen Anne, who had no surviving heirs.[1] The Act of Settlement, however, foresaw this and declared that Princess Sophia, the granddaughter of James I and currently the Electress of Hanover and Duchess of Brunswick-Lüneburg would be the heir. She died just before Anne, so it was up to her son, the first of the dreary Georges to come to the rescue.

With George begins the Hanoverian Royal Family and taken as a group they were barely creditable. George succeeded to the throne after the death of Queen Anne in 1714. When he moved to London after becoming king at the age of 54, he brought his half-sister, Sophia von Kielmansegg, and his mistress, Melusine von der Schulenburg, nicknamed 'the Elephant' and 'the Maypole', with him.[2] His wife, Sophia Dorothea of Celle, whom he had divorced and imprisoned for infidelity was not brought to England for the great plunder.

The Elector of Hanover and Duke of Brunswick and Lüneburg is now George I in our story. To his credit, he had some good qualities and though he spoke poor English, he had more of an understanding of British politics than most biographers think. He presided over the gradual constitutional changes in the government that led to the concept of rule by parliament and a cabinet as opposed to the old theory of 'divine right.' In addition, he was a major supporter of the composer George Frederick Handel both in Hanover and later in London. However, on the minus side of the ledger, he and his retinue seemed interested only in milking the royal treasury for as much as they could. Besides avarice, George I also had the distasteful habit of hating his heir. This was an issue he passed down to *his* heir, George II.

George II succeeded his father in 1727. He too, was not native to England, though he spoke the language better than his father. He had married the lovely and lively Caroline of Ansbach in 1705 and had seven surviving children. She, like her husband, hated their son and heir, Frederick the Prince of Wales, to the extent that she made no objections when George II threw Frederick out of the palace.

'Poor Fred', the Prince of Wales had something of a chequered youth. He had been left in Hanover at the age of 7 while his parents went to England as heirs to the throne. When he at last came to England, he hardly knew his parents. Young Fred, like most Hanoverians, was a spendthrift and a womaniser with several illegitimate children. An interesting sidelight about Frederick is that he nearly became the first Prince of Wales to marry a Lady Diana Spencer. In his case, this was the granddaughter of the influential Sarah Churchill, the first Duchess of Marlborough.

He eventually settled down with Augusta of Saxe-Gotha-Altenburg and had nine children. What upset his parents was that he headed up the political opposition and bothered the Parliament for money. 'Poor Fred' died at the age of 44 to his father's no great regret. It was Frederick's eldest son, George, who finally succeeded his highly unattractive grandfather in 1760.

And herein lies the tale.

George III as he was styled, is the same monarch that 'lost' the thirteen colonies and was also thought to be mad. In truth, he had only two significant periods of 'madness', probably brought on by porphyria (sometimes called the royal disease), but the second period lasted for over ten years. Before all these troubles he was a normal if unimaginative king who did his duty and married Charlotte of Mecklenburg-Strelitz. Together, they had an enormous brood of nine sons and six daughters. It was only logical to conclude that with such a large family of children, there would be heirs aplenty for the next generation, but that was not the case. The sons of George III ate too much, spent too much, 'wenched' too much, and for the most part evaded their royal responsibilities. The Duke of Wellington called them 'the damnedest millstones about the necks of any government that can be imagined'.[3]

The eldest son, yet another George, was born in 1762. He is best known for having presided over the period of English history known as the Regency. This was during the time of his father's second bout of psychosis. The most intelligent if eccentric of George III's nine sons, he was also hugely in debt, and a notorious womaniser. In 1785, he contracted an 'illegal' marriage to the unsuitable Maria Fitzherbert. Unsuitable because, though she was lovely and self-effacing, she was twice widowed, and a devout Catholic – the Act of Settlement again. When his father went 'mad', he was nevertheless placed in the position of being the prince regent. He had set aside his 'wife' Maria and reluctantly married Caroline of Brunswick in 1795. Frankly, he needed the money.

The couple barely managed to produce a daughter, Charlotte. Unfortunately, George loathed Caroline and the story goes, only 'came near' her once, and only after he got thoroughly, blubberingly, drunk, so there were no more children. He was no great prize, himself, being stout and at this point, not the handsome prince he had once been. More to the point, however, he supplied the needed heir.

Charlotte, who was George III's first legitimate grandchild, grew up to be a pretty and popular princess. Her childhood had been difficult, and she was much left in the care of servants and governesses. Her parents, who lived apart, were not congenial and Charlotte was often put in the middle of their various conflicts. She grew up an excitable 'tomboy' with a father that tried to control her and an absent mother. The prince regent tried to interest her in marrying William, the Hereditary Prince of Orange, but Charlotte was lukewarm about him. Eventually she consented and negotiations began on the marriage contract, but ultimately Charlotte had little interest in marrying him and broke off the engagement, mostly because she had no desire to live in the Netherlands.

Several other men did captivate the princess, however she eventually settled on the tall and very handsome Prince Leopold of Saxe-Coburg-Saalfeld, the youngest child of Duke Franz Friedrich Anton and Duchess Augusta. He was said to be charming and elegant, though others thought him 'cold and formal in manner, collected in speech, [and] careful in action....'[4] Actually, those don't sound like bad attributes for someone looking for the main chance, and Leopold definitely was. Indeed, when the couple were engaged, Parliament voted the prince an allowance of £50,000 a year. The prince regent opposed the marriage because he simply didn't like Leopold, but the young man's physical attributes and the fact that Charlotte was convinced that he actually liked her were too strong to resist. Charlotte was at least as stubborn as her father and after a protracted period, the prince regent relented, and the young people were allowed to announce their engagement in 1816.

The couple were married in May of that year and unlike her parents, Charlotte had contracted a true love match. She became pregnant in early 1817 and contentedly awaited her child's birth. Her doctors, concerned that she would not carry to term, bled her and limited her diet.[5] Consequently, when her labour started in early November, her health and strength had been severely compromised by this (even for then) outdated treatment. The poor princess suffered a difficult labour for two days and delivered a still-born son. It appeared that she was recovering, but started to bleed, which the doctors were unable to stop. She died on 6 November 1817. Her sad and probably unnecessary death was considered a national tragedy, but now, the race was reignited to the finish line – and that finish line was the sought-after heir.

There were two dynastically married sons of George III in front of Victoria's father. Frederick Augustus, the Duke of York and Albany and George III's second son, spent a career in the army. Like his brothers he had mistresses, but at some point woke to the fact that heirs must be provided for the next generation. He married the small and plain Princess Frederika Charlotte of Prussia in 1791. It was a loveless marriage and once it was evident that it was also to be childless, the couple found that they were happier living apart. The duke went back to his bachelor ways while the duchess did good works and went to church.

Next was William who eventually succeeded his brother, George IV, to become William IV. A man who had spent most of his life in the navy, he was considered coarse, severe, and like most of his brothers, he was eccentric, clownish and impecunious. He had an abundance of children from a Mrs Dorothea Jordan, an actress, but none of the ten (!) were legitimate. They lived together in domestic bliss until the issue of an heir was forcefully brought to bear.

Thus, in 1818, after leaving Mrs Jordan flat, the middle-aged William managed to persuade Adelaide of Saxe-Meiningen to marry him. She, too, was described as plain, evangelical, even the first of the Victorians, but nevertheless good natured and appealing.[6] More important, she was half his age so therefore an excellent candidate for childbearing. Sadly, though the couple were, against all odds, very happy together, she was unable to give him any children that survived.

In the end, the fourth son, Prince Edward, Duke of Kent and Strathearn, also woke up to his duty and deserted his very long-time mistress Madame Julie St Laurent. Edward was a 'tall, stout, vigorous man, highly coloured with bushy eyebrows, a bald top to his head, and what he had, carefully dyed a glossy black.'[7] Though he had lived with Julie for nearly thirty years, there were no children nor probably other 'by-blows' from this son.

He was trained in the army and had visited many of Britain's bases throughout the world, including Gibraltar, present-day Canada, and Nova Scotia. In Gibraltar, he had been extremely brutal as an officer and relieved of his command. Nevertheless, he was a liberal and admirer of the socialist Robert Owen and even had some social conscience. He was modest in his tastes and was considered reasonably temperate – no small thing for a son of George III.

However, like his brothers, he was in constant need of money. In fact, he lived with Julie in Brussels because it was cheaper than London. In addition, Parliament was getting tired of financing the lives of irresponsible princes and threatened to pull the plug unless these middle-aged men made some sensible marriages that might have, as Queen Victoria was later to call them, 'results'. The duke married Victoire of Saxe-Coburg-Saalfeld, the elder sister of Leopold of Saxe-Coburg and Gotha. Thus, the Duke of Kent became the clear frontrunner of the race.[8]

Victoire was the second wife and now widow of Emich Karl, 2nd Prince of Leiningen. She was the mother of two children, Karl and Feodora, who were attractive and more importantly, robust. She was 31, obviously fecund, and seemed like a good bet. She took a bit of wooing and made no decision the first time the Duke of Kent asked for her hand in marriage. After the death of Princess Charlotte, matters became more urgent, and Edward pressed his suit. For Victoire, it had been the choice of a pleasant widowhood or marriage to one of the lesser of George III's sons. Now, however, there was a chance to be in the enviable and far more fortunate position of being the mother of the heir.

According to Leopold's political mentor and most trusted advisor, Baron Christian Frederick Stockmar, Victoire was, 'naturally truthful, affectionate and friendly, unselfish, full of sympathy and generous.'[9] Victoire's brother, Leopold urged her to accept the duke and she did so. Happily, for them both, it was a congenial and even loving marriage. Unhappily for them both, it was quite short.

The couple were married first at Coburg at Schloss Ehrenburg, the seat of the Coburg family and next on 29 May 1818, at Kew Palace in a double wedding ceremony with Kent's older brother William and his bride Adelaide of Saxe-Meiningen. It was not long before the new duchess discovered she was pregnant and now the wait would begin.

They had gone back to live in Germany at Amorbach because it was cheaper, but when the duchess was in her seventh month decided to return to London since an heir naturally should be born in the country. It can't have been comfortable or convenient for the mother-to-be, but nevertheless, the pair made it to London in time.

In the early morning of 24 May 1819 at Kensington Palace, Victoire gave birth. She was helped by a certain Fräulein Siebold, a medical doctor who had accompanied the duchess from Germany. The doctor would return to Coburg three months later and help deliver Albert, who would much later become the Prince Consort.

After a comparatively short labour in which her husband was at her side, the duchess brought a little girl into the world. According to her father she was a model of 'strength and beauty combined',[10] and her mother wrote that she was 'a pretty little Princess, plump as a partridge.'[11]

When she was born, she was somewhat far down the line of succession, but that line would very quickly shrink. The naming would also be an issue. Her godparents were: Tsar Alexander I of Russia as well as the Prince Regent, the Dowager Queen of Württemberg, George III's eldest daughter, and the baby's maternal grandmother Augusta, Dowager Duchess of Saxe-Coburg-Saalfeld. However, it was really all up to the prince regent who had vetoed Charlotte, Elizabeth and Georgiana saying his name should not come before the Tsar of Russia.

Apparently, the regent disliked Edward and Victoire immensely since they had been friendly to poor Caroline of Brunswick. In revenge he dragged his feet on the name and in the end it was decided upon during the actual christening ceremony. She was named Alexandrina, and – almost as an afterthought – after her mother, Victoria, since a second name was needed. The baby would be known throughout her childhood as 'Drina' and later as Victoria. However, for simplicity's sake we will refer to her as Victoria.

Several months later, as the modern monarch she would become, the baby Victoria was vaccinated against smallpox. Sadness quickly came into the life of the little family when the duke died suddenly. The baby was 8 months old when the Duke of Kent contracted pneumonia. Like his niece Charlotte before him, he was made weak by bloodletting and primitive medical procedures and died 23 January 1820.

So it was that Victoria never knew her father.

The first royal baby to be vaccinated, Victoria's life would see astonishing achievements from a primarily agrarian economy to an industrial revolution, a great if unwieldly empire, to the beginnings the modern world. Mark Twain said that little Victoria would see 'more things invented than any other monarch that ever lived'.[12]

And that would be the least of it.

* * *

Kensington Palace is beautifully situated in Kensington Gardens. It was here where Victoria, her mother, and her half-sister, Feodora, would stay for much of her childhood. The death of Prince Edward, Duke of Kent, devastated the family and to make matters worse, George III died only days later, leading to the ascension to the throne of the prince regent. Victoire and her daughters were now faced with a king who had disliked his brother, and therefore by association, her.

At that point, the Duke of Kent's equerry, John Conroy forcefully took over the Kent family. John Conroy was an Irishman and a staff officer in the Royal Horse Artillery. He was described as overbearing, scheming and with a 'coarse, self-satisfied charm.'[13] In addition, he believed that his wife, Elizabeth, was the illegitimate daughter of the Duke of Kent.[14] This bizarre belief is given as an explanation of his autocratic behaviour toward Victoire and her children, but like many of the men of the day it was a simple, even natural, thing for him to bully women. Having said that, the duchess relied heavily on him and so it is likely that he believed he was entitled.

In 1826, when Victoria was 7, her beloved 19-year-old half-sister Feodora was packed off to Germany to marry Ernst I, Prince of Hohenlohe-Langenburg, making her small family circle even smaller. The issue was that the young and attractive Feodora might have caught the eye of the ageing George IV, who continued to hope for an heir and might have considered marriage.

It was best, her mother thought, to get her away, though Victoria was devastated by the loss. The pair were devoted to one another and that would never change. Victoria idolised her pretty, older sister and the two often wore matching dresses despite the large gap in their ages.[15] Even after Feodora left for her marriage, they maintained a lengthy correspondence that carried on for the rest of their lives. Indeed, later, their families would intermarry. But for now, this was a loss of perhaps the only companion near her age that Victoria actually liked.

Both sisters had loathed Conroy and the influence he had on their mother and in their household. That the duchess seemed to be somewhat blind to her daughters' dislike of the Comptroller was unsurprising. Victoire had had enough of the buffeting around that had given her one loveless marriage and another that had potential, but was cut short. She was a foreigner in a foreign land and her late husband's family despised her. She was left to run a household that contained something that was tenuous and delicate at the time – the heir. It wouldn't be a stretch to say that she was resentful of her position and that she was bossy and no longer the generous, sympathetic and affectionate character that Baron Stockmar had described. It was all a question of survival in an environment that was fraught with many foolish, resentful and in some cases, mentally unstable people.

An interesting side note to this is that Victoria's half-brother, Karl, who apparently met her in 1825 (he'd been in school in Germany) got along very well with Conroy. He allied himself with the equerry against little Victoria which caused her to despise her half-brother. Later in life this was mended to the extent that she awarded him the Order of the Garter, but at the time, it certainly added to the little girl's anger and bitterness toward her mother.[16]

The affect it had on the growing child is obvious. Very early on, Victoria was insistent on getting her own way, was impatient, had issues with temper and frustration, which as a very small girl might have been charming, but as she got older it was considered obduracy.[17] In addition, Victoria was mostly kept away from children her own age and so had little idea how to get along with her peers.

While her mother was struggling with outside forces and herself being controlled by Conroy, her daughter saw her as being manipulated by what was fast becoming a malevolent presence. Conroy was utterly paranoid and thought Victoria's food was being poisoned by devious servants. He also distrusted the Hanoverian brothers completely and so, with his influence, the duchess kept Victoria away from her uncles who sincerely wanted to see her.

To feed his obsessive suspicion, Conroy instigated what was called the 'Kensington System' – which simply meant that all matters pertaining to Victoria were in complete control by himself by way of the duchess. This included her governess, Baroness Louise Lehzen reading all her diary entries, being in attendance to the youngster all day and she was the one who had to hold the princess's hand when she descended stairs.[18]

Those fears were transferred to Victoria's mother who was completely under his sway. In addition, Victoria slept in her mother's room every day of her life until she became queen. As she got older, she had an increasing sense of isolation. In fact, between the duchess and Conroy, Victoria was kept away from family, playmates and virtually everyone except her governess, and Conroy's daughters. No wonder she was, as we would term it today, poorly socialised. Perhaps, the only positive thing that Conroy did, as far as Victoria was concerned, was to give her mother a King Charles spaniel called 'Dash'. Dash would quickly belong to Victoria who absolutely adored the creature, to the point of dressing him in clothing and bathing him herself.

Conroy didn't help matters either – he never took any steps to ingratiate or even be pleasant to Victoria. At one point when she was about 16, he tried to force her to sign a document that would guarantee him the post of her private secretary when she became queen. By then so much damage was done that she, even on a sick bed with typhoid, would refuse to sign such a document and resented him and her mother even more. The relationship between Victoria and her mother would not be mended until much later. The consequence of this was that Victoria was always on her guard, was completely self-controlled and 'precociously prudent and precociously secretive.'[19]

The mitigating influence throughout Victoria's fraught, manipulated and cocoon-like childhood, was Baroness Lehzen. Lehzen, as Victoria called her, loved her charge, and gave her a great deal of demonstrative affection. Louise Lehzen was born in Hanover and was the daughter of a Lutheran Pastor. She came to the Kent household in 1819, first in the position of Feodora's governess, but later, having moved with the Kent's to England, she eventually became Victoria's governess and as it was appropriate, George IV awarded Lehzen with the title 'Baroness' in 1827.

It was several years later when Lehzen slipped a piece of paper in a book called *Tales of the Kings and Queens of England* that revealed to Victoria that she was the heir. She is said to have 'exclaimed, "I am nearer to the throne than I thought" and burst into tears.'[20] Lehzen supervised Victoria's education which was wide and varied. Indeed, Victoria was far better educated than most girls of her time, even of the aristocracy. She learned Greek, Latin, French, German and what was called 'passable Italian'. She read French literature, and she had an ear for music and very much loved to draw and paint watercolours. She was taught economics, geography and politics.

The important thing was that after a slow start, she learned to love knowledge. Most historians also agree that the great importance of

Lehzen for the future queen is that she taught her independence and how to be forceful to carry out her own decisions. Though this obstinacy of mind put her at great odds with her mother and Conroy, it was the stiffening of her spine by Lehzen that gave her the strength to be her own person at an early age. In addition, she taught Victoria to be kind to others. In one of her earliest diary entries she talked about how Lehzen was firm to her but kind and taught her to 'own [her] ... fault in a kind way to anyone, be he or she the lowest'.[21]

By all accounts, Lehzen herself was not interested in money or appointments. She simply loved her charge and wanted to be with her. When Victoria was too old to have a governess, and when she became queen, Lehzen was her closest ally, her right-hand and a staunch support. Sadly, for her, she would not get along well with Victoria's young husband when he came along and would be sent back to Germany in 1842.

One of the few highlights of Victoria's childhood was visiting her Uncle Leopold at his English residence, Claremont.[22] Leopold lived there until something much better than being a grieving widower came along. It should be stated that as a young man, he mourned a short time and then had several mistresses before his second marriage. He had been offered the Kingdom of Greece, which had become an independent kingdom by way of the London Protocol of 1830, providing it was ruled by a Christian Prince.[23] Leopold refused that throne, but in April 1831 was offered the throne of the newly independent Belgium. This he happily accepted and so, Leopold became a king after all.

He felt that it was his place to guide and mould his little niece and did so. Certainly, an astute man such as he knew how important a niece on the throne of England would be. Nevertheless, Victoria loved Leopold like a father and that was the place he occupied in her life. When he left Claremont to go to Belgium, there was a definite gap for Victoria and she would see him only seldom, but the two exchanged copious correspondence until his death in 1865. Until the end of his life, Victoria always valued his opinion though he was frequently pedantic. He had advice on European politics, education, statecraft, and the way in which Victoria should conduct herself as queen. He answered her questions 'with the utmost care, and, at least in the early years, instructed as best he could'.[24]

Leopold remarried in 1832. His new wife was Louise of Orléans, the daughter of King Louis Philippe I of the French and his wife, Maria Amalia of the Two Sicilies. Louise was twenty years his junior, yet he outlived her. They had three children, including the infamous Leopold II of Belgium and tragic Charlotte, who, for a time was Empress Carlotta of Mexico.

Leopold would become one of the master manipulators of his family. During his lifetime he was able to accomplish the marriages of siblings, children, and other family members so that Chancellor Bismarck soon called Coburg the stud farm of Europe. There would be Coburgs in Portugal, Brazil, Romania, Sweden, Norway, Russia, Bulgaria, Mexico and, of course, Great Britain. While later, Queen Victoria was called the 'Grandmama of Europe', Leopold was certainly the uncle. It began with convincing his sister Victoire to marry the Duke of Kent, but really gained momentum when he convinced Albert and Ernst, his Coburg nephews, and the sons of his elder brother, to visit their cousin Victoria.

But there is still a little more to tell before we get to that momentous occasion.

* * *

Later, when George IV died, the family was confronted by yet another king who thoroughly hated the duchess. The next brother, William became king in 1830. The king and Queen Adelaide were very fond of their niece Victoria and would have liked her to appear more frequently at court. However, the duchess disliked the king as heartily as he disliked her, and thought the court was full of vulgarity and vice, and so the young princess was kept away from all her relatives. The feeling was mutual, and William and his wife detested the duchess and Conroy vehemently. This really came to the fore when the duchess insisted on precedence at the coronation. Since this wasn't granted, Victoire and Victoria did not attend.

In truth, William seemed a simple man who loved being king. He often walked out among the people and during his first appearance as king, he happily accepted a kiss on the cheek from a streetwalker.[25] As Victoria got older, she was invited to various functions at the court and made an excellent impression on the king and queen, but, again, the fly in the ointment were the duchess and her Svengali, Conroy. As William IV's health failed, he himself had determined that he simply would not die until Victoria was old enough to become queen without a regent. At that point, if there had been a regency the obvious candidate would have been the duchess who was under the sway of Conroy, or 'that Mephistopheles' as Uncle Leopold called him.

The duchess had made what the king considered some highly offensive demands when he took the throne. She wanted to be called the Dowager Princess of Wales, though her husband had never been a Prince of Wales – these were those irksome and overblown requests of precedence. In addition, there were arguments about Victoria's names. The king thought them both foreign sounding and wanted the duchess to adopt more English names.[26] Initially, the duchess acquiesced, but then thought better of it. After all, her daughter had her name. The king argued that no queen had had these names before, but nevertheless, Victoria's name remained.

The duchess also irritated the king by taking young Victoria for 'progresses' around the country and introducing her as the future queen. It was her intention that the visits would promote the young princess's popularity. However, the king responded to those progresses by saying that he hoped Victoria's succession would be very much in the future.[27]

The quarrels came to a head in August 1836 when the king invited the duchess and Victoria to attend Queen Adelaide's birthday celebration. The addendum to the invitation was that they should also stay for the king's birthday since both had been born in August. The duchess insulted the king and queen by arriving after the queen's birthday. This was not helped by her taking a suite of rooms in Kensington Palace without the king's permission.

At the birthday dinner on 21 August, William, in a rage, made the following speech:

> I trust in God that my life may be spared for nine months longer after which, in the event of my death, no Regency would take place. I should then have the satisfaction of leaving the royal authority to the personal exercise of that young lady, the heiress presumptive of the crown, and not in the hands of a person now near me, who is surrounded by evil advisors, and who is herself incompetent to act with propriety and the station in which she would be placed.[28]

It was horribly awkward, and young Victoria burst into tears. The duchess called for her carriage and walked out, dragging Victoria with her. Things were patched up the next day, but there was still enough anger, resentfulness, and bitter recriminations to go around. Ultimately, Victoria always knew that the king meant well, though he was 'odd, very odd and singular.'[29]

The king, however, got what amounted to his last wish.

William IV died on 20 June 1837. He'd been ill since the beginning of the month and wanted to see one more celebration of the victory of Waterloo. This he managed, but he died two days later. Victoria was woken up and got out of bed. Perhaps for the last time, her hand was held as she came down the stairs to receive the Archbishop of Canterbury and the Lord Chamberlain, Lord Conyngham, who gave her the sad news that the king had expired after midnight. Victoria recorded in her journal: 'I am *Queen*.'[30]

Chapter Two

'I beheld Albert....'

The first thing Victoria did was get a room and bed of her own. In fact, she said to her mother: 'dear Mama, I hope you will grant me the first request I make to you, as Queen. Let me be by myself for an hour.'[1] After the oppressive influence of Conroy and his Kensington System by way of her mother, the young queen had had enough. She wanted to be alone; she wanted to break free of Conroy and her mother and, at long last, that wish would be granted to the 18-year-old. Most satisfactorily, however, she gave Conroy an allowance and completely banished him from her presence.

Victoria[2] had, with great poise and dignity, accepted the news of the king's death with grief and with expectation and no doubt a little excitement as well. She wrote a letter to her Uncle Leopold and then, four hours after she found out she was queen, met Lord Melbourne, the prime minister, and told him that she wanted him and his colleagues to remain in office. He showed her the speech he had written for her to be read to the Privy Council and was dismissed. Later, when she read the speech to the Council, many were amazed at the self-possession of this young girl. That evening, Lord Melbourne had dinner with the young queen and so began a relationship that moulded the first years of Victoria's reign.[3]

William Lamb, 2nd Viscount Melbourne, was the Whig prime minister at the time of Victoria's accession to the throne and was to be her prime minister for the next four years. Melbourne, a politician since his twenties had been married to the notorious Lady Caroline Ponsonby who had a very public affair with Lord Byron. By the time he was prime minister, his scandalous wife had died many years before and he was a man alone.

Melbourne was an extremely charming and handsome man, and the queen would succumb to him as she would succumb to many handsome men in her life. Melbourne, however, had something to give – he 'tutored her in the world of politics and [instructed] … her in her role' as queen.[4]

He was extremely cultured and educated and acted as a sort of guardian to her.

Before Victoria's marriage, her diaries are full of 'Lord M' as she affectionately called him. She acknowledged that she was very young and inexperienced, but she always wanted to do what was right. He, doing his duty as her prime minister, saw her nearly every day and often more than once a day, taking meals with her and advising her on everything under the sun.

That he may have been a romantic ideal for the young girl is probable. Here was a man who had an extremely sad and tragic experience with a wife that had abandoned him and his son for the poet Lord Byron. That he forgave his wandering wife must have also been a tender model for young Victoria. That she was not the most forgiving and tender of people made her admire him even more. She no doubt thought that it was a kind of punishment for Lady Caroline that their son was mentally challenged and died as a very young man. Victoria, who in many ways was very forceful and self-contained for her age, was also very naïve about life and in particular men. She, in turn, was at once his queen, a daughter figure, and 'the last love of his life'.[5]

She was certainly lovely with the freshness of youth. Portraits of her at the time perhaps romanticise that beauty and innocence, but there is no doubt she was attractive. Victoria was quite tiny even by the standards of the time. She was under 5ft tall and had grown into a graceful, slightly plump figure.[6] She had the Hanoverian blue eyes, and a small slightly hooked nose. She always knew she was pudgy and no beauty, but at that time of a great new Victorian era, the country saw her with their heart and not their eyes.

Melbourne was among them; he grew very attached to her, and their sessions were the highlight of his last years in government. The two shared confidences like gossipy girls, talking and laughing about this one or that one of their mutual acquaintances. But, nevertheless, Melbourne was in a position to form the adult queen. In some cases, he was wise and in others, not so. However, one of the great things he taught Victoria was tolerance in all its forms. Under his tutelage, she grew into a person who, for that time, was fairly free of prejudices and discrimination on the basis of race or religion, and who understood that people could only do and be what they were.

There were those who felt that his sway wasn't as efficacious as the queen did. While he was extremely sophisticated, she was not, having been more or less isolated for her entire childhood. He also predisposed her to having Whig politics which, since the monarch was supposed to remain neutral, created many problems. It later made her dealings with prime ministers of the other party extremely difficult as we shall see. Because of this, some historians feel that despite some of his astute tutelage he made her life more difficult instead of easier.

Once Victoria became queen she moved to Buckingham Palace. Her mother and the duchess's household, though invited to move with her, were placed as far away in the palace as Victoria could make them. Her relationship with her mother did not improve even with Conroy gone, and she saw her mother only in public. Her mother, who was not as circumspect as her daughter, saw their estrangement encouraged not only by Lehzen, of whom she had been extremely jealous, but her new mentor, Melbourne.

A respite from all the petty household jealousies and even the scandals to come came when the queen was crowned on 28 June 1838. The coronation was celebrated for two days with fairs, concerts and fireworks. She wrote a long and detailed description of the day in her journal remembering it as the 'proudest of my life'.[7] It is interesting to note that in the journal, she also recounts a great deal about the festive dinner party conversations. They talked about who was there and even gossiped gently about them and Lord Melbourne was 'amusing' about what the ladies wore. Though she didn't sleep the night before, she stayed up late to watch fireworks and finally went to bed after midnight.

While Melbourne escaped all the scandals in his life due to the respect his fellows had for him, the same could not be said for his young pupil, the queen. There was the unfortunate case of Lady Flora Hastings and later the Bedchamber Crisis. In both circumstances, it was the young queen's impetuousness and immaturity that got her into trouble. Having said that, it should be remembered that in 1839, when both happened, the queen was not yet 20.

First Lady Flora.

Born in 1806, she was the daughter of the 1st Marquess of Hastings and Flora Mure-Campbell. Lady Flora was a talented and educated woman who wrote poetry and had a stinging wit. Lehzen smarted under her ridicule, making fun of her because she liked caraway seeds. She served the Duchess of Kent as a lady-in-waiting and because she was part of Victoria's mother's household and a Tory, Victoria disliked her. But the queen really needed no help in that direction as she believed that Lady Flora was also a creature of Conroy and a participant in the hated 'Kensington System'. As such, she was to be scorned.

Early in February 1839, after Lady Flora returned from Scotland to London in the same carriage as Sir John Conroy without a chaperone, Victoria noticed that the woman's waistline was thickening. Since her marital status had not changed it was thought that she was pregnant without the benefit of marital bliss.

Around this time, Flora began to complain of nausea as well as the distended stomach. She went to Sir James Clark, Victoria's physician, who apparently didn't have the knowledge to correctly diagnose the problem. In truth, Sir James was a little strange in some of his theories and remedies. For Lady Flora's malady his thought was to prescribe rhubarb and ipecacuanha pills[8] as well as rubbing liniments containing opium.[9] The majority opinion seems to be that Sir James was incompetent, indeed, Lord Clarendon said that he wouldn't trust a sick cat to him,[10] yet he remained as physician-in-ordinary to the queen until 1860.

As others began to notice her waistline, Victoria's senior Lady of the Bedchamber, Lady Tavistock, whose claim to fame was being the inventor of afternoon tea, took it upon herself to inform Lord Melbourne about the situation. Lord Melbourne told her to watch and keep quiet. This advice could hardly have been worse, since whatever was happening was going on in a court of a young, unmarried and highly impressionable queen.[11] And, Victoria in her blissful ignorance, had gleefully decided that Flora was pregnant and Conroy's mistress.

Eventually, Lady Flora consented to an internal examination. This was undertaken in the presence of Victoria's physician, Sir James; Lady Flora's physician, Sir Charles Clarke; Lady Portman, a lady of the household; and Lady Flora's maid. One can only imagine the indignity of such an examination at the time. It was considered indelicate and exceedingly humiliating. However, to Lady Flora's credit, she submitted to it and the doctors concluded that she was a virgin and not pregnant. Later it would be known that Flora was suffering from a cancer that would kill her in June of that year.

In February, after the medical examination, Victoria had written a letter of apology to Flora. She went to see her about a week after the doctors' visits and the two women agreed that for the sake of the Duchess of Kent, all would be forgiven and forgotten – but that did not quiet the whispers. Though Lady Flora was exonerated, much of the situation and rumours continued to swirl around the household. Melbourne and the queen shared some of the responsibility for this, not missing any swipe at Conroy and, by association, her mother, whom she agreed with Melbourne was 'a liar and a hypocrite'.[12]

The scandal itself lasted for a few months and eventually found its way to the newspapers. Lady Flora decided to write a letter to *The Examiner* and proclaim her innocence and that saying she was in the 'family way' was spread around by 'a certain foreign lady'.[13] And, since Lady Flora was found to be virtuous, the villain of the piece was the young queen, whose popularity plummeted with this disgrace and would not recover for several years. Indeed, at Ascot that year she was actually hissed at by several ladies. The newspapers, too, were less than flattering to the new queen about this situation. It was also thought that the Tories would use this as a cudgel with which to bludgeon the Whigs, and by strong association, the queen, and her court.

Just before Lady Flora's death, Lord Melbourne's government fell over the issue of slavery at the sugar plantations in Jamaica and its abolition. This was a major blow to young Victoria who wrote that she cried so much and was not sure she would have the strength to go on without 'Lord M'.[13] The problem was that Victoria had unwisely been indoctrinated by Melbourne to be a very strong Whig and it was exceptionally difficult for her to change. Remembering that she was not quite 20, the idea of being above politics was too challenging for her.

The Tories came in and the queen was forced to call in the leading Tory at the time – the Duke of Wellington. He, however, was old and deaf and declined the job. At the old duke's suggestion, Victoria called Sir Robert Peel, who did not decline. He was not the charming and fatherly man that Melbourne was and had great difficulty gaining the queen's confidence. That he was a reserved man, even his friends admitted, and perhaps a bit shy, but this was interpreted by the young queen as being cold and unfeeling.

It was in relation to this change in prime ministers that another scandal came to pass – the question of the Ladies of the Bedchamber. This of course had ramifications not only for the queen's household, but for the political life of the nation at large. It was predicated on what should have been a simple thing: the queen was requested by Sir Robert to change certain ladies in her household who held strong oppositional political (read Whig) views. This was traditional and not an onerous demand. The queen, however, saw her ladies as a personal issue, not a political one.

Victoria did not wish to dismiss any of the ladies who had been her support during her unhappy time under the thrall of Conroy. Melbourne had told her that 'none of your Majesty's Household, except those who are engaged in Politics, may be removed. I think you might ask him for that'.[14] He also, wisely, advised her to get rid of her dislike for Sir Robert. After several interviews with Sir Robert, the queen informed him that she was keeping *all* her household, even the ones who were married to Whigs. Sir Robert felt there was nowhere to go from there and he stepped away. 'Lord M' was to stay, at least for now.

The only good news at this point was that Sir John Conroy, at last, quit the duchess's household entirely. He decided to move to Italy where he could live like a foreign luminary. On 1 June he notified Lord Melbourne of his intent. The only void when the family left was in the duchess's household and her heart. She missed Conroy's entire family. Some at court hoped that his leaving would promote a reconciliation between the duchess and her daughter, but at that point it didn't happen. Added to that loss, the duchess was feeling wretched because her friend Lady Flora was dying.

As May turned into June, Flora was more and more ill, plainly wasting away. At the beginning of July, the queen paid one more visit to the sickroom. Still convinced that Lady Flora *was* with child, Victoria was shocked to see Flora's emaciated form. She was lying on a couch, deathly thin and swollen. The two women reconciled, Victoria not realising or perhaps not wanting to realise how serious her condition had been the entire time of the scandal. Was she remorseful for what she had put Lady Flora through? It has been said that Victoria experienced nightmares for many years afterwards. Being much older and more mature, Flora certainly realised at the time that Victoria didn't understand the ramifications of the situation.

When Flora died on 5 July 1839, there was one more ignition of the scandal. There was an autopsy after the death, and it was proven that she had never been pregnant but had a liver tumour. Because of the tumult, 5,000 people attended her funeral. Fearing that they might be stoned, the queen nevertheless gamely sent representatives to the funeral. There was no such disturbance, but Lady Flora's family were understandably very angry and bitter. The queen tried to send money to Flora's maid, but it was sent back by Lady Flora's mother. Her brother challenged Lord Melbourne to a duel, though it probably didn't happen.

As the young queen turned 20, she had weathered these two scandals. Lord Melbourne would stay as her prime minister until 1841, and the Hastings and Bedchamber affairs would fade. She would regain her popularity when she married and had her first child.

So now, as many young women do at her age, it was time to think about the next step in her life. Not trusting her mother, and no longer being under the thrall of Conroy and Melbourne's influence beginning to diminish, it was time to look for support, comfort and maybe even happiness from another quarter.

* * *

On 10 February 1840 Victoria married Prince Albert of Saxe-Coburg and Gotha. As in most things in her emotional life, she was madly in love with the handsome young man. But how did she get from not being ready to marry at all, thinking that she was too young, and not wanting to think about it for several years at least, to this celebratory day?

In May of 1839, she wrote in her journal: 'This day I *go out of my TEENS* and become 20! It sounds so strange to me!'[15] It sounds like something any young girl would write. The excitement of becoming an adult, though she had had to deal with adult things for several years after being wrapped in cotton wool for the first eighteen, must have been thrilling and puzzling. It had to be a strange and exhilarating feeling. There were some reasons for her to shy away from marriage. She was enjoying life and having too much fun with various other young men who came to visit. She was getting her bearings as an adult and the scandals and the wrangles with her prime ministers had been so difficult to handle.

The main point is that like most independent young women, she had an aversion to being hurried.

To backtrack a little, young cousins had been visiting by the boatload before Victoria became queen. They were mostly Coburg cousins, sons of Victoire's brothers. There was Princes Alexander and Ernst of Württemberg, the son of Victoria's Aunt Antoinette of Saxe-Coburg-Saalfeld and her husband Duke Alexander of Württemberg. Victoria was 14 years old when they came to visit, and she wrote that Alexander was very handsome, and Prince Ernst was very kind.

Two years later another couple of princes came calling – Ferdinand and Augustus. They were the sons of Prince Ferdinand of Saxe-Coburg-Koháry and his Hungarian wife, Princess Maria Antonia Koháry de Csábrág et Szitya. She thought both princes very handsome and amiable, but they had a problem. In order to marry the Princess Maria Antonia, who had a massive fortune, Prince Ferdinand, a younger son after all, had to convert to Catholicism, which he did. Therefore, the youngsters were not eligible.

King William IV, however, was not in favour of any of the Coburg cousins, most likely because of the duchess. He was more interested in the idea of Victoria's marrying Prince Alexander of Orange-Nassau, the second son of King William II of the Netherlands and his wife, Anna Pavlovna of Russia. The party of the king and his two sons, the elder William, also arrived to visit Victoria in May 1836.

There was a ball given to which yet another suitor for the young princess was present – Prince George of Cambridge, the son of Prince Adolphus, Duke of Cambridge (another of George III's many sons) and Princess Augusta of Hesse-Kassel. Victoria's opinion of the Netherlander 'boys' was that they were both plain and dull.[16] As for George Cambridge, he thought his cousin quite plain, and she disliked him.

Albert and Ernst of Saxe-Coburg and Gotha made their first visit to Kensington Palace in 1836 when Victoria was just 17. Ernst was not really in the picture as he was the eldest son and would inherit the Duchy of Saxe-Coburg and Gotha, but Albert, who was about three months younger than Victoria, was Uncle Leopold's prime candidate for the job. There was a small bruhaha about having so many princes visiting under the roof of the unmarried princess, but ultimately, it was a non-issue.

Princess Feodora, Victoria's sister, had an opinion about the Coburg princes. She liked Ernst better than Albert. She thought Ernst 'so honest and good-natured', though Albert was 'much handsomer and cleverer, too'.[17] During this visit, Albert, just a teenage boy after all, was unused to all the courts, dinners, and entertainments and was often sleepy or sickly. His brother Ernst was much more charming and had a way with women. In all, it wasn't the most satisfactory of visits – certainly not with the outcome that Uncle Leopold wanted, so though Victoria liked them both very much, marriage was not on her mind. It is safe to say that it probably wasn't on Albert's mind either as he told the young princess about his aim to study in Brussels and do some travelling.

Another cousin, Charles II, Duke of Brunswick, interested her a little in the summer of 1836.[18] He was the favourite of the old king at the time because of his aversion to the Coburgs. Young Charles had already been deposed in his own country in a revolution being called corrupt and misguided while his brother took over. The young man went to live in London and had danced with Victoria at the ball for the 'Orange men' (the princes from the Netherlands). Victoria wrote about admiring his hairstyle and his courtiers, but cooled off quickly enough thinking him very eccentric and unfortunate.

Young men continued to call after Victoria became queen – and not all of them were relatives. One who made a very strong impression on the young woman was young Tsarevich Alexander Nikolaievich (later Tsar Alexander II). He had been sent on a tour of Europe by his parents and met Queen Victoria, who was just one year younger than he. She became somewhat enamoured by him and wrote in her journal that he was very good-natured and spoke excellent English. She also described him in detail, handsome with blue eyes, a nice mouth, how well he danced etc. But ultimately, he came and went. Of course, that could have never been a match since he was to inherit the imperial crown.

Ernst and Albert made a second visit to the court in Fall 1839. Victoria was well aware of what her uncle wanted in this regard and chaffed under it. She wrote to her uncle that no assumptions of marriage should be made and that she did not want to marry for several years at the least. However, 'two more reluctant guests to the English court … could not be imagined'.[19] The reality was that, based on the first meeting in 1836, neither of the young people were particularly enthused. Both were quite disinclined to gratify their uncle's wish.

What a difference a few years would make.

* * *

Prince Albert of Saxe-Coburg and Gotha was born 26 August 1819 at the bucolic Schloss Rosenau in the forests of Coburg. He was the younger son of Ernst I, Duke of Saxe-Coburg and Gotha and his wife Princess Louise of Saxe-Gotha-Altenburg. His brother Ernst, who was about fourteen months older than him, would eventually inherit the Duchy. It must be said that the two brothers could not be more different. While Ernst was the consummate lady's man, a charmer, energetic and full of fun, Albert was quiet, studious and, at least as a youngster, seemed languid and unobtrusive. Nevertheless, they were educated together and supported each other during major family dysfunction.

Their father was constantly unfaithful and Princess Louise, sick of dealing with it, left Coburg in 1824. Though she herself had some flirtations, the fault does seem to lie more with her husband. The couple were divorced in 1826. According to historian Stanley Weintraub, a condition of the separation and divorce was that the boys may never see their mother again. Louise quietly married one of her lovers, Baron Alexander von Hanstein. Tragically, she died of uterine cancer in 1831. Albert was said to be crushed at the loss of his mother.

Nevertheless, the boys continued their education with tutor, Christoph Florschütz. Unlike a lot of strict tutors in those days, Herr Florschütz was warm and affectionate to the two boys. It was just before the first visit to their cousin Victoria that Leopold and Duke Ernst thought about Albert as a possible candidate for her husband. Though that first visit didn't perhaps go the way the older men would have liked, she did, nevertheless, see qualities in Albert that she liked. But at that point, Victoria hated the idea of marriage being imposed on her. She wrote to her uncle:

> I must thank you, my beloved Uncle, for the prospect of great happiness you have contributed to give me, in the person of dear Albert. Allow me, then my dearest Uncle, to tell you how delighted I am with him, and how much I like him in every way.[20]

She was quick to stipulate to her uncle and to Lord Melbourne that she wouldn't be interested in the idea of marriage for several years yet.

The vision of Albert as a humourless 'stick-in-the-mud' was not only widespread, but it is undoubtedly a modern perception as well. But imagine if you will, a child whose mother is gone when he is a mere 5 years old and who is brought up by tutors with his brother. He was taught at an early age to repress loneliness, emotion and feeling. True, Duke Ernst, their father, remarried in 1832 to his niece, Duchess Marie of Württemberg, but by then the two young boys were almost too old to benefit from a feminine influence. Besides which, the marriage was not a success and the couple elected to live apart.

Contrast that with the wildly emotional and impulsive upbringing that Victoria experienced among the erratic and eccentric royal family, as well as her mother and Sir John Conroy. We have seen some of the arguments and cruel games that the duchess played with her royal brothers-in-law, and the bitter competition between members of the household.

Two such different personalities seemed incompatible; however, someone was needed to rescue the girl-queen from herself.[21] Or as historian Lucy Worsley writes: 'Victoria needed a man about the house.'[22] That remark may sound flippant, but the truth was, Victoria needed the support from a younger man, and with Lord Melbourne on his way out, his parenting was no longer what the young woman needed.

When the Coburg princes visited for a second time, then, it was quite a different thing. Albert had grown up; he was no longer the sickly teenager who could hardly stay up passed nine in the evening. He was far more sophisticated, and manly than before. He was also anxious to get on with his life. His student years were over, and he was exasperated with the queen's hesitation, aware that there were other claimants for her hand.

During the intervening three years, he had travelled throughout Europe and many who saw him socially wrote in letters and diaries that this young man was possibly the handsomest in Europe. When the queen beheld him for the second time in October 1839, she couldn't help but agree. She was filled with emotion and *strongly* attracted. She famously penned: 'I beheld Albert – who is beautiful.' She wrote as if he were a holy apparition.

During that visit, they rode and played music together. Ernst became ill, but Victoria, enjoying Albert's company so much, didn't notice. A few days into their visit, Victoria informed Lord Melbourne about her change of heart about marrying in a few years. She wanted to marry Albert, and he told her she could consider it for a while. She took one day and made her decision.

However, because of her position, Victoria had to be the one to propose. She called him into her 'Blue Closet' one of her most private audience chambers, took his hand in hers and, as she wrote: 'I said to him that I thought he must be aware *why* I wished them to come here, and that it would make me *too happy* if he would consent to what I wished [to marry me].'[23] She never did anything by halves and now wrote in her journal how much in love she was, how kind and affectionate he was and how lucky she was.

It's interesting to note that the prince was coming to England to put an end to the waiting game. His patience was exhausted, and he had heard of her idea of waiting a few years. Albert had no wish to wait any longer for her to make up her mind and had every intention of telling her so and withdrawing from the situation. Later, Victoria wrote that she was angry at herself for having left him dangling for as long as she did.

Albert left in November of that year to spend the last three months of his single life in his beloved Coburg. When he went home, he had a long talk with his Uncle Leopold and the king's advisor, Baron Stockmar. Stockmar had been on Leopold's staff in the army and accompanied him to England when he married Princess Charlotte. He was a canny and wise man who had engineered Leopold's ascendency to the Belgian throne and was therefore invaluable. In future, Stockmar would also be a close advisor to both Prince Albert and Victoria throughout their marriage.

The never-to-be-forgotten day, as Victoria might have written,[24] dawned on 10 February 1840. Victoria was fully cognisant that this was her last day as a single woman, indeed her last day of sleeping alone.

As was completely untraditional for queenly brides, Victoria wore cream silk and Honiton lace. For some, it appeared sombre and even drab, but it was a tradition started and brides from then on wore white or various gradations of the colour. She received a gift of flowers from her mother, who, since Conroy had left the court, was slowly coming back into her daughter's good graces. Victoria also received the gift of a small ring from Lehzen. She was indeed very simple looking as she went to St James's Palace to be married. The old Duke of Sussex gave the bride away, crying copiously as he did so and throughout the ceremony. He had been Victoria's favourite uncle. After the ceremony, she embraced her aunt, the Dowager Queen Adelaide, but merely shook hands with her mother.[25]

Afterward, the couple changed and travelled to Windsor for their honeymoon. The following morning, Victoria was rapturous. She wrote: 'we did not sleep much….'[26]

Chapter Three

'...only the husband....'

And so, the queen was married.

At first, she was overwhelmed by the emotions she felt for this very private and reserved man. He was not used to being a public figure and would never be comfortable with it. And conversely, the public was never quite comfortable with him. He was a foreigner and a German. Many thought he was there for the money and yet others thought he was nothing but a Coburger stud, which didn't amount to much.

However, it must be said, it wasn't for nothing that Coburg was called the stud farm of Europe. In fact, Hugh Auchincloss wrote, tongue firmly in cheek, that the 'principal industry of the German States in the nineteenth century was the production of marriageable princes and princesses', and many of those spouses came from Coburg.[1] Nevertheless, the queen was ecstatic and from that auspicious day heralded the start of a life that produced nine children, saw ten prime ministers and the acquisition of two more homes.

As the young couple got to know each other, they were a study in contrasts. It seems probable that the designation 'Victorian' with its implication of priggishness and prudery belonged more to Albert than Victoria. He was undoubtedly a prude and would eventually insist that everyone in the court, including Cabinet Ministers be beyond moral reproach. He had a horror of sex without marriage, possibly because of what he saw with his father and mother. A more immediate reminder was his brother Ernst, who was Albert's opposite and already afflicted with venereal disease.

While the queen loved dancing, social events and staying up late, Albert was less robust; he didn't enjoy these spectacles and was all for a quiet supper and early bed. Victoria was passionate and argumentative while Albert, in marital battle, withdrew to the side-lines. In a passive-aggressive fashion he went to his writing desk and scribbled letters and made lists of his points and why he was right.² Albert believed that the monarchy should be politically neutral while, Victoria continued to be a very strong Whig.

During the early time in the marriage, Victoria stressed that she was head of state, and withheld documents of state from the prince. Her rationalisation was that she felt Albert had little experience in such affairs. Victoria was either unable or unwilling to share the power of her position with her new husband.³ Albert would obviously feel useless by this restriction and little time would pass before he did his best to fight it. It also seemed that between Stockmar and Lehzen's ubiquitous presence, as well as Lord M's, Albert was just an afterthought.

Albert came into a household still divided between the Duchess of Kent and the Lehzen faction. The truth was, with Conroy gone, the duchess was hopeful of an improved relationship with her daughter, though that would not happen as quickly as she might have wished. Albert saw this and thought a good connection with her mother was desirable. He also saw that a household that was controlled by Lehzen was a bad idea.

Almost right away, the thing that Victoria dreaded most happened: she fell pregnant. Despite going on to have nine children, she was never reconciled to what she thought of as a miserable and animalistic condition. She was extremely frustrated and irritated that the pregnancy had occurred so soon after her marriage, just a few months after the wedding. The queen was observed by the court to be in what she described in her journal as an 'interesting condition'.⁴

Another major incident early in their marriage was the first attempt to be made on Victoria's life. On 10 June 1840, while the royal pair were riding in an open carriage, a young man shot at them twice. Had he been a good shot, the second bullet would have hit the queen. Luckily, the slow-witted Edward Oxford was a terrible shot. The crowd captured him right away and he was quickly brought into custody and confined to an insane asylum. Victoria showed a great deal of sangfroid in this episode and the couple would immediately continue to show themselves. They rode about in an open carriage without hesitation.⁵ Sadly for the queen, it would not be the last such attempt. There would be at least seven more in the coming years, the last being in 1882.

Contrary to her poor cousin Charlotte, Victoria had an easy first pregnancy. She was neither bled nor starved and the obstetricians were most careful, not wanting a repeat of the former tragedy. Her labour began early in the morning on 21 November 1840 and a team of doctors were notified: Sir James Clark, Dr Charles Locock as well as several others. Albert was present throughout the ordeal and ultimately, the queen told everyone that she felt little pain. While Albert was present inside (and would be present at all the queen's births), the Duchess of Kent was made to wait outside the room. As the morning progressed and the birth wasn't happening quite as quickly as the doctors hoped, there was some consternation, but by early afternoon, it was all over.

The queen was told, 'Oh, Madam, it is a princess.'[6] She was heard to say, 'never mind it will be a boy next time'. They named the infant Victoria Adelaide Mary Louisa, but she was called 'Vicky' or 'Pussy' in the family. Just a few months after she was born, she was made Princess Royal, an honorary designation given to the eldest daughter of the monarch, at the pleasure of the monarch. She was the apple of her father's eye and both her parents' confidante. More children came at intervals: Albert Edward (Bertie), the heir (1841), Alice (1843), Alfred (Affie) (1844), Helena (Lenchen) (1846), Louise (1848), Arthur (1850), Leopold (1853), and finally, Beatrice (1857). They were a fascinating clutch of children – several had close relationships to their parents, particularly Albert, the others less so, but they and their progeny would continue to engross historians.

* * *

Lord Melbourne suspected that Lehzen was instrumental in encouraging the queen to keep Albert away from state business. Indeed, as she herself was increasingly shelved, Lehzen was desperate to hang on to any authority she had with the queen.[7] She resented that Albert pushed a reconciliation between the queen and her mother. And Albert, wanting to assert his power, decided to get on with the job of getting rid of Lehzen. He labelled her the 'house dragon'.[8]

As time went on, Albert began to be shown state papers and was slowly able to take control of running the household. Lehzen had been doing it in a completely inefficient manner and the queen easily gave the responsibility to her husband. As the queen had more pregnancies, fatigued both before and after, Albert took over more and more. He pointed out ineffective measures in running the palace and even in the nursery and was able, by summer of 1842, to accomplish his goal. Lehzen ostensibly retired because of her health and left with a carriage and a small pension in September of that year to live in Hanover.

By this time, Victoria had had her second baby and the long sought-after boy was born. Prince Albert Edward was born 9 November 1841 to great celebration. The fact that 'Bertie' as he was called by the family proved to be completely unlike his father was a regret and disappointment to both parents. Albert adored his first daughter Vicky, and unfortunately for Bertie, she was bright and inquisitive, and her intelligence outshone all her subsequent siblings. Regrettably, Bertie always knew that his father wished Vicky had been a boy, and so the heir. As much as they absolutely avoided any comparison to their Hanoverian uncles, Victoria and Albert did appear take on one of their nastier traits – hating their heir. At least this is what it looked like to the outside world because of their constant criticism and obvious disappointment. His parents loved Bertie as best they could, but because of his lackadaisical attitude toward his studies, his short attention span, and his complete lack of curiosity, he would never quite compare to Vicky. What is more, Bertie was always aware of this.

Albert began to take over the duties of a private secretary to his wife and began to work strenuously on a program of education for their children. He wrote memoranda to his mentor and advisor Baron Stockmar about his thoughts on the subject. He wanted them to be well-educated and the queen agreed with this completely. He was particularly interested in the education of Bertie, and in this, though Albert was scrupulous and well-intentioned, he was hardly successful. The young prince rebelled against all the strict schedules that Albert made out for him and consequently was a constant source of despair for his father.

As well, Prince Albert was very interested in England as a constitutional monarchy and spreading those kinds of liberal ideas throughout Europe. In particular, they focused on the German states, which Stockmar and Albert felt would soon unify. Albert thought that the ideal would be the familial uniting of ruling families and that he could be instrumental in doing this through such marriages and alliances.

And speaking of politics, it was Albert who gentled Victoria enough to be reconciled with Robert Peel as her next prime minister. During Peel's ministry, Victoria replaced some of the Whig ladies of the bedchamber, also because of Albert's influence. In fact, during this secret negotiation,

Peel confided to Lord Greville that he was 'charmed with her'.[9] It appears that as the queen had taken on Lord M's politics, she would now take on her dear Albert's. It was at this time that she learned 'outward impartiality … towards her prime ministers'.[10]

So, after a time, Albert began to find his place in the labyrinthine royal household. And once he did, he never stopped working. Nevertheless, throughout his life in England he had to tread lightly as the consort of the queen. No one could manage to forget that he was a German and a foreigner. He talked of his loyalty to his old home, which may have fed these feelings.

Albert's goal of affecting a reconciliation between Victoria and the Duchess of Kent was ultimately quite successful. With Conroy gone, the duchess seemed happy in the role of doting grandmother. She truly loved her daughter and got along splendidly with Albert, who apparently loved his aunt. For the duchess it was as though all the conflict was just a bad dream from which she had now awoken. As for the queen, she wondered how she could have ever been alienated from her mother and blamed Lehzen.[11] This appeared typical of her responses to difficult situations. Once the dispute of whatever kind was mended, she seemed to forget that she had any part in the cause.

However, perhaps one of Albert's greatest contributions to the British Royal Family was his institution of middle-class virtues. He was uncomfortable with sophisticated society parties and occasions and much preferred his private life with his family and his work. So much so that some historians call him 'Albert the Good', which sounds, yes, priggish. And Victoria, who was conservative in her views on the role of women, followed his lead in this. She considered him the head of the household and she was the wife. Instilling those middle-class virtues is what many historians feel has preserved the monarchy into the twenty-first century.

Very important to the young and increasing family was to find a house of their own that they could retire for privacy and to get away from London life. They particularly liked the idea of a place by the sea, and they inspected several properties. However, it was the prime minister who found the property called Osborne House on the Isle of Wight. The royal couple paid for and owned Osborne privately and it would be the scene for much of their family life in spring and summer.

Albert and Victoria loved the area. They felt protected by the isolation of an island and adored the views overlooking the beautiful bay and The Solent. The Osborne house that exists today was built between 1845–1851 and designed by Prince Albert and architect Thomas Cubitt. Cubitt was famous for having developed Belgravia and the façade of Buckingham Palace. It was an Italianate structure built in the palazzo style with two belvedere towers and terraces, built in this style because it reminded Albert of the Bay of Naples. In 1853–4, a complete Swiss Cottage was taken apart and brought from Switzerland over to Osborne. It became a life-sized playhouse for his children where they could learn to cook and garden and understand how ordinary people lived.[12]

The couple also loved the Scottish Highlands. The queen more so since she was a great admirer of Sir Walter Scott and his novels. They had visited several times and eventually decided that they wanted a home there as well. The queen particularly liked the remoteness of the highlands. 'Not a house, not a creature near us, but the pretty Highland sheep with their horns and black faces.'[13]

In February 1848, Lord Aberdeen arranged for Prince Albert to take over the lease of Balmoral and the house was purchased in 1852. As in the case of Osborne, it was felt that a new and larger residence must be built there. The construction was completed in 1856 and, like Osborne, it is the property of the Royal Family. A young guest, the queen's grandson, Wilhelm of Prussia, present in the late 1870s, described the building as not lofty or large, but comfortably appointed. The highlands, he said, were wildly magnificent and the highlanders had a great sense of humour, unlike the English.[14] Though it was never a popular residence for the queen's household, Balmoral was the place that Victoria felt her happiest and freer than she did elsewhere.[15]

As noted above, in the following years Victoria and Albert's family increased with alarming regularity. Alarming because the queen hated to be pregnant and was notorious for not liking babies. It wasn't an observation from others, she said so herself. She thought they looked like frogs. As they grew and became little people, she was more loving, and seemed to have gotten over that original aversion with her grandchildren. It may, however, be unnecessary to say that she very much enjoyed the process that went into making babies, but was more dubious of the final product itself.

Victoria also grew to lean more on Albert and needed his support. Although they were both stubborn people and there were vociferous disagreements, she grew to depend on him more and more. In some ways, as historian Lucy Worsley suggests, she became a typical nineteenth-century wife. While this is certainly true, she was, in other ways, the opposite of what became known as Victorian.

During this time, male doctors and other social commentators talked about an idea called 'The Cult of True Womanhood or Domesticity'. This provided that the woman was to be the moral centre of the home. It was for her to teach religion and to furnish a secular education for her children. She was tasked with making the home a serene and private place for her husband as he tangled with the public industrial world.

In the royal household, it was Albert who supervised the education of their children. It was Albert who imposed his strict, middle-class morality on them, and it was Albert who directed the running of the household. So, in some ways, Victoria and Albert were turning these theories on their heads. Both took private as well as public roles.

Publicly however, Albert was also a progressive and a reformer. Early in his marriage, he became the President of the Society for the Extinction of Slavery and took on other roles as time went on. In 1847, he was elected Chancellor of the University of Cambridge. He wished to modernise the so-called 'Oxbridge' system and bring it into the nineteenth century. He was interested in revising the curricula for the times and wanted what were considered contemporary subjects, such as history, economics, and modern languages.[16]

* * *

1848 was a fraught year.

Europe was breaking out in revolutions in France, in Hungary and in the Kingdom of the Two Sicilies, due to widespread economic problems. Britain, too, was at the height of its working-class Chartist moment with a 'Great Meeting' at Kennington Common, London, calling for political reform (i.e., one man one vote and the secret ballot, as well as other demands). It was also the year of the great potato famine in Ireland that killed millions, with millions more emigrating.

Though these varied demonstrations were mostly democratic and liberal in nature, England and her monarch were able to avoid the brunt of them because of the repeal of 'Corn Laws' and only sporadic support of revolution. As well, the Chartists were starting to lose support.

Albert, as president of the Society for Improving the Conditions of the Labouring Classes, made a speech that took the approach that the rich were the benefactors of the poor. Much like Andrew Carnegie's Gospel of Wealth, which felt that it was the responsibility of the rich to care for the impoverished, Prince Albert felt that it was up to the highest to take care of those who 'have most of the toil and fewest of the enjoyments of this world'.[17]

It should be noted that though Albert dedicated his life to Great Britain, he would always remain a German at heart and cared deeply about its future. He saw a Germany united and allied with Great Britain in constitutional governance – and he saw Britain as the example that Germany should follow. This would certainly influence his choice in his favourite daughter's mate.

Probably the crowning achievement of Albert's life was the Great Exhibition at the Crystal Palace in 1851. This was the precursor to the World's Fairs that would take place at intervals for years after. It was here that civilisations from everywhere on the known globe could exhibit science, technology and the best of their achievements and cultures. Prince Albert was the prime mover of getting this exhibition off the ground; he was a man who believed firmly in science and technology.

In early 1850, fundraising began for the endeavour, and in March the prince made a speech in London at a banquet given by the Lord Mayor in which he stated how pleased he was that his 'suggestion' was received with such gratifying results. There were many bumps along the way, not the least of which were the complaints about where the exhibition would take place – which was the south-east corner of Hyde Park. There were many nay-sayers who said it would be a failure, but it was not. What it showed at the time was the ingenuity and greatness of the British Empire. That she, at that time, was the most wealthy, advanced and powerful country on earth.

A beautiful steel and glass edifice, designed by Joseph Paxton, housed nearly 1,300 exhibits. The royal family as a group visited three times and the queen many more. The opening was 1 May 1851, and the queen,

Prince Albert, their two eldest children, Vicky and Bertie, as well as nearly half-a-million spectators witnessed the great event.[18] Victoria described it as one of the wonders of the world. Many said it was as Prince Albert intended, a celebration of peace.

* * *

The birth of their youngest son Leopold in 1853 was momentous for two reasons. It was the first time that the queen accepted chloroform to ease her delivery and second, after a time, it was determined that Leopold suffered from haemophilia. Although it was puzzling to the royal couple that he was born with this congenital disease, there are several theories. It could have been a gene that simply mutated in the queen, or, that it was simply not detected or known in little boys who had died as infants or toddlers in previous generations. Some historians have even postulated that since Victoria passed down such a gene that hadn't been visible in the royal family before, she might have been illegitimate, or Albert might have been illegitimate. This, however, appears to be extremely far-fetched.

Whatever it was, Leopold managed to grow up with the disease, marry and have children. Two of his sisters, Alice, and Beatrice, who was the last of the couple's children born in 1857, were carriers who passed it down to their sons and daughters. Since Louise was childless, it isn't known if she had the gene.

* * *

From October 1853 to March 1856, Victoria had to deal with something she, thankfully, did not have to deal with most of her reign – war. The Napoleonic Wars ended in 1815, and the Boer wars came at the tail end of the century. The Crimean wars, which started over the stewardship of religious places in the Ottoman region of Palestine, had grown into a conflict between Russia and Britain, France, the Ottoman Empire and Sardinia. The war was won by Britain and its allies, but ineptly prosecuted by them. Moreover, most of the casualties of the war were from disease and wounds rather than actual battle casualties. William Howard Russell made his reputation reporting this war for *The Times* of London and its 'utter incompetence'. This reporting contributed to the fall of Lord

Aberdeen's (the prime minister at that time) government. It was also avidly followed by the queen who encouraged and heartened the troops as much as possible. Parenthetically, it was Russell's reporting that encouraged the indefatigable Florence Nightingale to organise a band of nurses to go to Scutari Barracks in Turkey to nurse the sick and wounded. Victoria was clearly in awe of Miss Nightingale and would receive her later.

* * *

Albert continued his program of overwork. By the late 1840s into the 1850s he had lost his youthful beauty. He'd begun to lose his hair and his figure was not as slim as it had been. He had aged prematurely even for those days, and as mentioned he was never as robust and strong as the queen. Though, in appreciation for all he had done for her and the country, the queen made him officially the Prince Consort in June 1857; nevertheless, he suffered from depression, chills, fevers, stomach ailments and was known to be something of a hypochondriac.

Vicky, however, continued to be an endless source of great pride for him. The prince was extremely close to this child who had a great thirst for learning and never seemed to fail him. During the Great Exhibition, when Vicky was barely 11, she met her husband-to-be. Prince William of Prussia and his wife, Princess Augusta of Saxe-Weimar-Eisenach were among the visitors to this great showcase and they brought their son, Friedrich, called 'Fritz' in the family, who was nearly 20. Nevertheless, the two youngsters were attracted to one another, and began to correspond. Vicky was 'a fresh-faced little girl with sparkling blue-green eyes, completely unselfconscious, and full of a bubbling vitality'.[19] The queen and Prince Albert heartily approved of this handsome young man whom they saw as having much more liberal views than the typical Prussians.

Their next encounter was in 1855 when Vicky was 15 and Fritz 24. The pleasure they took in each other's company had not diminished and Fritz was emboldened to ask the queen about 'belonging to our family'.[20] Fritz admired what he thought was the informality of the British Royal Family in contrast to his strict Prussian one. The idea of belonging to such a family was extremely attractive.

The young suitor was told he would have to wait for Vicky to turn 17, but the couple were engaged in September 1856. Albert saw this engagement as a great step forward in his goal of uniting Europe through liberal monarchies. Likewise, Uncle Leopold certainly approved. It has been suggested that he had this idea very early on when Vicky was only 6.[21] The prince took this opportunity to instruct his daughter on the history of Germany as well as continuing to imbue her with his liberal principles and ideas of a constitutional government.

The young couple were married in January 1858, when Vicky was 17 and Fritz 26. Though Vicky was quite young to be married, she seemed to have no doubts about her husband. She was described as '[a]ll life and spirit, full of frolic and fun, with an excellent head, and a heart as big as a mountain'.[22] Their life together would be happy, but Vicky would have great difficulties with her in-laws and the stiff court at Potsdam and Berlin.

When she left, the prince consort felt her absence deeply. She had been his confidante, intellectual equal and she had a temperament he understood – unlike his wife's. However, Vicky did present the queen and Albert with their first grandchild the following year in January 1859. He was Friedrich Wilhelm Victor Albert, later to be Kaiser Wilhelm II. The forceps birth had been extremely difficult, and the child was born with a withered left arm which he spent his life hiding. This made him feel resentful and secretly inferior and made his mother feel extraordinarily guilty. Their relationship, therefore, was always problematic. Ironically, one of the assisting physicians was the incompetent James Clark.

With Vicky gone, the problem of their eldest son, Bertie, became more apparent. Not the student that Vicky was, he did not thrive when put through his educational paces. Instead, he was bored, distracted and continued to frustrate his tutors and his parents who always let him know this in no uncertain terms. In 1859, the young Prince of Wales reached his eighteenth birthday and had a lengthy continental tour in the charge of a governor, Colonel Robert Bruce, and Albert's private secretary, Captain Charles Grey. More beneficial for the young man was a tour he made of Canada and the United States in 1860. Beneficial because wherever he went, he was received with excitement and great affection despite America's being independent for less than one hundred years. Everywhere he went he was cheered with abandon. Even New Yorkers, jaded as they were even then, showed up in the multitudes to hail the young man.

New Yorkers were so impressed that a great ball was given in his honour on 12 October 1860. The event had so many gatecrashers that the floor of the building collapsed. Luckily no one was seriously hurt.[23] Despite his parents' doubts, the young prince was a royal celebrity on an international scale.

In the beginning of 1861, Bertie began a short period at Trinity College, Cambridge. And like a typical college student, he smoked, he drank and he caroused. However, the heir to the throne and the son of Prince Albert was not supposed to do these things; it was offensive to Albert's straitlaced sense of morality. There were constant letters back and forth about how Bertie must comport himself in a more 'manly' way.

By then, another royal marriage was in the offing. At the end of 1860, Alice, Queen Victoria's second daughter and third child, became engaged to the Hereditary Prince Ludwig of Hesse and by Rhine. Alice was 17 when Uncle Leopold had brought the young man with him to attend Ascot that year. Ludwig was tall and handsome and greatly attracted to Alice – he proposed, and she accepted.

Alice was a complex and intelligent young woman with a profound social conscience who would inherit many of her father's characteristics. That is, the tendency to overwork, being intellectually curious, striving towards social reform and ignoring the ravages of her own body when tending to her family. During the time of what would eventually become Albert's final illness, she would oversee nursing him and try her best to help her mother bear the emotional burden.

There was bad news in the beginning of 1861. The poor Duchess of Kent, who had for the decades of Victoria's marriage, finally been in her daughter's good graces, was now gravely ill. She had erysipelas and cancer and was in extreme pain. Despite a short operation the duchess did not rally and died on 16 March. Victoria was, of course, grief-stricken. After sorting through her mother's papers, she once again felt guilt and anger about what she considered the perfidy of Conroy and the jealousy of Lehzen. She blamed them for keeping mother and daughter apart.

Consequently, Victoria was in a state of emotional and mental paralysis and while her daughter, Alice tried to take care of her, Albert took on more and more of her duties. His demise, a man who was worn with work, depression, and a weakened state of health, may have been helped along by yet another event – a transgression by Bertie which some saw as his first love affair, or at any rate a young man sowing his wild oats. Others, however, would see him as falling into a moral decline – among them, his parents.

Bertie was serving at Curragh Camp in Ireland in the Second Battalion. As in the education of most princes, service in the military was thought to be the ideal. For a joke, his fellow officers smuggled the actress Nellie Clifden into the young prince's bed one night and the rest, as they say, was nature taking its course. Back at Cambridge, Bertie had certainly not told his parents about the adventure, but apparently Nellie, who was proud of the conquest, was not so discreet. In fact, she told it far and wide; so much so that it became gossip on the continent and from there got back to his very shocked parents.

The prince consort felt it was his duty to reprimand his son and letters went back and forth between the worried parent and the repentant son. Albert caught cold and was suffering from rheumatism, insomnia and the anxiety and worry that his eldest son caused him. Though forgiven, Albert found it necessary to rebuke his son in person and went up to Cambridge at the end of November 1861. They walked and talked about the failure in judgement and the real issue of Bertie's marrying before it was too late. Beside a cold and his mental agonies, Albert was possibly suffering the beginnings of typhoid.

Putting aside Bertie's moral transgressions, there were other matters clearly troubling the prince. In international affairs, he had become entangled with what would be known as the *Trent* Affair. The United States had been embroiled in a bloody and catastrophic civil war since April 1861. The Confederacy, because of the massive amount of cotton it supplied to France and England felt it could win if either of those countries would give her aid and diplomatic recognition. In November 1861 Jefferson Davis, the President of the Confederate States of America, sent several commissioners to London in the hope of getting the needed help. They had been aboard the British Mail Packet *Trent* bound for Britain, but the USS *San Jacinto*, commanded by Captain Charles Wilkes, intercepted the ship and removed the Southern commissioners.

This enflamed all parties on both sides of the Atlantic, to the point that war was possible and a stern ultimatum was issued to let the envoys be on their way. This was a close shave and caused a severe diplomatic crisis between the United States and Britain. Lord Palmerston, the prime minister at the time, called for a meeting of the cabinet. Britain made the following demands: reparations, the immediate release of the prisoners and a formal apology. It was pure chance that the Transatlantic telegraph cable was not working, and only worked sporadically for nearly ten years thereafter.[24]

After some manoeuvring, the prince consort got involved. He was able to suggest softening the language of a telegram that was ultimately sent from the British government to the Lincoln administration. Lincoln, who certainly did not want to risk war with the most powerful navy on earth, released the Southerners and issued a public apology without either country losing face. It was a masterly strategy which Albert accomplished on what would be his death bed.

There was one more thing that Albert was determined to do despite his failing health, and that was to begin the hunt for a suitable bride for Bertie. As we have seen, there were many legal requirements for a suitable spouse and Albert and Victoria realised in Bertie's case there would have to be several more. The young lady would need to be pretty to keep Bertie's roving eye in check, and she would need to provide stability. As historian Gordon Brook-Shepherd said, it was as though they were looking for a Protestant beauty queen and not just a Princess of Wales.[25] The parents looked at the various royal houses in Europe and enlisted the help of young Vicky, now the Crown Princess of Prussia. They looked at Princess Elizabeth of Wied, but it was thought she was too dowdy. How about Princess Hilda of Dessau or Princess Marie of the Netherlands, or even Princess Alexandrina of Prussia? But no! Either they were too delicate, not pretty enough, too slow witted, etc.

Vicky, who handled the duty as the other members of the family looked after the failing Prince Albert, had found one that was most certainly pretty enough: Her Royal Highness, Princess Alexandra of Denmark. Yes, Vicky would insist, she is the one and Bertie must not lose the chance at such a pearl. It is interesting that Vicky pushed for Alexandra when Prussia and Denmark were at each other's throats over the Schleswig-Holstein question,[26] but Vicky knew her brother and thought he would find the lovely Alexandra more to his taste than the young ladies of Wied, Dessau and even Prussia. However, that would have to wait.

Albert continued to be greatly saddened by his son's behaviour and was sure he, Bertie, was going down the same road that Albert's own brother Ernst had gone – or even one of the wicked Hanoverian uncles. The queen who wanted to agree with Albert in all things agreed with this. As December 1861 approached Albert was getting weaker and weaker and continued to push himself harder and harder coping with Bertie, the *Trent* Affair and other state business.

He muttered many times that if he became ill, he would not have the will or desire to fight. During this time, he was also sleepless with worry which of course complicated his condition. He ate little, he was feverish and even at times delirious. His doctor, Sir William Jenner, diagnosed typhoid fever, though more modern forensic diagnoses are possibly stomach cancer or Crohn's Disease.

He deteriorated rapidly with only brandy to sedate him. On 14 December 1861 with Victoria, Bertie, Alice, Helena, Louise and Arthur about his bed, he breathed his last late that evening. Victoria, hysterical, had to be led from the room.

Part II

Widowhood

Introduction

...and so, now we come to her long widowhood and the questions are many.

When Albert died, Victoria lamented that there was no one left to call her 'Victoria'. Were there men in this lengthy second half of her life and reign? Her husband gone, Lehzen gone, her mother gone, Stockmar gone in 1863, and Uncle Leopold gone in 1865. Did the queen seek to replace them?

Who would help her deal with prime ministers as Albert had done? The household? Who would deal with her nine children and forty-two grandchildren and their various and sometimes troublesome spouses? Who would be the man about the house, counsel her and lend support?

Most important, why didn't he fight?

To this last, she would never find a satisfactory answer.

However, she would spend her life memorialising him in every way possible. She would note his death day *every* year in her journal. There would be an Albert Memorial, an Albert Hall, there would be a multi-volume biography mostly written by Victoria, there would be compilations of speeches, and the poet laureate, Alfred Tennyson would compose a eulogy for Albert in a new edition of his poem *The Idylls of the King*.[1]

But what would she do without him? As it turns out, quite a lot.

Chapter Four

'My dreadful & overwhelming calamity....'[1]

Victoria's grief overwhelmed her so completely that for several weeks she was unable to write in her journal. She truly believed that her 'life as a happy one is ended!'[2] She was 42 years old and a widow and though she began writing again in the new year, trying to describe what life was without her 'beloved one' was difficult and highly emotional for her. Each entry was an agonised exclamation of her sadness, but even so each one had the unavoidable daily business. Perhaps she wasn't even aware that life went on, even if the colour and beauty were absent for her. She was fortunate to be surrounded by family and close friends, and she went through the motions, and made little effort to take solace; mostly, she felt bereft.

Albert was laid to rest with all due ceremony nine days after his death, but the queen was too grief stricken to attend. Bertie, who she had initially blamed for his death, was the chief mourner. The prince was interred in St George's Chapel at Windsor and later permanently so at Frogmore Mausoleum.[3] The queen gave orders that his room should remain the same, that his shaving water should be laid out, his linens changed daily, and his clothes should be put out as though he had just stepped out for a moment. This carried on until Victoria's death. She slept with his nightshirt in her arms, she knelt at his side of the bed before going to sleep and mourned him deeply for the rest of her life. Oddly, the room was used by Victoria for audiences, and this became extremely unnerving for some of her ministers.[4]

At this point, she remained lost, shocked, highly depressed, and moving like a sleepwalker. People commented on her self-possession during this calamitous time, but others observed that she was so composed because she just didn't take it in. The queen stopped making public appearances for state or social occasions and she rarely met with her cabinet and refused to open parliament. Later she would have to be persuaded to show herself to the people and prime minister, Benjamin Disraeli, and some members of her household may be credited for cajoling her out of her isolation, but that was after six long years of mourning in virtual seclusion.

Albert had been the lynchpin of her life. He had been everything to her: her husband, her private secretary, her guide, her educator, even her stylist. He had advised her and helped her choose hats and dresses as well as designing jewellery for her.

But even as she suffered the paralysis of sorrow, life did go on, though she hated the thought of it without Albert. She wrote at the time that nothing would ever be the same. She thought this for the remaining forty years of her life, although life did improve. However, no event went by without Victoria writing that she longed for Albert to be there. Perhaps nothing ever had the savour it might have had. On her Golden Jubilee twenty-six years later, she wrote that though surrounded by family, she was alone. The feeling that an entire world was lost would persist. However, despite what she wrote, eventually she would take pleasure in her family, her friendships, her queenship and her life again.

She was comforted by the presence of Uncle Leopold who rushed to her side after Albert's death. He wrote in the most affectionate terms that he would 'devote myself, with the faithful affection I have borne you from the first days of your existence, to be of use to you'.[5]

Most fortunate for her during this dreadful time was the presence of her beloved second daughter Alice, who had been her father's nurse and was now the queen's caretaker. The young woman shielded her mother as much as possible from cabinet meetings and petty annoyances that Victoria simply couldn't face. Alice even attended to her own wedding arrangements that had initially been started by Albert.

Fulfilling *his* wishes provided immediate consolation and distraction for the queen, so the wedding preparations continued. Since Victoria felt that weddings were solemn occasions, she saw no difficulty in having them and attending them while in her deep mourning. She was joined in this determination by Alice, who wanted to honour her father in thought and deed in all things.

Victoria, who was convinced the shadow of death was following the family, wrote that Alice's wedding would be horribly 'gloomy'. And her wedding on 1 July 1862 was an almost funereal occasion. Though the day was sunny and warm, Alice's brothers and sisters were weeping copiously throughout the ceremony – and not from the sentimentality of a wedding, but because of absent papa. Victoria, too, sobbed the entire time, though she thoughtfully sat away from the rest of the attendees so her face would not be seen. She wrote, perhaps disingenuously: 'It was a terrible moment for me … I restrained my tears, and had a great struggle all through, but remained calm.'[6]

Alice had been such a valuable daughter and while the couple were on their honeymoon, Victoria made plans of her own. Alice would have all her babies in England since Victoria mistrusted German physicians after the sad debacle of Wilhelm's birth. She also felt that since Ludwig was the heir and not the reigning Grand Duke, the couple would be able to spend most of their time with her, and little Hessians as well, when they came at intervals. Why, it would hardly seem as though anything had changed. In this, she was destined to be disappointed. Though immensely caring, Alice was ultimately a strong and determined figure who would build a life for herself and her family in Darmstadt. The queen would be extremely angry at Alice about this, thinking her selfish, unfeeling and impressed by her own position. Alice was hardly that – she was just individuating, an opportunity her younger sisters would struggle to have.

Victoria would not have been perceived at that time as a controlling and smothering mother. It was, in fact, completely natural, especially in upper- and middle-class families with a comfortable number of children, that one or two daughters would remain unmarried and stay home with the parents. This, for the obvious reasons of companionship and the duty of caring for them in their old age. The queen was no exception and looked forward to the thought that she had no end of useful daughters. If not Alice, then Helena – if not Helena then Louise – and so on. Eventually, it would be Helena, who practically lived with the queen when she married and the 'Benjamina' (the youngest) of her brood, Beatrice, who *did* live with her that would perform this duty.

It may seem odd that the queen needed this companionship since she had a sufficient household. That household included women who had served her in various capacities for decades, women who were in close and constant attendance, whom today we might even call 'best friends'. Her household was comprised of a hierarchy of women from Duchesses who served as Mistress of the Robes and wives of peers who served as Ladies of the Bedchamber, to daughters of peers who served as Women of the

Bedchamber. These women did not live constantly with the queen but had periods of 'waits', three or four times a year lasting two to four weeks. The queen was never without adequate company.

After the death of Albert, Victoria handed more and more of the administrative duties to various ladies of her household instead of doing them herself. She wanted intermediaries between herself and the outside world and used many in her household as messengers so she wouldn't have to deal with anything the least disturbing or controversial. Two key women, who might serve in the 'best friend' category seem the most significant. Both were Ladies of the Bedchamber: Jane Spencer, Baroness Churchill, and Jane Loftus, Baroness Ely. Both women were with the queen for over forty years and served as caretakers when she was in her deepest sorrow and were both trusted friends and confidantes.

Jane Churchill was the daughter of the Earl of Conyngham (one of the gentlemen who had come to the teenaged Victoria that fateful morning to inform her that she was now queen) and married to Francis Spencer, 2nd Baron Churchill. The Baron's father was the youngest son of George, 3rd Duke of Marlborough. She was considered discreet and had a great deal of common sense. She always put the queen's interests first and never dabbled in politics. One of her duties was to be the 'eyes and ears' of the queen, when the queen could not be present. Her reports were especially valuable to Victoria after the marriages of her elder daughters. Jane was despatched with Vicky and later Alice to make such reports through letters and later detailed conversations about each young woman's situation in their new courts.

Victoria wrote that when Lady Churchill accompanied Vicky to Berlin, she wrote daily and returned with 'every possible detail'. The Baroness described life at the palace in Berlin as extremely uncomfortable but could not speak enough about Vicky's happiness her 'success, & her admirable reception'.[7] The sad fact was that Vicky didn't do that well in the court of Berlin. She was highly intelligent, but completely tactless. She spoke directly with her in-laws, the old Kaiser and his wife, on myriad of matters without much thought of how such directness and clarity would be perceived. As a result, she was treated poorly by them, by the Chancellor von Bismarck and later by her three eldest children who were under the influence of the older pair and Bismarck. Many in the Prussian court resentfully called her '*die Engländerin*' (the Englishwoman). That she loved Germany with all her heart made no difference to the populace at large. Her son would say of her, 'She was always most German in England and most English in Germany.' Therein lay the problem.[8]

When Alice married, Baroness Churchill accompanied her to Darmstadt. Jane gave the queen a 'long account of everything. In general, it was satisfactory, but the improper tone of many as to her remaining much in England with me was much to be deplored'.[9] We can interpret that to mean that Alice was determined to make her mark in Darmstadt and not be in constant attendance on her mother, and she did. Alice would become a true *'Landsmütter'* ('Mother of her Country') to her subjects in Hesse.

Lady Ely was Jane Loftus, Marchioness of Ely. She was the daughter of James Hope-Vere and the wife of John Loftus, 3rd Marquess of Ely. Not only was she invaluable to the queen, but she developed strong relationships with others in the court as well, for example, Victoria's beloved friend the Empress Eugénie. At the time of her service, she was already a widow and during the aftermath of the prince's death, Victoria looked more to her for solace than Lady Churchill as she felt she would better understand.

Nevertheless, both Lady Ely and Lady Churchill were afraid of the queen. Lady Churchill was able to hide this, but apparently, the queen could bully Lady Ely 'mercilessly'.[10] Some thought Lady Ely had a want of dignity and tact and had 'neither specialised knowledge nor particular discretion for so important a role'.[11] She was nervous and injudicious and had an odd habit of whispering messages from the queen to others that usually resulted in misunderstandings. However, the queen relied on her deeply – she was loyal, devoted, and a tremendously hard worker.

Beatrice, Victoria's last child with Albert, whom she called 'Baby', was also one of Victoria's closest companions in grief. According to David Duff, one of Beatrice's biographers, the night that Albert died, the queen grabbed Beatrice from her cot and brought her to bed with her.[12] Whether things precisely unfolded this way, that night was the beginning of a dependence that would last the rest of the queen's life. Beatrice would always be with her, always be the useful daughter, even to the detriment of her own husband and children, and in the end would oversee her legacy.

But for now, she was the only one who could lift the queen's spirits even a little. Beatrice was a bright, good-tempered but bold baby. She said things that none of the other children would have dared to say and got no reprimand, but a chuckle from her parents. When Albert died, the doctors felt that Victoria should be with Beatrice as much as possible since she cheered her up.

* * *

The next wish of Albert's heart was to get the recalcitrant Prince of Wales married. As mentioned, the queen blamed Bertie for the death of his father, feeling that Albert should never have travelled to speak with or deliver reprimands to Bertie in a rainstorm at the height of winter. She was sure that the exacerbation of her consort's condition was because of this. She might have forgiven Bertie for this in the long run, but she never forgot it. She felt that he 'broke Papa's heart'[13] with his want of rectitude. Bertie, in his mother's eyes, was not Albert and never would be. Bertie did not have his moral character and would be a libertine who lived for pleasure, and as she wrote, reclined with a cigar in his mouth.

As for marriage, the young prince had been favourably if not enthusiastically impressed by Princess Alexandra of Denmark during a meeting that was engineered by Vicky. The couple were to meet at a cathedral in Speyer, Germany – she with her parents, and he with Vicky. He wrote to his mother describing her pretty face and her vivacious manners, but Victoria's impression was that he 'seemed nervous about deciding anything yet'.[14]

Bertie, at 20, was hesitant to marry and felt he was too young to have a family. This reluctance was quite admirable since he evidently knew himself better than his mother did. However, at that point he could not face the juggernaut of parental disapproval once again. In February 1862, after Albert's death, Victoria sent Bertie on a trip to the Middle East. It has been suggested that she sent him because she simply couldn't look at him and was disgusted by him. However, when he returned, he was more sanguine about the possibility of matrimony and even stopped in Paris to buy Alexandra some trinkets.

All that remained, then, was for the queen to meet the young lady in question. After the queen made a sad pilgrimage, accompanied by Bertie, to Coburg in September 1862 she proceeded on to Laeken in Belgium. The visit was ostensibly to see dear Uncle Leopold, but the queen also met with young Alexandra's parents, Prince and Princess Christian of Denmark, and 'Alix', as she was called in the family. Alix made an excellent impression on the queen. She wrote in her journal that she was 'lovely, such a beautiful refined profile, & quiet lady like manner, which made a most favourable impression'.[15] Bertie proposed and was accepted during that trip.

The couple were married on 10 March 1863 at St George's Chapel at Windsor. The queen's journal is full of her misery and suffering during that day. Why? Principally because, again, Albert was not there, and he was all she thought about that day. Though not stated in her journal entry, Victoria's other constant fear was the uncertainties of marriages in general. She felt it more for her daughters than her sons, but she always believed that one never knew how such unions would turn out.

As she had done during Alice's wedding, the queen watched from a private vantage point and welcomed the couple back to Windsor for luncheon. She wrote affectionately about her son and new daughter-in-law and capped off the day visiting Albert at the mausoleum which seemed to have the effect of calming and soothing her.

Alice had been heavily pregnant by the time of Bertie's wedding and gave birth to her first child just under a month later. According to her mother's wishes, she gave birth in the Tapestry Room at Windsor. Alice was delivered of a girl named, as all the grandchildren would be, after their grandparents. In this case it was Victoria Alberta Elizabeth, born 5 April 1863.

The queen was quite repelled by the fact that Alice breast-fed her new daughter. She thought it animalistic and repulsive. However, her new granddaughter would be one of her favourite grandchildren and later a trusted confidante. Little Victoria (who curiously never had a nickname in the family) would be among the early group of grandchildren born in the fifties and sixties. The queen, however, would continue having grandchildren into the nineties, even after the birth of her first great-grandchild.

Alix and Bertie did something that the queen and Albert had not done – they became leaders of society and as such they went to parties, balls and 'drawing-rooms'.[16] Alix began to draw a great deal of criticism from the queen for not being as bright and clever as had been hoped. Victoria worried that because she wasn't an intellectual, she wouldn't be able to hold Bertie, which in the long run she didn't. It should be pointed out, however, that this had nothing to do with Alix's intellectual gifts or lack thereof. Bertie was, and continued to be, a notorious womaniser who was deathly afraid of boredom above all things.

The queen also worried about Alix's health because amid the glittering excitement of the London season, the young princess very satisfactorily became pregnant almost right away. Another addition to the family came in January 1864 with the birth of another heir, Albert Victor, known in the family as 'Eddy'. He was premature and the queen blamed his precipitous birth on Alix's social life.

* * *

Soon after the death of the prince consort, the doctors, who were flailing in their attempts to pull the queen out of her anguish, hit on a solution that ameliorated her unhappiness. In 1864, Dr Jenner requested that Victoria's Scottish ghillie, John Brown, be brought to Osborne. For an extended period, Victoria kept to her two private residences, Osborne, and Balmoral. As a consequence, there were various rumours that the queen had gone mad and hysterical with grief. The doctors fumbled around for something to bring her out of her extreme sorrow and realised a partial answer was in front of them. Beatrice helped a bit with her babyish antics, but it was Brown, who had been Albert's ghillie at Balmoral from 1851 onward, and who was now promoted to be the queen's special servant and attendant, who seemed to comfort her.

Brown was the son of a farmer at Craithie, Scotland, and at the age of 23, came to Balmoral in 1849. He was strong, devoted, highly moral and treated the queen like a 'regular' person, to which, for some reason, she responded. He led her around on a pony quite often when Albert was alive and spoke very frankly and sternly to Vicky and Bertie when they were children. This contributed to the early resentment Victoria's children had for the Scotsman that would fester until his death. Brown, who had seen all the queen's children growing up, was used to liberties not taken by others in her retinue. The girls were able to laugh it off for the most part, but Alfred, called 'Affie' in the family, Leopold, and Bertie especially, felt free to be rude to Brown, whom they thought constantly overstepped.

To most, he was plain-spoken or brusque, ill-mannered, over-bearing and frequently drunk. He was said to take high commissions from tradesmen and take advantage of his influence with Victoria. To the queen, however, he was kind, solicitous and even chivalrous if the occasion demanded. Dr Jenner was convinced that he would cheer her up, and from then onward Brown was called the Queen's Highland Servant attending her not only outside, but indoors.

She wrote to her Uncle Leopold: 'Have *now* appointed that excellent Highland servant of mine to attend me always ... so unlike an ordinary servant and so cheerful and attentive.'[17] Brown had started out at Balmoral leading her around on a pony, but from her widowhood on, he became 'her shadow'.[18] He attended her everywhere she went, standing behind her chair at meals, at her carriage or on any journeys she took.

For Victoria, here was a man she could rely on, who would support her no matter what. She, in turn, would become his defender against all who would denigrate him out of jealousy or resentment – and many did. He appealed to her because of his highland simplicity – it reminded her of the relatively simple upper-middle-class households she kept with Albert at their private homes. She wrote, 'I like having ... good honest souls near me, who were so constantly with Albert.'[19] Here was another person who could lift the queen's spirits and was utterly devoted to her.

To give an idea how formality and hierarchy was more relaxed in the Highlands, Osborne, or the places where the queen felt most at home and perhaps closer to the days with Albert, one of Victoria's Ladies of the Bedchamber, Lady Charlotte Canning, told a new maid-of-honour: 'You will be delighted with your waiting at Balmoral or Osborne. You will see the Queen intimately, riding, dancing, playing, dining.'[20] But she went on to warn the novice that such intimacy would not be tolerated at Buckingham Palace or, for that matter, Windsor.

This was never the case for the man who freely called her a 'widow woman', or 'wummin' in his Scottish accent, to her face or entered her room without knocking. Many were angry or at least bemused at the liberties he took with the queen. Despite his high-minded principles, he would often come into Victoria's presence smelling like a brewery and might be found dead drunk and unable to accompany the queen on her drives.[21] For him, there seemed to be no walls of separation no matter where the court happened to be.

So many adjectives were used to describe Brown throughout her journals: good, loyal, honest, dependable, calm and what is seen is that as the years went by, he became her right-hand man. The queen constantly mentions him and he seems to be always with her, following her, in the box of the carriage with her. It must be noted that this seemingly intimate behaviour gave rise to gossip and rumour.

One historian takes the strong stance that Victoria was in love with him. Julia Baird perceives this as a love quite different than the one she had with Albert. With Albert she was always the worshipful pupil, but with Brown she was treated like a woman and not a queen.[22] There were even whispers that she had secretly married him, and she was sometimes called 'Mrs Brown' in the more exploitive 'rags' of the day. It was simply that he was a tall handsome man who was a comfort to her and with whom she felt contented. Most feel that though this relationship was close, it was most certainly platonic and any other thinking was inappropriate. The queen thought of him as a close and devoted friend.

So many disliked Brown or mocked him, but he did a service to the country by bringing Victoria out of her heartache and into life once again. His companionship and deep friendship in those last years of the 1860s lessened her sorrow enough that she worried about it and consulted with Gerald Wellesley, the Dean of Windsor. He advised the queen that there was nothing to be ashamed of and that it was all quite natural. She, however, would nevertheless feel guilty and undutiful that she was coming out of her deep morass of mourning.

* * *

It was a good thing though, as by this time, her people were getting restive. They wanted the queen to show herself on a regular basis once again. A few years was understandable, but even the Victorians, who made such a ritual of mourning, thought the queen's nine years of isolation excessive. She worked as hard as she ever did, but refused to take her place in society or in the public as she had done before widowhood. She would often not be seen for days except by her household and thought it was utterly inhuman that people expected otherwise. When urged to come out of her mourning by her children or her household, she would say it was not grief that kept her isolated but her workload.

She was begged to open parliament and said 'no' until finally in 1865 she at last said 'yes' to Lord John Russell. He was a member of the Whig party and had been her prime minster from 1846–1852, and later from October 1865 – June 1866. She protested, asking why would anyone want to see such a poor, broken and unhappy widow open parliament? But of course, she must have known in her heart that the people longed to see her.

So, on 6 February 1866, the queen appeared publicly to open parliament. She was extremely nervous, but was accompanied by Helena, or 'Lenchen' as she was called in the family, and Louise as well as Bertie and young Arthur. Her motivation, however, was twofold. She wanted an annuity for Affie who was turning 21 and about to be created Duke of Edinburgh, and to have parliament grant a dowry to Lenchen, who was to marry.

* * *

Victoria's travel schedule also began to solidify during those middle years of the sixties. She and her entire household spent Christmas at Osborne and went at least twice a year, including the end of summer, to Balmoral in Scotland. Initially, she went back to Osborne in the spring, but in later years, as her rheumatism bothered her more and more, she sought warmer places abroad.

She especially loved Florence and the French Riviera and holidayed in France most often during the last decade of her life. She and her household could be seen in Menton, Grasse, Hyères, and in Cimiez away from the city centre of Nice. In the late 1890s her last visits in the Riviera were spent in a hotel that been built especially with her in mind. The Hotel Excelsior Régina in Cimiez began construction in 1895 and was completed in 1897. The building is a fine example of the architecture of the Belle Epoque. After its completion, she stayed there, and came with a staff of over 100 people, which included her chef, her household, a dentist – and her own bed. Today there is a statue of the queen in the gardens.

Buckingham Palace was not a regular part of the routine, but she did spend some time there, usually when her attendance was required at a major event such as weddings or her jubilees, or even 'drawing rooms', when debutantes were presented. Her time at Windsor filled in the other bits of the year and usually it was there that she spent the sad anniversary of Albert's death.[23] She called Windsor Castle, poor sad old Windsor, but it was her home.

* * *

While Victoria's popularity was plummeting after Albert's death, her family continued to grow with the births of more grandchildren. Alice delivered another girl, 1 November 1864, this time in Bessungen, Darmstadt, at the Hessian family home where the doctors seemed competent enough. She was called Elisabeth Alexandra Louise Alice – the Elisabeth after her paternal grandmother. She was destined to become a grand duchess of Russia. Nearer to home was the birth of another boy for Alix and Bertie. George Frederick Ernest Albert was born at Marlborough House on 3 June 1865. He, too, was premature by a month. Interesting that Bertie's brother Affie said that the baby was on time. One wonders if Victoria, who wished to attend the births of her grandchildren, was told different dates so that she would miss the occasion. Was this something that Bertie would do to his mother who had only begun to soften her stance against him?

Later that month, the queen wrote to Bertie that she was not exactly happy about the name that the baby was given. 'George only came over with the Hanoverian family.'[24] Frederick was better, she thought, but not what she would have desired. That she mentions this shows how much she desired to distance her family with her Hanoverian predecessors. She further expressed the hope that the baby would be good and wise and thus not live up or down to the previous Georges. Luckily, as would be with all the grandchildren, he had 'Albert' in his names.

* * *

In August of that year, Victoria travelled to her beloved Coburg to unveil a statue of Albert. Her three younger daughters accompanied her. Lenchen was 19 years old at this point and the queen was looking around for a husband for her. Lenchen was considered one of the plainest of the queen's daughters, but in photographs, she looks a great deal like her younger sister Louise, though slightly more matronly. She was just beginning to have the stout figure that her mother already had, but she had a sweet and pliable nature. She was a talented classical pianist and held her own playing duets with professional musicians.

The queen had some specific qualifications for the husband of her third daughter. He must be a good man; he need not come from a reigning house, and he had to be willing to live with the queen. Victoria was most determined not to part with this daughter.[25]

Vicky and Uncle Leopold, who were now old hands at this sort of thing, were in on the search. Having been so successful with Bertie, Victoria was more than willing to listen to Vicky concerning candidates for her other daughters. There had been several contenders: Prince Henry of Hesse, Prince Ludwig's brother; Prince Albert of Prussia, the son of Prince Albert of Prussia and Marianne of the Netherlands; Prince Elimar of Oldenburg, the son of Augustus, Grand Duke of Oldenburg and Cecilia of Sweden; and, even a couple of Princess Alexandra's brothers.

However, Vicky made an especially good account of Prince Christian of Schleswig-Holstein-Sonderburg-Augustenberg, fifteen years Lenchen's senior. Victoria liked what she heard and invited the gentleman to Windsor without Helena's knowing the reason for the meeting. And evidently, though he looked more like a father than a suitor, Lenchen was positively disposed toward him, indeed, determined to have him.[26] After meeting him again at Darmstadt in August 1865, Victoria became more convinced that he was a good fit. He was, she wrote, 'pleasing & gentlemanlike'.[27]

At the beginning of December 1865, though Victoria wrote that it agitated her no end, Lenchen became engaged to the prince who had an impressive array of titles and no visible means of support. There were the usual cries in the queen's journal about how she felt so alone and how she wished Albert was there. Seeing these things written so often in the journal do give pause. The queen knew these journals would be looked at in some form for posterity, and perhaps she didn't want to be seen as getting over her great bereavement. However, the lamentations didn't stop her from mobilising a doctor and dentist to attend to the prince's smoker's cough and to fix his teeth. She wrote further that it was too bad that he looked so old.

As well, there were some political as well as familial headaches that came with such a match. As noted earlier, the German Confederation and Denmark were in conflict about the regions of Schleswig-Holstein and to which country they belonged. Because of that, the Danish Princess Alexandra of Wales had a strong prejudice against any of the German princes. Indeed, it was one of the reasons that earlier, Alexandra herself had been considered a politically inopportune choice before her engagement to Bertie.

The queen's children also took sides in this issue; Vicky and Fritz were good friends of the prince while Alix obviously was against it, and Bertie took her side. Princess Alice, too, disliked the match because she thought Christian was too old for her sister. Alice's opposition put her at loggerheads with her mother, who was angry about both that and the fact that Alice did not visit as much as was expected. Victoria now believed that Alice should be helping her sister Helena doing the social duties the queen refused to do, such as drawing rooms, and other court entertainments. Surely, she couldn't be so busy in Darmstadt? These feelings were exacerbated by the queen's antagonism to Alice's nursing her babies about which she never stopped obsessively complaining.

However, the big issue was the marriage. Alice was convinced that Helena was being sacrificed for the queen's needs rather than her own happiness.[28] This precipitated a very serious rift between the queen and her second daughter. The queen hated being frustrated in her matchmaking and if Alice was doing so, she must be 'jealous, sly and abominable'.[29] Considering that no one else who knew Alice thought that she was any of these things, it shows how annoyed the queen was. Alice was also intelligent enough to see how the politics of the match were conflicting – both the Prussians and Chancellor Bismarck and the Danes would be insulted in some way.

* * *

Before the big event another tragedy occurred in the queen's life. Her Uncle Leopold died on 10 December 1865. He had been ill for a short time but had lived to a comparatively old age and so the passing was not completely unexpected. The queen expressed her sorrow over and over in her journal and what a blow it was for her. Naturally coming only four days before the anniversary of Albert's death, Victoria was particularly gloomy. She did mention that it was Leopold's wish to be buried with Princess Charlotte of Wales, his first love. However, it was decided that this would be opposed by the Belgian people who needed to have their first monarch interred there. So instead, he was interred in the Royal Crypt at the Church of Notre-Dame de Laeken, next to his second wife, Louise.

Doing a quick survey of her journal entries on the crucial date of 14 December, the anniversary of Albert's death, Victoria had family all around her, even her sister Feodora comforting and attending her. Bertie, who had not been there in 1862 was present in the years after to give his mother comfort. She had written initially that she could not even look at him because of her anger, but this animosity had clearly dissipated. She noted that he came to Windsor *especially* on that day before proceeding to Brussels for the funeral of Uncle Leopold. The pattern for this day in perpetuity was a trip to the mausoleum, prayers, hymns, the placing of wreaths and quiet time with her family members.

* * *

The wedding of Lenchen and Prince Christian took place on 5 July 1866. The family continued to be divided about the match and Bertie and Alix had threatened not to come to the wedding. Alice, however, close as she was to her older brother, secretly beseeched him in a letter to attend pointing out that politics should not come before family obligations. Apparently, it was a good enough argument and the Waleses' attended.

The couple were married at the private chapel at Windsor and the controversies of their engagement did not spill over into their marriage which was placid. Contrary to what her sister and brother thought about Prince Christian, Lenchen truly liked him and they were quite happy together. They had four surviving children and lived just a short drive away at Frogmore House and would later live in Cumberland Lodge in Windsor Great Park.

Christian was so amiable and obliging a son-in-law that the queen thought him quite dull after a while. Watching him loitering about smoking outside, she wondered couldn't he find something else to do? However, to be fair he was given no occupation and what does a prince do? At some point, Christian was made Ranger of Windsor Great Park while Lenchen continued as her mother's companion and secretary as her daughter Helena Victoria would also do. Poor Prince Christian had his eye accidentally shot out by his brother-in-law, Arthur in 1891 during a hunting party. In the spirit of making the best of things, he had a false eye for every occasion and would often show them off to company; he even had an eye that was bloodshot if he was tired, ill or hung over.

However, Helena would distinguish herself. She had always loved nursing and science and would be a founding member of the British Red Cross.[30] Sadly, she was also a drug addict, according to the queen's physician, Dr Reid.[31] In those days, it was very common to take laudanum, which was a tincture of opium. Many middle- and upper-class women in the nineteenth century were addicted to laudanum including, among others, Mary Todd Lincoln, President Abraham Lincoln's wife. It was usually given to reduce pain, to help with sleep problems, agitation, or even periodic cramps. Eventually, Dr Reid was able to stop Lenchen's dependence.

It was also in that year that the queen began to refer to Brown as John Brown, Esq. This was certainly not the designation that a servant was entitled to, and there was much talk about this and the nature of the queen and Brown's relationship. The satirical magazine *Punch* got in on the act when it printed as an ostensive 'Court Circular':

Balmoral
Mr John Brown walked on the slopes.
He subsequently partook of a haggis.
In the evening Mr John Brown was pleased to listen to a bag-pipe.
Mr John Brown retired early.[32]

Chapter Five

'...we, authors, ma'am....'

During the early part of her mourning, Victoria's prime ministers could not be said to be of the greatest consolation to her. The queen's unwritten constitutional duties were to choose who should form a government, to encourage and warn, and to refuse the dissolution of parliament. The various prime ministers were there to inform her about what was going on in the administration of the nation's business. They met regularly to discuss these matters, but they seemed insensitive to the loss of her 'angel', as she usually referred to the late prince consort. From their point of view at that time, they wondered why they had to deal with her private mourning when there were problems of the state to consider. Their inability to understand the state of mind of the queen was an obvious error which continued even after Victoria was able to come out of the worst of her grief.

In the early 1860s, it was Lord Palmerston who went against the prince in stoking the flames of possible war with the United States over the *Trent* Affair and Victoria didn't like him. He hadn't shown the proper respect to Albert, and she felt that he had caused terrible problems in foreign affairs. Palmerston, it must be said, was a patriot who believed in an aggressive foreign policy that favoured Prussia over France. Much as she adored her husband's birthplace, Victoria had a marked favour for France. She and Albert had had a wonderful trip to France in 1855, visiting Napoleon III and Empress Eugénie as well as the *Exposition Universelle*. So much so, that when the emperor was overthrown, the Imperial family would be given sanctuary in England. The Empress Eugénie would become a very close and particular friend of the queen's during this time and continue until Victoria's death.

Mostly, as prime minister from 1860–65, Palmerston was not the compassionate presence she craved after the death of her husband. Although she wrote that Palmerston behaved well as prime minister, she also wrote that she could not like or respect him. He was certainly no 'Lord M'. Palmerston died in 1865 and for a year or so his compatriot in the Liberal Party, Lord John Russell, took over but was prime minister for a very short time.

In 1866, Lord Stanley, the Earl of Derby and a member of the Conservative party, became prime minister for several years. During his ministry the queen made it clear that she would do her best to attend public occasions, but it must be understood that it would only be during the day. As one historian wrote: 'To do the job that nobody asked of her, she would give up the job that everyone expected of her.'[1]

The queen opened parliament the following year at the request of Lord Derby as parliament was considering what would become the 1867 Reform Act. This act would expand the voting franchise in Britain and was hotly debated. The queen, however, wrote to Lord Derby that the exertion would be 'great, trying, and painful'[2] and cautioned Derby not to expect her to open parliament every year.

She was also especially annoyed about having to delay her summer trip to Osborne because she was obliged to receive the Sultan of the Ottoman Empire. Although the queen did what Lord Derby asked, this didn't prevent her from writing a long letter of bitter complaint to her prime minister. Her late husband had previously taken her to task for these endless complaints (which are constant throughout her journals and letters) about her various 'physical ailments', saying:

> We cannot, unhappily, bear your bodily sufferings for you – you must struggle with them alone.... [I]f you were rather less occupied with yourself (if that is possible) and your feelings (if that is possible) and took more interest in the outside world you would find that the greatest help of all.[3]

Without Albert there to scold her about such things, she felt free to indulge herself.

* * *

At the end of 1867, Victoria prepared for the private printing of *Leaves from the Journal of Our Life in the Highlands 1848–1861*. Described as:

> A record of the impressions received by the Royal Author in the course of these journeys, as might hereafter serve to recall to her own mind the scenes and circumstances which had been the source of so much pleasure. ... The book is mainly confined to the natural expressions of a mind rejoicing in the beauties of nature, and throwing itself, with a delight rendered keener by the rarity of its opportunities, into the enjoyment of a life removed, for the moment, from the pressure of public cares.

Although her eldest son called it 'twaddle', most likely because there were too many mentions of Brown, her editor and publisher maintained that it should be made available to the public. The queen assented saying that it would show everyone how simply she and Albert had lived.

She was thrilled at the positive reception the book received and wrote to Theodore Martin, Albert's biographer:

> The Queen was moved to tears on reading Mr Martin's beautiful and too kind letter.
>
> *Indeed* it is not possible for her to say *how* touched she is by the *kindness of everyone*.... What has she done to be so loved and liked?[4]

It was also at the beginning of 1868 that a new prime minister came into power and into the queen's life: Benjamin Disraeli. Lord Derby had written to the queen that he was ill at this time and couldn't discharge his public duties. He asked the queen to accept Disraeli. He would go down in history as her favourite prime minister.

* * *

Benjamin Disraeli was born in London in 1804. He came from a Jewish family that traced its roots to Italy and was possibly of Sephardic origin. His father left his synagogue when Benjamin was twelve years old and converted to Anglicanism. Many sources say that it was because of a dispute with the elders of the synagogue, but others say that Isaac D'Israeli, Benjamin's father, knew his children would get nowhere in society as Jews.[5] This is more likely in the climate of gentlemanly antisemitism in

England and especially in the government at the time. Many politicians, including William Ewart Gladstone sneeringly called Disraeli 'the Jew' behind his back. Other pejorative labels for him were 'oriental', 'exotic', a 'vizir', even a 'wizard' or a 'wandering Jew'. Disraeli's father had sense in converting his family, but there was no escaping his origins.

Those origins included his firm middle-class background. And so more labels were hurled at him such as calling him an audacious arriviste from 'low beginnings' ever striving to make something of himself. Interesting to note that during his long tenure in parliament, as a Tory and mostly in the Opposition, Victoria and Albert disliked him. They, too, thought he was a middle-class climber and upstart and most certainly not a gentleman. Victoria even expressed that he was peculiar and so 'Jewish-looking'. However, that was all to change when Disraeli became prime minister.

Disraeli had spent the early part of his life searching for occupation. He tried the law, but rejected it, and then turned his hand to writing novels, traveling and speculation in the stock market. He participated with the publisher John Murray in founding a newspaper that might rival *The Times* of London, but that proved a failure. Disraeli continued his literary career which had some success and during his life published nearly seventeen novels as well as poetry, and some non-fiction. He married Mary Ann Lewis, a woman who was twelve years his senior, and people concluded that he only married her to get out of the tremendous debt he had accumulated. She apparently knew this but also knew that Disraeli grew to love her, though they would not have any children. He at last settled on a political life, taking a seat in the House of Commons at the age of 33.

By the time he became prime minister, Disraeli was 64-years old. Unfortunately for him, his first term as PM would be unusually short. During this brief time, the queen changed her mind about him completely. He was able to make her feel closer to him than to any prime minister since Melbourne. Victoria wrote: 'He certainly shows more consideration for my comfort than any preceding Prime Ministers....'[6]

The correspondence between them was cordial and warm, though the letters have been derisively described as 'sickening in their sweetness'.[7] But Disraeli had the simple knack of always treating her like a woman, while she complained that his bitter rival Gladstone treated her like a committee. Their relationship was such that he presented her with his novels and she, of course, presented him with her publication *Leaves from the Journal of Our Life in the Highlands*. Disraeli, always the flatterer, called her the head of the literary profession and was heard to say, 'We authors, ma'am.'[8] To be fair to Disraeli, though, it would have to be said that he had truly enjoyed *Leaves*. He told Sir Arthur Helps that 'he had read it with unaffected interest. Its vein is innocent and vivid, happy in picture and touched with what I ever think is the characteristic of our royal mistress – grace.'[9]

And, of this flattery, sincere or no, perhaps Disraeli did compliment the queen overmuch, but it was because he understood women, or at least the woman the queen was, so much better than many of his predecessors. This, of course, apart from Melbourne, though Lord M's relationship with Victoria was as the fondness of a father, while Disraeli's relationship was of a strong though platonic affection. There were no fatherly feelings for Victoria on the prime minister's part but an association of genuine respect. Disraeli liked and valued intelligent women and felt that one could learn more from a well-informed woman than anyone. The queen was certainly well-informed.

Victoria felt that he made the business of state so much more interesting than some of his predecessors and she looked forward to her audiences. She was essentially a shy person and even more so because of her prolonged reclusiveness. Disraeli brought her out of herself. As her granddaughter Victoria Battenberg later wrote:

> Grandmama was essentially, what was called a womanly nature and her likes and dislikes were influenced by personal contacts. This was the secret of [Disraeli's] charm for her; he never overlooked the woman in the sovereign.[10]

Wisely, Disraeli saw that because the queen refused to go out in public even as the 1860s closed, this was not good for the monarchy or the government. There were republican whisperings afoot, and Disraeli wanted the queen to change her view of her role. The public wanted the pageantry that came with the monarchy, the show that is talked about all over the world even today, but Victoria still preferred to wallow in her mourning. Nevertheless, though he knew when to stop pressing her, he was able to persuade her to come out for military reviews, a breakfast, and even a garden party in June 1868.

The queen discovered that Disraeli loved flowers, especially spring flowers. She sent him some from Windsor to 'brighten his rooms'.[11] He especially loved primroses and so those were also sent as well as the violets. She would continue to send him flowers for the remainder of his life as a token of her strong and affectionate friendship.

Unfortunately for Disraeli, he was voted out of office by December of 1868 after a mere ten months. Victoria was upset when faced with the possibility of Gladstone and would never be as cordial with him as she had been with 'Dizzy', as both his friends and critics called him. She wrote in her journal that she shook hands with him, 'saying how truly sorry I was to part with him. He expressed his warm thanks.'[12]

Disraeli, however, would be back.

* * *

In April 1870, there was a significant shake-up in the queen's household. The queen's journal: 1 April 1870: 'Saw Sir T[homas] Biddulph[.] Col[.] Ponsonby is to replace for dear General [Charles Grey].'

Sir Thomas was the Master of the Household to the queen from 1851–66 and the Keeper of the Privy Purse. The privy purse[13] that he was responsible for was the queen's monies as allotted by the government.

Queen Victoria's previous Private Secretary, General Charles Grey had been Prince Albert's and when the prince died, Victoria commandeered him for that role. He was, incidentally, the same Charles Grey who had accompanied eighteen-year-old Bertie on his continental tour. He died in 1870 and in his place came a gentleman who had also been Prince Albert's equerry, Sir Henry Ponsonby. He held this post along with keeper of the privy purse until his death in 1895 and became an indispensable member of the queen's household and her life.

Ponsonby, who was born on Corfu in 1825 and, like his predecessor, was an army man who had fought in the Crimean war. He spent the American Civil War (1861–1865) in Canada and returned committed to service to the crown. In 1861 he married one of the queen's maids of honour, Mary Elizabeth Bulteel, who upon marriage had to give up her post in the household. They had an 'exceptionally affectionate' marriage and had five children. Nevertheless, the couple spent their lives in service and at the court of the queen.

Politically, both were Liberals; Mary was inquisitive, sometimes radical, and in some ways what we today might call a feminist. However, neither let their beliefs get in the way of the increasingly Conservative queen. The queen praised Ponsonby in a letter to Vicky saying: 'Colonel Ponsonby is a very decided Liberal, but he never has mixed in politics – and is very discreet.'[14]

He was, according to his son, 'a mine of information. Courteously impartial, he held the confidence of all politicians, Liberal or Conservative.'[15] Even Disraeli praised his objectivity saying: 'I can only say that I could not wish my case stated to the Queen better than her private secretary does it.'[16] In addition, he was a great admirer of William Gladstone, against whom the queen had a decided hostility.

Nevertheless, Ponsonby understood her. It was said that he knew how far to push her and no further. It has also been thought that he was her sounding board and that she, herself, understood how far she could go politically, and was realistic about it. His personality, with his sense of humour and his rationality, appealed to Victoria. He was, '[s]agacious, of keen insight, patient, understanding, and with a great range of knowledge, the Queen possessed in him not only a secretary but a counsellor of the highest worth.'[17]

Ponsonby has also been described as 'quiet, witty, cultivated ... possessed of a deep and sympathetic understanding of ... human nature'.[18] He had the wonderful ability to put nervous visitors at ease before an audience with the queen. He was tactful, energetic, patient and had the confidence not only of the queen but of her ministers as well.[19] Because of this, he became the man to whom others in the household, as well as members of her immediate family, applied when they had issues and messages to the queen that needed attention. He understood how to get things done with her and deal with myriad of matters diplomatically. He invariably tempered the tone of various dispatches to get the wanted result.

If that sounds like an ideal person to deal with the queen who was, at best, eccentric, stubborn, contradictory, emotional and always used to her own way, it was. He was highly adept at it, especially during the beginning of his tenure with Victoria, a time when republicanism and dissatisfaction with the monarch was on the rise. He could be said, along with Disraeli and Brown, to be one of the people who at last pulled the queen out of her deep mourning and back into the public eye. This certainly helped to beat back the republicans at Windsor's gates.

* * *

After Disraeli had been voted out, the queen dealt with a less than sympathetic prime minister in William Gladstone, son of one of the largest slave owners in the British Empire, Sir John Gladstone. Young William was born in Liverpool in 1809 and attended Eton College and Christ Church, Oxford. As early as his time in university, he was considered a great orator. He, too, began the study of law, but after some years, lost interest. In 1839, at the end of his brief law career, he married 'the beautiful'[20] Catherine Glynne. The marriage was described as a love match, and the couple had eight children.

He came into the House of Commons as a Tory, and later a Liberal, and continued either in office or in the Opposition for the rest of his life. From very early on, he disliked Disraeli and Disraeli returned his animosity. They were keen political rivals for most of the latter part of the century. He was prime minister four times, a chancellor of the exchequer, and really put together the Liberal party.

Gladstone was a zealous religious figure and ferocious in his morality. He roamed around at night looking for prostitutes to reform. Historian Stanley Weintraub thought these noble motives were nonsense, but nevertheless, the story persists. He may have been satisfying a strange sexual aberration, and it was well known at the time that he did these nocturnal promenades. Sanitised whispers may have reached the queen who, along with her other reasons for disliking him, might have found him untrustworthy in this odd endeavour. However, it must be said that Gladstone was a devoutly religious man, and his motives might well have been pure.

In all events, Gladstone accomplished a great deal during his four ministries. It is thought that he represented and drove most of the British progressive movements of the nineteenth century. One of his first accomplishments was abolishing the selling of military commissions. This had been a huge bone of contention after the Crimean war. Gladstone's intention was that men should be promoted on merit rather than just because they could afford to buy a commission.

Besides instituting reforms in the military, Gladstone also pushed for reforms for separating the Irish Church from the Church of England, and land reform in Ireland called the Landlord and Tenant Act 1870. Victoria, however, would never think of giving up any of her prerogatives, 'especially in the military area',[21] and, proudly calling herself the daughter of a soldier, was against these reforms. It is thought that this is the beginning of her great antipathy toward Gladstone, and it seems that nothing would ever change.

Victoria, who believed in a strong sovereign and military, resented the fact Gladstone treated her like a figurehead. Her basic political beliefs can be summarised: no income or death taxes, a strong House of Lords and a distrust of the 'lower orders'. And despite the fact she was head of the government, she did not believe that women should have the vote. Victoria felt that her position was unique and not predicated on her sex. Ultimately, though, no amount of wheedling or persuasion, even by the more congenial Disraeli, would have changed her mind about myriad of different issues, and Gladstone never tried. Indeed, these points and more put her in constant contention with him.

In perusing her journals, Victoria describes Gladstone as sensible, satisfactory, hopeful, and talks about how nice his wife is, all very lukewarm adjectives. It appears there was some part of her who believed she ought to like and get along with him. After all, Albert liked him very much and the two of them respected one another. Albert thought him a great intellectual and extremely clever. Other words she used to describe him weren't so positive such as arrogant, obstinate, and 'a very dangerous and unsatisfactory Premier'.[22]

Gladstone, who scorned a nuanced approach, treated the queen as though her opinion didn't matter as much as her signature. He disdained her pleasure in the pomp and ceremony of royal events and made her feel like a 'silly girl'.[23] Further, Victoria often said that Gladstone made her feel like he was the cleverest man in England, while Disraeli made her feel like she was the cleverest woman.

Gladstone, who had had a great deal of advice on how to handle the queen seemed to ignore it all. He lectured, he harangued, he pushed when he should have treated a matter lightly and tried his best to get the queen to appear in public again, which only made her want to step back more. Truthfully, it probably felt to Victoria like he was bullying her, and remembering that Conroy tried the same thing, it is no wonder she didn't respond to him.

Victoria sometimes said she would rather abdicate than have Gladstone as prime minister and was usually quite irritated by the end of their meetings. The irony is, Gladstone was one of her biggest defenders and a strong monarchist. They rubbed along through four ministries; daggers drawn but never really thrust.

* * *

All told, the 1860s had been a terrible decade for the queen. Initially, she was lost without the support and advice of her beloved Albert. However, as time went on, things improved, and she pulled herself together. By the end of the decade Victoria was starting to do more, and to enjoy some of the public events that her subjects had expected of her – despite complaining that she didn't.

And because the worst of her grief was receding, even *that* was something about which to be sad. Indeed, she often bemoaned that she was a poor widow and grumbled about overwork and shattered nerves. Certainly, without Albert as a moderating influence, she saw no reason not to indulge herself even more. Nevertheless, many observed that Victoria was able to laugh again and enjoy life. Her health was generally good, and she had numerous people helping her with the workload.[24]

* * *

There were more grandchildren during this fraught time. Vicky expanded her brood with two daughters and three more sons. Charlotte, called 'Charley' in the family, was born in 1860 (and would be the first grandchild to present Victoria with a great-grandchild). Henry, born in 1862, would marry a first cousin, and two other boys who unfortunately did not survive childhood. Also added to the group was a daughter, Viktoria, known as 'Moretta', born in 1866.

In 1868, Alice had the long hoped for boy, after producing three daughters for the Grand Duchy of Hesse. The baby called Ernst Ludwig was born at the Neues Palace in Darmstadt, on 25 November. Her daughter Irène had been born in 1866 and there would be more children later. Alice's first three girls: Victoria, Elisabeth, called 'Ella' in the family, and Irène were considered beauties, but also very boisterous, to the point that the genteel families in Darmstadt did not allow their children to play with them. 'The Three Graces', as they were called, were really just lively and energetic and weren't worried about public opinion. They were content enough and encouraged to enjoy their own company.

Alix and Bertie added three girls to their family. Louise (1867) who was sickly; Victoria (1868), whom the queen called a 'red lump'; and Maud (1869), the last of Alix's living children. The queen complained to her daughter Vicky that they were going 'on like rabbits in Windsor Park!'[25] These three British princesses would be called 'Their Shynesses' or the 'Whispering Wales', as they were the opposite of their Hessian cousins and not at all lively.

Helena and Christian had two sons during the decade, Christian Victor, who would have a tragic destiny, and Albert.

It goes without saying that Victoria adored her grandchildren, though she could be as critical of them as she was of her own children. However, she was far more tolerant of them while they were babies than she had been of her own nine. Probably because they could easily go home.

* * *

Though the queen wrote affectionately about Bertie in her journals, his behaviour as the heir continued to be troubling for her. Certainly, he had married a beautiful woman who was devoted to him, but the marriage did not provide the stability his mother and father thought he needed or hoped he'd have. As time went on, though the pair were often in society together, Bertie not only travelled without Alix, but became a prominent 'man about town', seen at parties and other social occasions without his wife. Alix, it must be said, was not the most intellectual of people; even her mother-in-law had commented on that, and was hardly stimulating company. Though the prince, too, was scarcely a cerebral person, he enjoyed the sparkling company of beautiful, witty, and intelligent women.

He caused a scandal in 1870 when he became a witness in the divorce trial between Sir Charles and Lady Mordaunt. It was the first time that any Prince of Wales had been called to a court of law since the reign of Henry IV back in the fifteenth century.[26] He protested his innocence in any sort of impropriety and did so forthrightly. Nevertheless, just being called as a witness was the scandal itself. It didn't help that there were letters and evidence of private calls.[27] However, it was eventually established that these letters were quite innocent and friendly. After the prince protested his innocence of any sexual conduct toward the lady, Ponsonby wrote: 'London was black with the smoke of burnt confidential letters.'[28]

The queen, when it was proved that it was a mere indiscretion, supported Bertie with her love and sympathy. He was quite gratified to have it and was fulsome in his thanks, but that is as far as it went. Bertie was, in simple terms, a ne'er do well. He had no occupation because his mother would not give him one. He was easily bored and needed constant distraction. According to Royal Historian Theo Aronson, he poured the energy into his love life that he might have put into work, which was and would be prolific throughout his life. He certainly could have found better occupation than society, women, hunting and a voracious appetite for food and drink. Perhaps, had he done so, his mother might have been persuaded to give him more, or at least *something*, to do. Blame may fall obviously with his upbringing and his parents, but there comes a point in one's life where that rings hollow.

Where was Alix in all of this? She was hardly the ignorant spouse some might suppose. She knew of his infidelities, which were legion, and poured herself into her children, which in some ways infantilised them. The princess had suffered a long and severe illness before and after the birth of Louise, her eldest daughter, in 1867. Several days before the baby's birth, Alix suffered from an attack of rheumatic fever and acute pain in her leg and hip. Afterward, Alix was in constant pain for several months, and only began real improvement in April of that year and was at last up and around by the summer. During this time, Bertie put his desk in her sick room so he could do his letters while keeping her company, but was mostly bored and as ever looking for distraction. 'Now all of London … knew that whilst his wife lay sick in Marlborough House, the Prince had been amusing himself elsewhere.'[29]

Most unfortunate was that it had lasting effects for the Princess of Wales. She had a stiff knee and walked with a limp for the rest of her life. In addition, she was showing the signs of what would become profound deafness from a condition called otosclerosis. This made her even more isolated from the glittering London society that Bertie loved, and she retreated into herself, her children, and her pets. Having said that the princess was not a great thinker, she had hitherto learned by listening to the brilliant and interesting people around her. This was now lost to her and unfortunately, she wasn't a reader. None of this excuses the behaviour of the feckless prince, but it does perhaps explain some of it. In the end, Alix said, perhaps naively, 'He always loved me best.'

* * *

Bertie's indiscretions and the queen's continued isolation made for a less popular monarchy as the decade ended. The queen had initially been defended in the press for her beautiful devotion to her dead husband, but it did not last. Gladstone observed that the queen was invisible, and the heir was not respected. It was argued in various newspapers that when she was needed most, she was six hundred miles away at Balmoral, and that this gave her 'enemies' reasons to rejoice.

Apparently, her association with John Brown did not help her popularity and the press had a field day churning out little titbits of gossip and sometimes coarse hearsay whenever they fancied. Even the most sensible thought her association with the gruff and overbearing highlander was at the very least indiscreet and at the most highly inappropriate.

Added to domestic worries, Chancellor von Bismarck began to assert Prussian militarism in Europe. The Franco-Prussian war began ostensibly because Bismarck and a united Germany backed Prince Leopold of Hohenzollern-Sigmaringen (the Catholic branch of Prussia's ruling Hohenzollern family) as a candidate for the Spanish throne. That throne had been vacant when Queen Isabella II had been deposed and the French naturally felt threatened by the idea of Hohenzollerns on the thrones of both Germany and Spain.

The candidate was withdrawn, and the French made an informal demand during a private conversation that such a candidacy would never again be proposed. This informal meeting was described in a telegram called the Ems Dispatch to Bismarck who then edited the conversation in such a way that both Germany and France were insulted. The French were provoked into declaring war. Hostilities commenced on 19 July

1870. In truth, the point of the war was for Germany to challenge France's dominance of Europe.

The queen noted that the 'enthusiasm in Germany seems to be very great'.[30] Vicky, as the Crown Princess of Prussia was in the very thick of things, and the queen was extremely distressed by this. She worried deeply about both her daughters in Germany but at least, unlike the Austro-Prussian War of 1866, her daughters were on the same side. Vicky in Potsdam and Alice in Hesse were both feverishly working in hospitals for the war wounded. The queen's other daughters were also doing their bit, working on behalf of the London Committee for Aid to the Sick and Wounded – established to help the soldiers on both sides of the conflict. Nevertheless, she wrote '[t]o have to stand by & see this terrible conflict, without being able to do anything to avert it, is most painful & distressing'.[31]

Even more distressing to Victoria was that the French army was defeated, her friend Napoleon III was captured, and his empire fell. A third French Republic was established, and this too, fed into the republican rumblings. The ex-emperor, his wife Eugénie, and their only child, 14-year-old Louis Napoléon, the Prince Imperial, sought refuge in England in 1871. Victoria wrote in her journal about receiving the emperor upon his exile and how poignant and different it was from their very happy and successful visit to England in 1855.

Thereafter, the queen would often visit them at their house in Chislehurst outside of London, but the emperor died soon afterward at the beginning of 1873. The empress and Victoria remained good friends after Napoleon III's death and Eugénie would later be the godmother of one of Princess Beatrice's children. It was also at this time that King Wilhelm I of Prussia, Vicky's father-in-law, became the first German emperor or Kaiser, ruling over a united Germany.

A few friends from her childhood and youth had also passed away in that crucial year of 1870. The incompetent Sir James Clark died in June of that year; he had been with her when all nine children were born, when the Duchess of Kent died, and of course when Albert passed away. He had been her doctor for thirty-five years and despite his mistakes she called him a dear, kind, and intimate friend.

In September, Baroness Lehzen died at the great age of 85. The queen, who had not visited her old governess and friend in eight years, noted this several days later in her journal and seemed to have reconciled any bitterness she had towards that lady:

> Though latterly her mind had not been clear, still there were days when she constantly spoke of me whom she had known from the age of 6 months. She had devoted her life to me from my 5th to my 18th year, with the most wonderful self-abnegation, never even taking one day's leave! After I came to the throne she got to be rather trying & especially so after my marriage, but never from any evil intention, only from a mistaken idea of duty & affection for me. She was an admirable Governess, & I adored her, though I also feared her. I feel much that she too is gone.[32]

These deaths put a close to the queen's childhood and youth as Victoria, seemingly, smaller and rounder – lonely but never alone – entered her fifties.

Chapter Six

Family Matters

As the new decade opened, it became apparent to all that the queen was at last going to pull herself out of her melancholy and prolonged mourning. She, however, was going to do it in her own time. No one could make her see sense until she, herself, saw it. Her prime ministers had tried with limited success. Her daughter Alice tried but was strongly rebuffed for making such intimations, as were her other children at various times. They, in desperation, signed a joint letter to her about this very thing, but she wasn't interested in their opinions on what she considered a personal matter.

Her adult children, who clearly didn't understand her well, were not much comfort to her. She expressed it this way: 'Only very occasionally do I find intimate intercourse with them either agreeable or easy ... I am used to carrying on my many affairs quietly and alone.'[1] She went on to say that she had always been used to the company of adults and wasn't around young people enough to take pleasure in their company (read: her children). It was a shame for them, especially the ones who remained unmarried and still at home during the major portion of her grief. It never occurred to her that they might need her help in processing *their* heartache. It must be said, though, that Victoria certainly knew herself well and minced no words.

What continued to be unavoidable were the seemingly happy occasions – her expanding family as weddings and births continued. Though Victoria never really wanted daughters to leave, in the late sixties her three eldest daughters had married and now discussions began about possible spouses for her next daughter Louise.

Louise had been another somewhat useful daughter, acting as her mother's secretary during those last few years since Lenchen became a married woman and a mother. But Victoria knew this daughter well enough to know that her usefulness was a temporary stopgap until

Beatrice came of age in 1875. Louise, who had a mind of her own, wanted more than to just be her mother's companion and had a restless energy about her that irritated Victoria.

Louise was stifled in her adolescence by her mother's protracted mourning and would never be content to sit by her mother and write letters and pick out knitting. She was completely different than her sisters, Helena and Beatrice, in her intellectual curiosity and that she wanted to participate fully in public life outside the palace. So, it was obvious that she would not be the compliant miss that her mother needed, and it was felt that something must be done. The queen made the decision that the sooner she was married, the better.

Louise was quite possibly the most independent-minded of Victoria's daughters. She had exhibited an extraordinary talent for art and particularly sculpture, which up to that point had been considered a masculine art. The talent, however, was so undeniable that she was able to procure her mother's consent to take classes at the National Art Training School. Though it had hitherto been unheard of, the princess went off to her art classes each morning. There, her excellent abilities were fostered by an association with Joseph Edgar Boehm, the Hungarian sculptor, who became a close personal friend – and as speculation had it, even closer than that.

Louise was considered the most beautiful of the queen's daughters and not just because she was a princess, but also because her looks were celebrated in society along with other reigning beauties. She was taller and more slender than her sisters with a lovely oval face. She loved the Bohemian society in London and was considered something of a flirt. There were rumours of crushes on her brother Leopold's tutors, and even deeper romances, but no actual confirmation that we know of. Historian Lucinda Hawksley speculates that the rumours of her having an out-of-wedlock child in 1867 from one of the tutors may be true and makes the argument quite logically, but again there is no hard evidence.

Louise balked at the fact that her mother rarely permitted her to go to any social events and longed for the company of creative people. Though she was intrigued by feminism, she knew it was her duty to enter into a traditional marriage, and so suitable spouses were proposed for her. There was talk of her marrying Alix's brother, Frederick, the Crown Prince of Denmark, but Victoria dismissed that as being politically undesirable.

The Prussians might be insulted. There was also mention of the same Prussian prince, Albert, who had been considered for Lenchen, or even the Prince of Orange, but they and other foreign princes were ultimately vetoed.

Finally, it was decided that Louise should not marry a foreigner. The queen, quite rightly, lamented that European alliances were worthless since wars could tear families asunder no matter who was married to whom. She believed that they no longer had any political importance. In addition, the British public and parliament were getting tired of supporting the various princes who had been presenting themselves for the last century, therefore the search for someone nearer to home commenced. Louise was also enthusiastic since she had expressed a wish to marry and spend her life in Britain. Though no royal had married a countryman since the sixteenth century when Henry VIII's sister married Charles Brandon, Duke of Suffolk, Louise hoped to break that cycle.

The fellow Briton would have to be aristocratic at the very least, and if not a duke then the son of a duke. Finding such a 'someone' was not as easy as might be thought. A lot of the aristocrats turned their noses at the royal family since they felt themselves more royal and aristocratic than the 'Coburgers'.

John Campbell, the Marquess of Lorne, known as 'Ian' in his family and later the 9th Duke of Argyll was put on the 'short list' of candidates who would be considered. He had a great deal going for him and seemed to be an ideal choice. His family was the head of the substantial Campbell clan and so the young man had a sizable fortune of his own and would not be a drain on the British public. He was educated at Eton, the University of St Andrews, and Trinity College, Cambridge. He had a poetic and artistic bent as well as a facility for modern languages and history. Because of all this, it was hoped he would challenge Princess Louise intellectually. He was physically attractive, which doubtless would have appealed to the artistic Louise – it certainly appealed to her mother. Not for either of them a Prince Christian type who looked more like a wizened uncle than a suitor.

Lorne became a member of the House of Commons and was a Gladstonian Liberal. Here, Bertie had objections because he felt that marrying someone with a particular political bent was wrong for the royal family. Never mind, of course, the queen's strong Conservatism at this point, or that she had been an overt Whig in her youth. Nonetheless, this was a consideration. The other, more important, consideration for the more sophisticated Bertie was the fact that there were whispers that Lorne had homosexual affairs. Consequently, he may not have wanted his sister involved with him.[2] Still another practical consideration that Bertie had was the difficulties that the pair might have as virtual 'semi-royals' and the arguments of precedence that might come from such a marriage. The Prince of Wales was hardly a snob, but he understood that many others were.[3]

Louise had a long and difficult time making up her mind. In the end, after initially saying no, she changed her mind and consented. Hawksley debunks the idea that this was a great love match, though other historians have called it so. The truth of the matter was that while her siblings did not necessarily approve of Lorne, in fact the Prussians saw the match as quite bizarre, Queen Victoria very much did approve.[4] That was all that was needed and would ever be needed. She once quoted if the queen had approved the match, what had other people got to say? In all events, she was a staunch supporter of 'new blood' in the family because of the genetic weaknesses that were evidently present and Louise, who wanted her own life in England and away from the court at Windsor, went along with it.

There was the obstacle of having to open parliament again, which in the decade since Albert's death, the queen did very reluctantly. Since she was asking for a dowry for Louise as well as grants for her second to youngest son Arthur, who would be coming of age that year, it was a necessary evil. The republican movement was at its height and Victoria's popularity was at its lowest ebb, but nonetheless, the queen took up what she considered a distasteful task. Her prime minister at the time, Gladstone, a strong monarchist despite himself, made sure she received the dowry and the grants, notwithstanding their mutual dislike.

The marriage took place 21 March 1871. Lorne appeared in full Campbell apparel, kilt and all, and no doubt gained his mother-in-law's further approval, loving as she did, anything to do with her beloved Scotland. Interesting to note that Victoria gave her daughter away on that sunny Windsor day and not some male relative, though Bertie was on Louise's other side and Albert's brother, Ernst the Duke of Coburg, on Victoria's other side. Unlike previous weddings, she did not sit weeping in the background, but was front and centre with her daughter. The queen knighted her new son-in-law after the ceremony and gave him the Order of the Thistle.

* * *

Louise was a popular and lively princess so that helped with the queen's declining popularity somewhat, but it wasn't enough. In the late summer of 1871, the queen fell seriously ill. She was tired all the time, had a sore throat and there was a painful abscess on her arm. She wrote in her journal: '22 August 1871. Never felt so ill since typhoid at Ramsgate in 35.'[5] Eventually, Joseph Lister, an expert in the experimental field of bacteriology and infections, was sent for. He gave Victoria 'whiffs' of chloroform and lanced her arm. He then treated it with carbolic spray – an antiseptic. It wasn't cured overnight, however, and that and a gouty foot left Victoria in pain and despair.

It happened that Alice's family was visiting the queen at that time, so she was able to do a great deal of the nursing for her mother. The state of the queen's health was kept from the ministers by her own physician, Sir William Jenner, so they were left to continue their speculation about her sanity. This conjecture had been going on during the entire first decade of her widowhood. Many of her subjects wondered if the queen had lost her reason.

Two major incidents happened toward the end of that year that helped the queen's popularity rise once again. After Victoria was finally well enough to go to church and get back to her duties, another more heartrending event happened. Just after the Prince of Wales's thirtieth birthday he became feverish and was diagnosed with typhoid. Initially, it appeared to be a mild form of the fever but soon worsened appreciably. The prince's fever was very high and he became confused, delirious, and as the queen termed it 'wandering in his head'.

Since Alice was still in England, she was on hand to do the nursing when the prince became seriously ill. Coincidentally, during the prince's illness, all four of Alice's children became ill. They were sent to Buckingham Palace, having contracted whooping cough, but Alice went immediately to Sandringham and Bertie's sickbed. She joined Alix and Helena who were also doing the duties. As an acknowledged expert on typhoid, Sir

William Jenner was despatched to Bertie's side and along with the sisters and Alix, looked after him during the long illness.

The queen, with a rare empathy for her eldest son, hesitated to visit because she didn't wish to agitate him, and so she stayed at Windsor with her grandchildren who had easily recovered from the whooping cough and were now with their grandmother. Alice's eldest daughter, Victoria, wrote that they had wonderful memories of playing hide and seek in the large halls and behind huge pieces of furniture; playing with their aunts' and uncles' wonderful toys and generally making much more noise than their grandmother could stand.

At the beginning of December, it looked like Bertie was improving though not out of danger. However, as these things go, he got worse again. This happened several times – the roller coaster of serious illnesses. The queen was informed that she should come to see her heir and was now periodically visiting him. When he was not feverish, he was tremendously appreciative of her presence.

Victoria was told of the enormous number of well-wishers around the country who were concerned about Bertie and was extremely grateful. She wrote, '[t]he feeling shown by the whole nation is quite marvellous & most touching & striking, showing how really sound & truly loyal the people really are'.[6]

On 13 December, the melancholy anniversary of Albert's death was approaching, Victoria was told that there was no hope for the prince and that he was close to death. That night, in his wandering and coughing, Bertie looked at the queen who was sitting by his bedside and asked who she was, but before she could reply he said: 'It's Mama. It's so kind of you to come.'[7] Victoria noted this in her journal and may have been surprised that he was so happy to see her. For once, she stayed at Bertie's bedside instead of being at Windsor for the anniversary on 14 December, though she noted how sad she was not to be at the mausoleum.

By the beginning of January, Bertie at last began to steadily improve. Victoria was advised that a public Thanksgiving Service for the prince's full recovery was a good idea since the public had been greatly concerned for their future monarch. The whole family, excepting Vicky and her brood, attended, as well as the ex-Emperor Napoleon and his wife Eugénie. Though Bertie was not completely well, and it was not a state occasion, it became one in all but name. During the procession, at Temple

Bar the queen raised Bertie's hand and kissed it which made the crowds wild with joy. The service was held at St Paul's and the queen noted 'the deafening cheering never ceasing for an instant'.[8] And later, 'I went upstairs & stepped out on the Balcony with Beatrice & my 3 sons, being loudly cheered. — Rested on the sofa after taking some tea. Could think & talk of little else, but today's wonderful demonstration of loyalty & affection, from the very highest to the lowest.'[9]

It can be safely said that from that day, the republican movement was all but dead.

* * *

It is ironic, however, that the following day, there was another assassination attempt on the queen. Either some equerries or John Brown stopped the youngster with a pistol. According to Victoria's journal, he may have just wanted her to sign a petition or document, but of course was stopped quickly. Victoria gave all the credit to Brown in preventing this attempt. It was to Brown that she believed she owed her life and safety, though her own son Prince Arthur, who was also present, certainly played a role. Unfortunately, this had the effect of subduing the groundswell of her renewed popularity. Brown was so unpopular with the public that Victoria's commendation did little good.

* * *

The idea of giving Bertie something truly important to do was floated around after he recovered from his illness. Ponsonby wrote a comprehensive memorandum about the various proposals for the Prince of Wales. They fell into the categories of: Philanthropy, Arts and Sciences, Army, Foreign Affairs, and India. He put this together with the help of the prince's private secretary and Gladstone. However, Gladstone complained to his wife that Bertie had absolutely no attention span. Victoria thought that art and possibly foreign affairs might do, but she was sceptical. It seems that all anyone could agree on concerning Bertie was that he was enormously charming. And, though this should be seen as no mean accomplishment, the queen was never disposed to make use of her heir. Whether right or wrong, in the end, no one seemed to think he had the sense of responsibility or the endurance to maintain interest in anything for very long.[10]

Meanwhile, Vicky had given birth to her fourth daughter, Margaret. Victoria wrote her congratulations and wrote further: 'I don't dislike babies, though I think very young ones rather disgusting ... but when they come at the rate of three a year it becomes a cause of mere anxiety for my own children and of not great interest.'[11]

And, whether she liked it or not, there were three that year. Margaret, called 'Mossy', had been Vicky's fourth, as another daughter – Sophie, though nicknamed 'Sossie' – had been born in 1870. In June 1872, Alice gave birth to *her* fourth daughter, called Alix or 'Alicky' in the family. Alix was not a nickname as it was for the Princess of Wales, but her given name. Alice complained that they murdered her name in German so instead of calling this daughter Alice, they settled on Alix. In August, Helena gave birth to her last living child, Marie Louise, who joined her brothers and older sister, Helena Victoria who was born in 1870.

Along with its births, that year also had several deaths, which compounded Victoria's sadness. In early autumn her beloved half-sister, Feodora of Hohenlohe-Langenburg, died of scarlet fever. The sisters had always been close and corresponded constantly. Victoria supported her with an allowance that financed her travel to Britain for visits. Unfortunately, even Feodora's visits courted controversy. Feodora's daughter Adelaide was married to one of the counterclaimants to the Duchy of Schleswig-Holstein, so it was hardly surprising that there was a coldness between her and the Danish Princess of Wales. It made for very uncomfortable family parties and eventually Victoria had had enough and forbade talk of the contested duchy during family gatherings.

Victoria took comfort in the fact that she had taken a lightning trip to Baden-Baden in April to see her dying sister one last time. She lamented in her journal:

Can I write it? My own darling, only sister, my dear excellent, noble Feodore is no more! She is at rest & in peace since 2 this morning. What a fearful loss! Darling precious sister, whom I hoped so to go & see! I stand so alone now, no near & dear one nearer my own age, or older, to whom I could look up to, left! All, all gone! How good & wise, beloved Feodore was, so devoted to me, so truly pious &

religious. She is gone to that world she was so fit for & entered it, just sleeping away. What a blessed end! but what a loss to those who are left! She was my <u>last</u> near relative on an equality with me, the <u>last</u> link with my childhood & youth.[12]

Truly, now there was no one to call her 'Victoria'.

In addition to this sad event, Disraeli's wife Mary Ann died. Victoria was of course very aware of her illness and when she died, the queen wrote, 'Poor Mr Disraeli has lost his faithful and devoted partner.'[13] Disraeli had lovingly asked for a peerage for his wife when he resigned in 1868. The queen, at first reluctant, ultimately granted his wish and Mary Ann became Viscountess Beaconsfield in her own right. This was a great favour and Mary Ann was ecstatic over the elevation. No doubt it gave her great comfort during her final illness.

The loss of Disraeli's wife gave monarch and former prime minister one more connection and reason to commiserate. Lastly, her dear friend the ex-Emperor Napoleon III died at the beginning of 1873. He had had three operations to remove a 'stone' in his bladder but did not survive the last one. Victoria had a great regard for him and considered him and his empress true friends. She wrote in her journal about the good times they had during their visits back and forth. Now Eugénie, too, was a sad widow. The ex-empress would become a fixture at Victoria's court.

* * *

An exotic interlude occurred in June 1873 when the Shah of Persia, Nasr-Ed-Din, visited London. Naturally, it took a great deal of persuasion for the queen to meet with the visiting dignitary, and somehow, Gladstone was able to extract a promise from Victoria to receive the gentleman. It seems that it was deemed highly politic to do so, given the always tense issue of Russian imperialism in what was called at the time the Near East.

Happily, the queen was pleasantly surprised by the manners of the Shah and his extensive retinue. During a somewhat awkward reception throughout which, the queen wrote in her journal, she felt quite shy, they made presentations and exchanged orders. Afterward, the queen gave a large luncheon where she remarked that he ate only fruit and drank ice water. The retinue visited the Crystal Palace of which the Shah was most impressed.

Victoria also commented that he was taller and thinner than she had first supposed. What she was most pleased about, however, was that the Shah had had her book *Leaves From the Journal of Our Lives in the Highlands* translated into Persian and complimented her on her literary endeavour as well as expressing a wish to visit Scotland.[14]

* * *

A very important and interesting marriage took place in January 1874. Alfred (Affie), Victoria's second son, who had been made the Duke of Edinburgh in 1866, took a wife. Affie was considered by many to be the handsomest of the queen's sons. Like his brothers he had the Hanoverian protruding eyes, but they were a clear and brilliant blue. Because he was a naval man and spent a great deal of his life at sea, he had a deep tan which enhanced those eyes. There is more resemblance in his face of the young and handsome Albert, but none of the children really got Albert's stunning good looks.

Affie was thought to be the most intelligent of Victoria's sons and was 12 when he entered the royal navy. He was a second son and needed something of an occupation and so like many royal princes, he was consigned to the military. He went on his first long voyage when he was 14 years old, and as a youngster got along well with his shipmates no matter their rank or walk of life. He also made a good impression on people at the various stops during these voyages and was enormously popular throughout the empire. Indeed, he might have been an extremely popular prince, but events conspired against him.

Affie had a much better relationship with Albert than his elder brother Bertie, and he was hit very hard by Albert's premature death.[15] He, like Victoria's other children, was not really helped in his grief by his mother. He knew from an early age, however, barring a birthing miracle, he would be the heir to his childless Uncle Ernst, the Duke of Coburg. Since he shared a love of Coburg with his father, he was quite satisfied with that idea. Other options were open to him: the newly independent Greeks offered him their throne, and later the Bulgarians would offer him their principality, but his father and mother had wanted him to be Duke of Saxe-Coburg and Gotha and Albert's wishes were sacrosanct.

Sadly, for Victoria and Gotha, as Affie approached his twenties, he seemed to be more like his elder brother, sowing his wild oats and having affairs with society beauties, and less like the affable boy he used to be. As she had not understood Bertie's adventures, and Albert was too rigid to tolerate them, this would be demonstrated in Affie's case as well. Victoria continually despaired of her second son in her journal and felt he was beyond redemption. She wrote that he was 'ungracious [and] reserved ... which makes him so little liked'.[16] 'In addition, he was dour, moody and generally irascible. Many commented upon his 'badness' and lack of charm, though it wasn't a universal opinion. Others thought him 'very quiet and grave'.[17]

As the time came for him to marry, he had some ideas of his own. He had been interested in marrying his cousin Frederika of Hanover, but Victoria objected because of double relationships and the hereditary blindness in the family. The queen had some interest in Princess Dagmar of Denmark, Alix's sister for Affie, but she, instead, married the Tsarevich Alexander Alexandrovich, later Tsar Alexander III. By 1871, Affie had made his choice and informed his mother. He would ask Tsar Alexander II for the hand of his only surviving daughter, Her Imperial Highness, Grand Duchess Marie Alexandrovna.

Was it a love match? Certainly, Affie initially enjoyed the company of the gregarious teenager. She was not conventionally pretty, but she had lots of brothers and had a way of making young men feel comfortable. Marie was enormously rich and certainly had a very lofty idea of her own importance – after all, she *was* the only daughter of the Tsar. This would later get her in trouble with Queen Victoria when she would insist on having precedence above Alix, the Princess of Wales. Marie reasoned that she was an *Imperial* Highness, so of a far more exalted rank. Victoria, who initially did not want to give her precedence over her five daughters finally gave in and gave her precedence directly after Alix.

Moreover, Marie's parents were not altogether happy at first about the match. Perhaps they thought that the only daughter of the Tsar of All Russia could do better than a second son. Certainly, the tsar felt his daughter was too young and so the young couple were made to wait a year.

Her mother, the tsarina, felt she wouldn't like England – and in that she was correct.

Victoria seemed at best lukewarm with the choice. Marie was younger than the prince by over nine years, but at least she wasn't Roman Catholic, something that could not have been tolerated. However, she was Russian, and the queen's opinion of Russia – that it was autocratic, dangerous and with an atrocious climate – hadn't changed much since the Crimean War. She was keenly aware of the instability and insecurity of the ruling family and in that she was completely correct. Marie's parents, however, felt a similar distrust of England. The queen was aware of their reservations and put it to the fear of the loss of their only daughter.

Then there were issues about where the queen would meet her future daughter-in-law. Victoria wanted the tsar to bring his daughter to Scotland to meet her and the tsar refused. Eventually a compromise was reached, and all met in Cologne, Germany. Victoria was furious and said that she had been on the throne twenty years longer than the tsar and didn't like being treated like a little 'princess'. It is at this point that the idea of becoming Empress of India might have appealed to her, though it was not suggested until several years later. She clearly hated someone, even the tsar, pulling rank on her.

The British people seemed to approve of the match because Marie wasn't another impecunious German. Indeed, the Russian Imperial Family was one of the richest in the world and the tsar gave his daughter an immense dowry, a yearly income and many of the Imperial Jewels. However, as time went on, Victoria was able to take each Russian as they came and would later admit to liking many of the Romanovs for themselves.

Ultimately, despite the whole precedence issue and feeling that the tsar wasn't respectful to her, Victoria came to like her daughter-in-law very much: 'I have formed a high opinion of her; her wonderfully even cheerful satisfied temper – her kind and indulgent disposition, free from bigotry and intolerance & her serious, intelligent mind … makes her a most agreeable companion.'[18]

The wedding took place 23 January 1874. The couple were married in St Petersburg and the queen was not in attendance. With her opinions about that country, one could hardly have expected her to travel such a long way. However, that did not stop her from getting many reports and accounts about the ceremony and festivities from Bertie and Vicky who did attend. She wrote a long description in her journal:

> My mind entirely taken up with today's great event & I felt it very trying to be absent! May God bless our Child & make him happy … — Walked out with Beatrice & planted a tree in remembrance of the day.…
>
> Received telegrams from Bertie, Vicky … saying all had gone off extremely well & the 2 marriages had been very impressive. Heard also that the Banquet for 800 people was over, which was followed by a Ball, all most magnificent. After this the young couple were going to leave. Thought so much of them. May they be happy & keep their happiness longer than I did mine! —[19]

The couple returned to England several months later. Victoria was excited and expectant and continued writing positive things about Marie. She liked her new daughter-in-law but remarked that no one liked Affie; he was a difficult character, who later became an unhappy alcoholic, and it can't be said that the couple were deliriously blissful after a time.

Marie, as her parents expected, disliked England, and complained a great deal about the food and the climate. The comparison to the splendour of Russia, the massive palaces, the glorious colours of the buildings, the vastness of *everything* made London, her mother-in-law's palaces, incredibly disappointing, even bourgeois.

Meanwhile, the new Duchess of Edinburgh was enlarging her family. Affie's son and heir, Alfred Jr. was born at Buckingham palace in October 1874. He was followed a year later by Marie, who was born at Eastwell Manor in Kent where the family resided until Affie's eventual succession to the Duchy of Saxe-Coburg and Gotha. And in quick succession came Victoria Melita, born in 1876 in Malta, where Affie was stationed as part of his naval duties. Victoria noted that Victoria Melita or 'Ducky' as she was known in the family was her '16th grand daughter & 25th grandchild, born on little Ernie's birthday'.[20] Ernie was Ernst Ludwig, Alice's son, who had been born on the same date in 1868. A fourth daughter, Alexandra (called 'Sandra' in the family) was born at the Rosenau in Coburg in 1878.

There would be one more daughter born in 1884 called Beatrice or 'Baby Bee'.

Because of Affie's naval career the family moved around quite a bit. Eventually, Affie was made commander-in-chief of the Mediterranean Fleet which was based in Malta. Marie, who hated England and ultimately did not get along well with her mother-in-law, loved being in Malta where she was the first lady of the island.

And, after a while, Victoria's positive feelings about her daughter-in-law changed.

* * *

The following month there was excellent news for Victoria. Her beloved Disraeli was returned as prime minister.

Poor Gladstone, for all his great respect for the monarchy, he just couldn't convey it to the person of the queen. They had a major dispute about what employment might be sought for Bertie while Prince of Wales. Gladstone had grandiose views of the prince serving as a sort of viceroy in Ireland and giving a boost to the monarchy for its Irish subjects. When approached with the idea, the queen would not hear of it. Gladstone pressed and pressed and *pressed* about the issue and at last, in exasperation, Victoria wrote that when she had a strong conviction about anything she was generally right. Gladstone finally backed down. His party was having problems of its own, the Liberal party was losing support and in February 1874, he made the decision to dissolve the government.

When he took his leave of her, the pair talked about the results of the election and what had gone wrong. They were both surprised at the results and how the Liberal party had plummeted in popularity. After Gladstone left, the queen wrote that she found the interview most 'trying'.

Chapter Seven

'...we, authors, ma'am' redux

The despised Gladstone was gone.

Victoria breathed a sigh of relief. No more would she be pressed by his abhorrent ideas; she knew best for the country and certainly her family, and specifically Bertie. In particular, she hated being dictated to, which Mr Gladstone tried to do. Mr Disraeli, naming her 'the Faery Queen', was back, and all seemed right with the world. If the above seems a breathless exaggeration, it wasn't by much. Historian Theo Aronson goes as far as to call it a 'romantic partnership'.[1] Added to the fact that Brown continued to be a factor in her life, the queen felt safe, secure, esteemed, protected, and loved.

To say that the exotic prime minister and his 'Faery', despite being choleric and more and more overweight, got along beautifully is an understatement. It was noted that their audiences often exceeded the allotted hour, and laughing and gaiety could be heard from the room. Their discussions were in fact so delightful that often the queen would have to be reminded that she had another appointment.

In contrast, the queen had experienced great relief if her audiences with Gladstone were less than twenty minutes. She was happy not to hear his endless lectures, his subversive views, and his entreaties to go out in public. Indeed, in her mind, the only thing that the two prime ministers had in common was their reverence for the monarchy – although she no doubt thought, in Mr Gladstone's case that might be questionable.

Victoria also felt that when it came to the business of the state, Disraeli didn't leave anything out as others had done before him, so she trusted him implicitly and explicitly. He, she would say, told her everything.

It was also during the mid-century and into the 1870s that the queen became involved in what she called the completion of the Reformation. She felt that Roman Catholicism was encroaching upon Britain once again and that there were too many conversions into the Catholic faith.

In addition, she preferred a simpler service and enjoyed the Scottish Presbyterian church to the high Church of England.

Gladstone had opposed what he termed the authoritarianism of the church and its lack of liberality. However, he did oppose the Public Worship Regulation Act that was passed in 1874 because it cleansed the Anglican church of all and any rituals that smacked of Catholicism. It was a swim upstream for the Liberals who were against the act because they believed in the separation of church and state, but they were out of power. Disraeli, when he was in the Opposition and when he was in in power, was for it, while the queen, who was the head of the church was strongly for it.

But the queen's interest lay more in foreign affairs, and her attention was easily directed there. Disraeli, who believed in the Imperial dream, knew what he was doing when he deftly pointed her in the direction of India. In November 1875 the Khedive of Egypt, Isma'il Pasha, who was deeply in debt, wanted to sell his shares of the Suez Canal, which comprised 44 per cent, in order to settle them. The canal, which had taken ten years to build, had been completed in 1869. It was built by Ferdinand de Lesseps and owned by Egypt, France and Britain. Disraeli, with an eye to protecting all routes to the East, was able to persuade Victoria that the British government should buy the shares worth £4 million. The Baron Lionel de Rothchild lent the government the money and the purchase was made. The canal shortened the journey to India by approximately 5,500 miles and therefore was a much-desired link.[2]

With the queen's prompting, Disraeli now introduced The Royal Titles Act which would add on to Victoria's titles 'Empress of India'. To the queen's chagrin this was hotly debated in parliament, with the opposition coming from some in the Liberal party. Their reasons were that none of the previous prime ministers were asked to do this and that it would change the queen's titles altogether. She wrote that this would certainly *not* be the case, but there were mutterings that the titles 'queen' and 'king' were grand historic titles, while 'emperor' and 'empress' were autocratic, despotic, foreign-sounding and altogether negative. In truth she had been informally the Empress of India for as long as the sub-continent had been a crown colony, but Victoria wanted to make it official since it irked her that her daughter would be an empress, and her Russian 'brother' was an emperor.

In conjunction with this debate, Bertie at last had an assignment that he could enjoy and that would produce positive benefits. He decided it would be a good idea were he to tour India. Though the queen instinctively thought it was never a good idea to let Bertie do anything he wanted to do, Bertie was able to persuade Disraeli to champion the idea.[3] Disraeli, who certainly appreciated the idea of Imperial gestures, as opposed to the despised Gladstone who was firmly on the side of European liberalism, put it to the queen and wisely left it with her.

Discussions and questions ensued: should Alix accompany him or not? She certainly wanted to but was persuaded that it was too difficult a journey for a woman. Of course, there was that other reason: Bertie might wish to flirt (and more) with women during his time away from home. Questions about who was paying: not the queen. Who would accompany the prince? Certainly, only people of whom Victoria approved. However, at last all was settled and from November 1875 to March 1876, Bertie and a large entourage, toured India.

It was highly successful, and the prince made an excellent impression wherever he went. It seemed that one of the positive traits he learned from his mother was a relative lack of prejudice against people with different religions and skin colours. He remarked: 'because a man has a black face and a different religion from one's own, there is no reason why he should be treated as a brute'.[4] The prince assiduously reported back to his mother so that by a certain point she got tired of his descriptions of animals, jewels, and ceremonies. A highly successful tour with cheering crowds wherever he went, perhaps the most poignant note was a large sign with the message: TELL MAMA WE'RE HAPPY.

The debates about the queen's title continued. There were arguments about the precedence of the titles, possible changes in currency and even consultations with other colonies. Should there also be a Duke of Canada or Australia? Was Disraeli pushing her into this, did she want this? The Opposition kept pounding. Although it was never used in Britain, the bill did at last pass and Victoria was declared by parliament Queen-Empress on 1 May 1876.

It would be formally announced in India, in what would be known as the Proclamation Durbar,[5] 1 January 1877. It was in Delhi and under the auspices of the Viceroy, Lord Lytton that it all came to pass. This completed the transfer of control of India from the East Indian Company to the Crown. Victoria was now Queen of Great Britain and Empress of India.

Disraeli also got his award. He was elevated to the peerage in August 1876 and sat in the House of Lords as Lord Beaconsfield.

* * *

The queen and her 'Dizzy' had a decidedly more serious difficulty to ponder in the mid- and late seventies. That was the very real and dangerous 'Eastern Question'. Put simply, it was the rivalry between the two great empires, Britain and Russia, over the disintegrating 'sick man of Europe', the Ottoman Empire. Both large powers were determined to thwart the other over this issue. Russia was interested in what land it might be able to grab from this slow dissolution, and Britain was just as determined not to let them get anything, worrying as they did about how it would affect their access to their empire in Asia, and more specifically India. There had been several wars already fought over this issue and it continued into the late nineteenth century.

Victoria was very pro-Turkish for the above reason, but also because of her entrenched animosity towards Russia. However, the Turks were committing terrible atrocities against Christians in Bosnia, Herzegovina, Serbia and Bulgaria, which angered Gladstone and the Opposition. Gladstone who wrote several pamphlets about what the Turks were doing was also making powerful speeches about the matter in parliament. It was difficult for Disraeli to support the crumbling and erratic Ottomans, but the queen was convinced that the Russians were pushing their fellow Slavs to revolt and therefore what was happening was terrible but not unexpected.

All the scattered uprisings and instabilities caused Russia to declare war on Turkey in April 1877. Victoria was livid; this was just what one could expect from the 'Russian bear', as she thought of the tsar. She would be happy to go to war against the 'scoundrel' (meaning the tsar) herself and she wanted her household to share the beliefs. To say that she was annoyed that Ponsonby sided with Gladstone over the matter is an understatement. In her little retaliation, she used her son Leopold and Lady Ely to communicate with the ministries. She even thought of moving Ponsonby's position elsewhere in her household, but he was adamant that if she did, she would lose him. Ponsonby kept his position.

The war dragged on for over a year. The British warned the Russians not to march into Constantinople and when it looked as though they might, Britain sent ships to that area as well as moving troops from India to the Mediterranean. Although Dizzy encouraged the queen's anger and bellicosity toward Russia, he used it to finally get the cabinet to agree to this 'showing of the flag'. It was enough to get the Russians to sit down and negotiate a peace called the Treaty of San Stefano which gave independence to Romania, Serbia and Montenegro and further ended Ottoman control of the Balkans. One by-product of the treaty was the transfer of the Island of Cyprus to Britain, which gave Britain even more security in the Mediterranean, but control of a most troublesome and divided island.

In 1878 at the Congress of Berlin, Disraeli and Chancellor von Bismarck met in person and hammered out alterations to the treaty that furthered Britain's interests in that area and kept the balance of power in Europe. Bismarck was extremely impressed with Beaconsfield and said: 'Disraeli *is* England'.[6] Certain lands were moved around taking into consideration only what was best for Europe, not the Balkans. In the process, the Russians would not get what they most desired – access to the Mediterranean. Was it a long-range cause of the First World War? Maybe. But, for the moment, British naval supremacy was maintained, and the queen was very happy with Dizzy, as was the rest of the country.

It can't be doubted that while Brown gave her basic care, Dizzy gave her emotional and intellectual support. It is interesting to note that Disraeli always treated John Brown with respect, which is more than the queen's household and family did. The queen, who never wavered in her affection for Brown, valued Disraeli's regard for her favourite. Disraeli even asked about Brown in the letters he wrote to the queen, and she never forgot his consideration.[7]

Disraeli also did something else which was very important, and that was to show Bertie the respect that the prince expected and never received from his mother. Unlike some in the queen's household, Disraeli treated him as someone who should be kept well-informed about matters of state. It is thought that Dizzy appreciated Bertie's skills as a diplomat and as someone who understood the running of the state far more than Victoria gave him credit for. Because of this, Victoria, too, slowly began to see her son in a more positive light.

* * *

Princess Alice continued to expand her brood in the 1870s. In October 1870, she gave birth to a second little boy, Friedrich, or 'Frittie'. Frittie suffered from haemophilia and died after a fall out of a window when he was just a toddler. Little Alix was born in 1872, and the last of the Hessian children, Marie or 'May', was born in 1874.

In the winter of 1878, Alice's daughter, Victoria complained of a sore throat. She was quickly put to bed with a hot water bottle and a physician was sent for who diagnosed diphtheria. The entire family, excepting Alice and little Ella, quickly came down with the dreaded disease. Desperate to do something, Victoria sent her personal physician, Sir William Jenner, to help the beleaguered family. The queen, who received daily and sometimes hourly reports, wrote: 'I am miserable …. Poor dear Alice, and she so delicate herself.'[8]

Alice threw herself into nursing her four sick daughters and remaining son. She was going from sick room to sick room soothing fevered brows while the family physicians tried to match her twelve-hour schedules. Tragically, little May died of the disease in mid-November. Alice held back telling the other children about the death of their sister, but eventually told her remaining son Ernie, who was slowly convalescing from the illness. To comfort him, she gave him a kiss and with that, Alice came down with the disease.

The illness and exhaustion took their toll on Alice and as 14 December, her father's death day, came around, there was no improvement. The queen continued to receive nearly hourly reports on the health of her daughter, and there seemed to be a rally; however, by later that morning, as Victoria wrote:

This terrible day come round again! … When dressed, I went into my sitting room for breakfast, & met Brown coming in with 2 bad telegrams; I looked first at one from Louis, which I did not at first take in, saying: 'Poor Mama, poor me, my happiness gone, dear, dear Alice. God's will be done'. (I can hardly write it!)

… All, in the house, were crying & in great distress. — Telegrams streaming in, all day, from all sides. Hardly able to answer them. … That this dear, talented, distinguished, tender hearted, noble minded, sweet child, who behaved so admirably, during her dear Father's illness, & afterwards, in supporting me, & helping me in every possible way, — should be called back to her Father, on this very anniversary, seems almost incredible, & most mysterious!'[9]

The evening before, Alice had been conscious, and had visits from her family as well as Sir William. She died in her sleep, early that morning.

Victoria's first child to die during her lifetime.

Alice left a widower and five children. Her eldest daughter, Victoria, was 15 years old, and she took over the family with the help of her sister Ella and various aunts and uncles. Most importantly, the queen wrote lovingly to her granddaughter, 'Think of me as your mama.'

The queen's relationship with Alice had always been a little bumpy. This child, who was so much like Albert, had also had an iron will when it came to her children and husband. She was first lady of Darmstadt for most of her time there and felt it her duty and obligation to be present in the Grand Duchy. It took some time for Victoria to understand that.

Like her father, Alice was an incredibly hard worker and unsparing of herself. During her time in Darmstadt, she founded the Alice *Fraüen Verein*, or Women's Union, she founded an orphanage, a girls' school, a home for unwed mothers and an insane asylum. She was an avid follower of Florence Nightingale and her women's union trained Red Cross nurses according to Miss Nightingale's methods as outlined in her *Notes for Nursing*. Alice nursed in both wars in which Darmstadt took part: the Austro-Prussian War of 1866 and the Franco-Prussian War in 1870. She was a true first lady of Hesse.

Nevertheless, Alice and her family did visit Britain. In fact, it was during a trip that Alice gave birth to her first child, Victoria. She was beloved in Britain, as people well remembered her sacrifice and love while caring for the prince consort, and the support she was to her mother thereafter. She also had a robust correspondence with the queen, and the bumpiness felt in the early years of her marriage gave way to something of an understanding by Victoria of the position held by Alice.

In truth, Vicky and Alice may have been the only daughters who were truly permitted to grow up. Because both lived far away, their mother had to acknowledge their duties and their growth from British princesses to in one case an empress, and in the other a grand duchess. She eventually learned to treat both women like adults, so unlike the way she treated the daughters and sons who lived with her or close to her.

* * *

Though the queen mourned her beloved daughter deeply, there were always distractions. Disraeli encouraged the queen's love of empire and foreign affairs and in 1879, all Britain turned to South Africa. At the time there were problems between the Dutch settlers, the 'Boers', and the indigenous population, the Zulus. The Boers were incredibly cruel in their warfare against the Zulus, killing both women and children. The Zulus routed the Boers and Britain felt it necessary to send reinforcements to the settlers.

The young Prince Imperial, Louis Napoléon, a graduate of the Military Academy in Woolwich, insisted on being part of the forces, although, he had to get special permission since he was the hope for the future of the Bonapartists. When Princess Beatrice was just 15, she was observed talking to the prince and it was thought that she had a tendresse for the young man. Though he was a Catholic, there were people who thought the two might make a match of it and so rumours started. He was handsome and melancholy looking, so perhaps she was in love with him, or perhaps not. Louis Napoléon was devoted to two causes: to redeem his father, and to regain his throne.[10]

When Beatrice married in 1885, her daughter was named for her mother and the ex-empress – whether because she was a good friend of the family or for more romantic reasons, the truth will never be known; it is known, however, that she had a photograph of Louis Napoléon on her desk at her death at the age of 87.

In the end, Louis Napoléon got his wish. He had his mother plead with Victoria for him to be able to take part in the action and she reluctantly acquiesced. Tragically, on the morning of 1 June 1879, the prince was killed. His troop had been ambushed by the Zulus and the prince was unhorsed. Nevertheless, he fought valiantly and was speared multiple times.

This was yet another death for the queen who had been very fond of the young man, with his sad eyes that looked exactly like the ex-empress's. He was one of the few people who was never afraid of Victoria and was never anything but himself around her. She wanted him to have a magnificent funeral with all the trimmings. Disraeli disagreed since he did not want to offend France, but in this, the queen was insistent. These disagreements put their close relationship under a small cloud – but it very soon was mended.

Foreign politics continued to be a worry. The Viceroy of India wanted to turn Afghanistan into a friendly buffer state between the expanding Russian empire and British India. He was more or less successful, but only after Afghani troops stormed the British Mission in Kabul, killing all the members there. Eventually, the Afghanis would be defeated, but was it futile in the end? Was the imperial lion souring? Disraeli certainly didn't think so and the queen agreed with him.

* * *

Arthur, the queen's third son, was by all accounts her favourite. Named after the Duke of Wellington, Arthur attended the Royal Military at Woolwich and graduated a lieutenant in the Corps of the Royal Engineers in 1868. From then on, he had a distinguished military career serving all over the empire in India, South Africa and Canada. In 1874, Prince Arthur was created Duke of Connaught and Strathearn.

Arthur was probably favoured by Victoria because she didn't expect great things from him and so was continually pleased. As the third son, he was a less complicated and morose creature than Affie, not ill like Leopold and not the heir, like Bertie – from whom Victoria expected much and was repeatedly disappointed. That didn't prevent the queen from constantly instructing him on what he should do and what he should not do – nagging, in fact – but she always considered him her most precious object.[11]

On 13 March 1879, Arthur took a bride. Vicky, the indefatigable matchmaker, introduced him to his future wife: Princess Louise Margaret of Prussia, the daughter of Prince Frederick Charles of Prussia who was a cousin to Vicky's husband, Fritz, and Princess Maria Anna of Anhalt-Dessau. Louise's parents were estranged; their marriage had been extremely unhappy, and Frederick Charles was a brutal drunkard and a bully to his children.

The queen was not initially pleased with Arthur's choice. Why marry a girl from a broken home, she thought? Why not look around more? But really, why should Arthur, who was so good, marry at all? The queen thought the princess rather unattractive and wanted Arthur to meet other prospects. However, Arthur was firm and 'Louischen', as the queen would call her, was his choice. In fact, she was extremely attractive, and her two daughters were among the prettiest of the queen's granddaughters. Vicky and Fritz came for the wedding which took place on a sunny day in March.

The queen was much more cheerful on this wedding day than she had been during others, especially those of her daughters. As she expressed it in her journal, she wasn't 'parting with my dear child … it is to see, a dear or excellent son give me a daughter … whom he so dearly loves!'[12] In other words, she wasn't losing a son, but gaining a daughter. And one that she found more and more attractive as time went on. By all accounts, it was a love match, which made it all the better.

A few months later, the queen's first great-grandchild was born. Feodora of Saxe-Meiningen, born 12 May 1879, was the daughter of Vicky's daughter Charley, and her husband Bernhard III, Duke of Saxe-Meiningen. Victoria put a short note in her journal: 'Excellent accounts of Charlotte.'[13] But says little else about the birth. Possibly because Charley was always at odds with her own mother and was considered an extremely difficult child. Vicky was extremely hard on her, telling her mother that Charlotte was stupid and ugly.

Like Bertie, Charlotte was hardly stupid – nor, as photographs show, ugly – and realised that she could never please her mother and so went onto the side of Willy and Henry and their paternal grandparents, Vicky's in laws, the old Kaiser and his wife. In any case, it is nearly certain that Charley and her daughter Feodora suffered from the dreaded porphyria that had been passed down through the British Royal family. More interested in Berlin society than expanding her family, Charley refused to have more children.

Little Feodora, a particularly sad only child, constantly suffered from ill-health. She married but was fated to have an unhappy life due to illness and depression, so much so that she committed suicide 26 August 1945.

* * *

More immediate to the queen was the results of the election of 1880. Because of domestic issues, what should have been an easy win for the Conservatives turned out the other way. The returns announced a Liberal victory, and the despised Gladstone was back in power. And no sooner was he there than the queen wrote that he was a 'half-crazy enthusiast ... ruining all the good of 6 years [of] peaceful, wise government.'[14] The Boers, the Russians and Afghanis were no doubt forgotten.

Dizzy was old and asthmatic at this point, and so was happy to give up the mantle. The queen, of course, would have kept him forever, but that was not to be. She had to accept his resignation, but they continued to meet and dine together until Dizzy was too ill to do so. On his death bed, he was asked if he would like a visit from the sovereign and he famously replied: 'No it is better not. She'd only ask me to take a message to Albert.'[15] Benjamin Disraeli died 19 April 1881. The queen wrote:

I am most terribly shocked & grieved, for dear Ld Beaconsfield was one of my best, most devoted, & kindest of friends, as well as wisest of counsellors. His loss is irreparable, to me & the country. To lose such a pillar of strength, at such a moment, is dreadful! Just this day, year, Ld Beaconsfield left Windsor, having resigned, which he felt so much, & so did I, but I was full of hope he might be my Minister again.'[16]

He had no wish for the state funeral that the queen might have given him, but a simple one to be buried next to his wife, Mary Ann. The queen placed a memorial tablet over his pew at his seat at Hughenden and sent a primrose wreath to his grave which bore the inscription 'His favourite flower ... A tribute of affection from Queen Victoria.'[17] Victoria could not attend, but she sent her three sons to the ceremony, and she visited the graveyard alone four days later.

Disraeli's political contributions were many and varied but for the queen, he provided a deep and even passionate friendship filled with emotion that satisfied Victoria's equally impassioned nature. Along with John Brown, he brought her out of mourning and made her visible once again to the public. He made her an empress and in doing so made his 'faery' happier than she had been since the death of Albert.

According to Theo Aronson, '[B]y treating her as a great queen and an attractive woman, Disraeli re-fashioned Victoria.'[18] Disraeli created a romantic Shakespearian world where Victoria could be 'the faery queen' and in doing so gave her an identity that was independent of her husband, her mother, and the other counsellors in her past. He showed the reclusive and sad 'widow of Windsor' a way out where her identity depended on no one else but herself and the woman she was becoming and thus restored her self-confidence. She emerged as the true Queen-Empress and despite all the flowery flattery of which Dizzy was adept, their relationship was a loving one and a true meeting of two very different minds.

She had metamorphosed from Melbourne's student to Albert's consort, to at last, 'the Queen-Empress before whom Disraeli swept his deepest bows. [T]he impressive object of an empire's worship....'[19]

Chapter Eight

'...the queen's stallion....'

Whether she would admit it or not, Victoria had moved on. She would always mourn the loss and absence of Albert, but the last vestiges of agonising grief were truly gone. There was still Brown there to give her a tipple of whisky in her tea, but she was moving into the phase that many historians called her apotheosis, the stunning twenty years when she was the true queen-empress, Victoria *Regina et Imperatrix*. That glorious time when the light of the British Empire shone its brightest. And she was able to do it all on her own.

And, whether she liked it or not, she now had to deal with Gladstone and there were few around to sweeten the pill. He was in office from 1880 until 1885, then for a brief period in 1886 and then he was gone into the Opposition for the rest of the decade.

At the start of the decade Britain had to deal with the First Boer War. It was a conflict over the British annexation of the Transvaal and the resentment of the Boer residents over taxation. Gladstone preferred self-determination over imperialism and eventually the Boers were given their 'qualified' independence. The queen was not pleased with the outcome and thought it would set a dangerous precedent. Would her empire become unravelled now that Gladstone was at the helm? She was more encouraged with his dealings with Egypt. The country was unstable and after a short war in 1882 in which her son Arthur took part, the British army took control of the country and stayed for forty years. The outcome was control of the Suez Canal which was so important for secure routes to India. During this war, Victoria noted in her journal that Arthur was safe and well, and had proved himself a brave soldier. She often expressed to him that she wished he was the eldest and was extremely annoyed that he was not made Commander-in-Chief of the army later.

* * *

It appears from many of her biographers, that Louise's marriage was not one of domestic harmony. In her first years as a married woman, Louise was certainly worried about her inability to conceive. Her first duty was the begetting of an heir for the eventual dukedom, but unfortunately this was not to be. The pair had no children and whether this was due to childhood illnesses on Louise's part or sexual disinclination on her husband's part we will never know. Louise, however, busied herself with good works and her art as time wore on. In 1878, Disraeli offered Lorne the office of Governor-General of the Dominion of Canada. This was an exciting opportunity that Lorne could not refuse, and the couple left for Canada in autumn 1878.

In 1880, after several years in Canada, Louise suffered a terrible injury in a sleigh accident. She was seriously hurt, and according to Historian Jerrold Packard, it was then that her marriage began to unravel.[1] Louise decided to go home to her family and left Lorne in Ottawa. The reason given for this decision was her health. Eventually, however, she did return to Canada in 1882, though not to the capital. Lorne resigned in 1883, ostensibly because of Louise's health and the damage that the cold Canadian winters did to her. Perhaps, as well, he might have wanted to save his faltering marriage.

* * *

The youngest son, Leopold, comes into the spotlight now. He was created Duke of Albany during the queen's birthday honours in May 1881. Her youngest-but-one was 28 years old and suffered from haemophilia. He was an attractive young man with a great zest for life. In photographs he maintains a slender figure, unlike his older brothers, and has a much more intelligent and soulful air. He had a way about him that was very 'taking', and many remarked upon his appealing manner. He liked people and wanted 'desperately to be liked'.[2] His mother was understandably over-protective of him, and this caused him to wish fervently to get out from under her wings.

Since a military career was out of the question, Leopold had a ferocious desire to learn. He was able to persuade his mother to let him study at Oxford, though rather than risk her wrath, he made this request by letter. It took her some time to come around, though she finally did – grudgingly.

Victoria didn't understand how he might be lonely, surrounded as he was by only his mother and his baby sister, Beatrice. She also made mention of needing a grown-up child around when company came to visit.

Leopold spent four years at Christ Church, Oxford, and left with an honorary doctorate in Civil Law. It was also at Oxford that he met the family of Dean Liddell, and in particular one of the daughters, Alice, who was the model for *Alice in Wonderland*. The entire family became Leopold's close friends, and he was extremely happy at Oxford. This royal son was considered a particularly clever and thoughtful person.

Victoria had always assumed that Leopold would not marry because of his condition. She had planned that he would stay with her forever as an unpaid secretary and companion, putting him in the dreary category of the 'useful' daughters. Leopold had no such intentions and though each declaration of independence was a struggle, he nevertheless had as much iron will as his mother. Because of his illness he had a feverish desire to live and grab every opportunity. His mother permitted some travel, and he travelled in Italy and visited his sister Louise, when she and Lord Lorne were serving as Governor-General in Canada.

The death of his sister Alice in 1878 affected him deeply. He was very close to the Hessian family and poured affection on his nieces and nephew. The loss of his sister left a gaping hole in his life, and he tried to fill it by spending time with the children of the family and his brother-in-law the Grand Duke. He never patronised the young family, and they grew to love and admire him greatly; in the case of Alice's son Ernie, even more than his own father, Grand Duke Ludwig, who always seemed to be out shooting whenever he was needed. Spending time with the Hesses also precipitated Leopold's wish to have a family of his own. And so, he began to search for a bride.

It was difficult as all were aware of his health issues. Not only the haemophilia that could likely be passed down, but also that he may well have had epilepsy. He had considered his second cousin, Princess Frederica of Hanover, but never proposed to her. Several other German princesses were considered, but they were teenagers when at this point Leopold was nearly 30 years old. He considered a young Englishwoman, Mary Baring, the daughter of Lord Ashburton, but she also was too young. He never proposed to Frances 'Daisy' Maynard', though she intimated that he did. She would later marry Francis Grenville becoming the Countess of Warwick, as well as one of Bertie's mistresses. Alice Liddell, whom some thought Leopold wanted to marry, became engaged in 1880, and so Leopold continued to look.

After Leopold received his peerage in 1881, he had been encouraged to consider the young Helen of Waldeck and Pyrmont as a possible candidate. They met for the first time at the Villa Westphalia and later again in Frankfurt. The couple were engaged in November 1882. The queen's reaction was characteristic. She wrote to Vicky: 'To me his marrying at all is a grief and a shock which I can't get over.'[3] In a typical turnabout, she then went on to say she was happy with his choice; she wrote that she had heard that Helen was 'so good and nice'.[4]

Princess Helen was the daughter of George Victor, Prince of Waldeck and Pyrmont and Princess Helena of Nassau. She was born in February 1861 at Arolsen, Germany, and her elder sister Emma was the wife of King William III of the Netherlands – albeit forty years his junior. The queen found her 'charming, so amiable, kind, friendly and cheerful. She would be very pretty were it not for her complexion which … is very red.'[5]

The pair were married 27 April 1882 at St George's Chapel, Windsor. The queen noted in her journal that she wore her lace and wedding veil for the first time since her own wedding. She was mostly concerned about how Leopold would physically get through the ceremony. Indeed, he was able to walk on his own up to the nave but was supported by Bertie and his brother-in-law Ludwig of Hesse at the altar.

The queen usually wrote on the morning of her children's weddings about how trying the day was going to be. The weddings of Alice and Bertie had been extremely mournful occasions for her. However, in this case she seemed about as happy for Leopold as she was capable of being at the thought of losing yet another useful child. She wrote:

This exciting day is all over, & past, like a dream, & the last, but one, of my children is married, & has left the paternal home, but not entirely, as he still keeps his rooms. It was very trying to see the dear Boy, on this important day of his life, still lame & shaky, but I am thankful it is well over.[6]

Leopold and Helen were happy together. Helen was attractive and intelligent and when Leopold introduced her to his Oxford friends, she was able to hold her own. He had chosen a woman who was 'generous enough to enter into his world, and intelligent enough to share it [.]'[7] His health was always a concern during their marriage, but Leopold wanted to live as normal a life as was possible.

He continued to assist Victoria with her work and was even allowed to have keys to the red dispatch boxes, which Bertie, up to that time, certainly was not. Leopold suggested himself as a candidate for the Governor-General of Canada or a lesser regional governmental post in Australia, however, the queen, and ultimately the government, refused to consider the appointment. All felt not only his health would not endure it, but also, he had not the experience for such postings. While Gladstone said that the princes should only hold decorative offices and leave the real work to those qualified to do it, the queen nevertheless still opposed Leopold's appointment. She felt that Leopold's first duty was to her. Arthur, at this point, was at a posting in India, and so she decreed that his brother must stay nearby until he returned.

The Albanys had two children: Alice, born in 1883 and Charles Edward in 1884. Fascinating that the queen, who thought babies ugly and frog-like, thought Alice quite beautiful and plump.

* * *

Several years before these events, Queen Victoria added another important member to her household. He was James Reid, later Sir James, who became Resident Medical attendant in July 1881 and would continue to be a member of the household until the queen's death. Dr Reid was from Aberdeenshire in Scotland and received his medical degree in 1872. At the time, the best medical schools were thought to be in Scotland, so his graduating with high honours from the University of Aberdeen was in his favour.

He was approached by a member of the queen's household and asked if he was at all interested in such a posting. He interviewed with the queen in June and was offered the post. The queen not only saw unimpeachable medical qualifications, but also saw other qualities that she liked, including 'shrewdness, tact, honesty and a great sense of humour'.[8] In addition, she liked the idea that he was a German scholar.

The queen relied on him for his rectitude as far as her health was concerned and eventually trusted his advice on other subjects as well. The story goes that when he was initially appointed, the queen did not have him dine with the household. She felt that he was 'below the salt'. Apparently, this did not bother Reid much and he began to have dinner parties of his own which were found to be much more fun and interesting than the queen's dull repasts. Eventually, the queen decided to have Reid dine with her and the household. He would work under Sir William Jenner as physician-extraordinary and when Sir William retired in 1889, he became physician-in-ordinary. Six years later, he was knighted.

As the queen grew older and more infirm, she would depend on Sir James more and more. Indeed, he would find himself doing commissions for the queen that were far outside the purview of his medical duties. He found himself often giving her advice about family matters and serving as an intermediary, a position he did not relish. In particular, he became very good friends with Sir Henry Ponsonby. According to Reid's biographer, a warm friendship grew between the two men based on their sense of humour, and no doubt the ways that they had to finesse issues with the queen. Ponsonby felt that Reid knew which health and family matters to take seriously – and which not to blow out of all proportion.

* * *

In 1882, Louise's erstwhile art instructor and sculptor, Joseph Boehm was commissioned to make a bust of the queen's best friend, John Brown. The talk of the household was that Brown was 'the queen's stallion'.[9] Though that was a rather malicious characterisation, as discussed earlier, Brown continued to be an important part of Victoria's life, at her side seven days a week, fifty-two weeks a year.

He never took time off, never softened his demeanour with others on the staff, the household, and particularly the family. Victoria's children continued to dislike him. Bertie in particular had shouting matches with him, but Victoria always defended him no matter what happened and no matter what he did. She certainly countenanced no complaints about him from anyone – ever.

Brown never shirked his duties toward the queen and reported to her even when ill. In early March 1883 he was suffering from chills and fever

Queen Victoria with Prince Albert and Princess Victoire, the Duchess of Kent, Victoria's mother, with L-R Albert Edward (Bertie), Victoria (Vicky), Alice with a blurry Arthur in front of her, Louise, Helena (Lenchen) and Alfred (Affie).

Queen Victoria's complete family. L-R Alice, Arthur, Prince Albert, Bertie, Leopold, Louise, the queen holding Beatrice, Affie, Vicky and Lenchen, 1857.

Vicky's wedding photo with her parents. Victoria was trembling, hence the blurry image, 1858.

Vicky and Prince Friedrich Wilhelm (Fritz) at the time of their marriage, 1858.

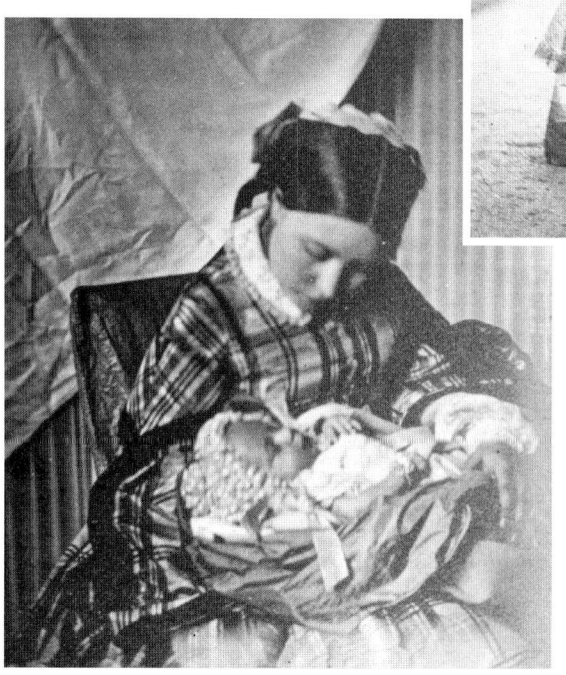

Vicky cuddling Wilhelm (Willy). She looks like a child herself, 1859.

Lady Jane Spencer, Baroness Churchill, a Lady of the Bedchamber who served the queen for fifty years.

Victoria sitting on bench with Arthur and Lady Ely, a Lady of the Bedchamber, standing.

Princess Alexandra (Alix), the queen, the Prince of Wales (Bertie) with a bust of Albert at the time of their marriage, 1863.

Victoria and John Brown.

Victoria's grown sons: L-R: Bertie, Affie, Arthur, and Leopold. 1881, Balmoral.

Lenchen and Christian of Schleswig-Holstein at the time of their engagement, 1865.

Lenchen and Christian's children: L-R Helena Victoria, Christian Victor, Marie Louise, Albert.

Benjamin Disraeli, the queen's favourite prime minister.

Sir Henry Ponsonby, Victoria's private secretary.

William Ewart Gladstone, Victoria's least favourite prime minister.

Bertie and family. L-R Maud, Louise, Albert Victor (Eddy), Victoria (Toria) (on floor), Alix, Bertie, and George.

Louise at the time of her marriage, 1871.

Victoria surrounded by Louise, Leopold, Lord Lorne, and Beatrice.

Affie and Marie at time of their marriage, 1874.

A group in Malta when Affie was stationed there. Standing: Marie, Princess Beatrice of Edinburgh (Baby Bee), Prince Ernst Ludwig of Hesse (Ernie), Prince Max of Baden, Victoria Melita (Ducky) and George. Sitting: Alfred (Affie, Jr.), Princess Alexandra of Edinburgh (Sandra), Affie, and Princess Marie of Edinburgh (Missy). c. 1891.

The Hesse and by Rhine Family: clockwise, Grand Duke Ludwig holding Princess Marie (May), Alice holding Alix, Elisabeth (Ella), Irène, Ernie and Victoria, mid-1870's

The Albany's: Prince Leopold, Duke of Albany, and Helen of Waldeck Pyrmont.

Arthur, Duke of Connaught and his wife, Princess Louise Margaret of Prussia.

Helen, Duchess of Albany with her children, Alice, and Charles Edward (*later* Karl Eduard).

Sir James Reid, the queen's physician.

Princess Charlotte of Prussia (Charley) and her husband, Bernhard III, Duke of Saxe-Meiningen.

Engagement photograph of Willy and Augusta Viktoria (Dona).

Hesses, Battenbergs and Romanovs: Knelling, Grand Duke Serge Alexandrovich, his fiancée Princess Ella of Hesse, standing Prince Louis of Battenberg, Princess Victoria of Hesse, and Grand Duke Ludwig IV, 1884.

Prince Henry Battenberg (Liko) and Princess Beatrice.

Prince Alexander of Battenberg (Sandro).

Princess Victoria of Prussia (Moretta) and Prince Adolf of Schaumburg-Lippe.

Victoria smiling with: standing, Princess Beatrice, Princess Victoria of Battenberg and Alice (future mother of Prince Philip).

Lord Salisbury, the queen's last prime minister.

The wedding of Beatrice and Henry. Back row, L-R, Prince Alexander Battenberg, Princess Louise of Wales, Princess Irène of Hesse, Princess Victoria of Wales, Prince Franz Joseph of Battenberg (FranzJos). Middle row: Princess Maud of Wales, Princess Alix of Hesse, Princesses Marie Louise, and Helena Victoria of Schleswig-Holstein. Front row: Princesses Victoria Melita, Marie and Alexandra of Edinburgh, Princess Beatrice, and Prince Henry. At Osborne, 1885.

Sitting at a tea table facing front: L-R Beatrice, Queen Victoria, and Prince Henry. Their three eldest children, Alexander (Drino), Victoria Eugénie (Ena), and Leopold. Mid-1890's.

Family portrait of Prince Henry of Prussia and Princess Irène of Hesse with L-R, Waldemar, Henry, and Sigismund.

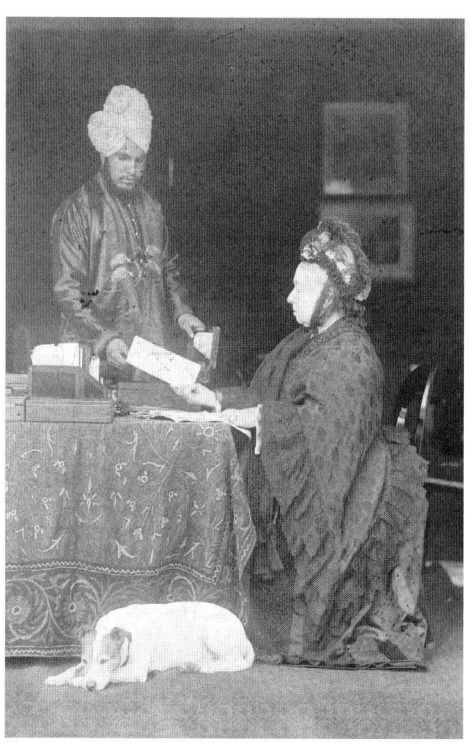

The Munshi, Abdul Karim, standing over Victoria handing her a paper.

Princess Louise of Wales and Alexander Duff, 1st Duke of Fife. Wedding portrait 1889.

A photo of a family in mourning. Sitting, Princess Victoria of Prussia (Moretta), Dowager Empress Frederick, Princess Margarethe (Mossy). Standing, Princess Sophie of Prussia and her fiancé Constantine (Tino), Duke of Sparta, 1888.

Princess Marie Louise of Schleswig-Holstein and Prince Aribert of Anhalt.

Prince Albert Victor (Eddy).

Prince George, Duke of York, and Princess Mary (May), Duchess of York with, L-R Princess Mary, Prince Henry ('Gloucester', seated) Prince George ('Kent', standing on chair), Prince John (being held by the Duchess) Prince Edward of York, later Edward VIII, and Prince Albert of York, later George VI (father of Queen Elizabeth II and grandfather of King Charles III).

Three Generations of heirs 1894. Standing, Prince George, Duke of York, Bertie, Prince of Wales. Sitting: the queen with Prince Edward of York.

Princess Alix of Hesse and Grand Duke Nicholas Alexandrovich (Nicky) at the time of their engagement.

Young married couples. Top row: Prince George, Duke of York, Grand Duke Ernst Ludwig of Hesse (Ernie), Crown Prince Ferdinand of Romania (Nando). Front: Princess Mary, Duchess of York, Princess Victoria Melita (Ducky), Grand Duchess of Hesse and Crown Princess Marie of Romania.

Princess Victoria of Wales (Toria), Bertie and Alix's unmarried daughter.

Princess Maud of Wales and Prince Carl of Denmark

The queen with family at Balmoral 1896. Seated, Empress Alexandra Feodorovna (Alix) and her daughter, Grand Duchess Olga Nicholaevna and the queen. Standing, Tsar Nicholas II of Russia and Prince Albert Edward of Wales.

A family portrait of the Duke and Duchess of Teck. Standing: Prince Alexander, Princess Mary, Prince Francis and Prince Adolphus. Seated: Princess Mary Adelaide of Cambridge, Duchess of Teck, and Francis, Duke of Teck.

Wedding portrait: Prince Alexander of Teck and Princess Alice of Albany, 1904.

but still came to attend Victoria, who had a swollen knee following a fall and temporarily needed to be carried around. Brown was ill enough to need aid in carrying her. As Brown became more and more ill, he was nursed by Dr Reid. He was diagnosed with erysipelas (a bacterial skin infection) of the face, which he had suffered from in the past, as well as the chills and delirium tremens.

Brown died from these last illnesses on 27 March at the age of fifty-six. Dr Reid's father died on the same day, but Reid stayed with Brown. Leopold, never an admirer of Brown – or his brother, Archie, who at one time had been an extremely cruel valet to him – was the one to break the news to his mother:

Leopold came to my dressing room, & broke the dreadful news to me, that my good, faithful Brown, had passed away early this morning. Am terribly upset by this loss, which removes one, who was so devoted & attached to my service & who did so much for my personal comfort. It is the loss not only of a servant, but of a real friend.[10]

Victoria was completely crushed. She wrote to Vicky, 'He protected me so – that I felt safe! ... I shall never be the same again.'[11] That is the key. For eighteen years he had made her feel protected, buoyed with a solid support. She likened the blow of his death to a reopening of old wounds that could only mean she counted Brown's demise as awful and demoralizing as her husband's.

Ponsonby wrote, 'with all his want of education, his roughness, his prejudices and other faults he was undoubtedly a most excellent servant to her'.[12] And, as if to corroborate that, Victoria wrote to Brown's brother, Hugh, 'I told him no one loved him more than I did or had a better friend than me: and he answered "Nor you – than me. No one loves you more."'[13] If there were anything secret or untoward, it is doubtful she would have written to his family in such a fashion. So, to speculation of a more intimate relationship or the rumours of marriage that went around – utterly ridiculous.

Tennyson provided a tribute for the plinth of the statue of Brown on the grounds of Balmoral Castle. 'Friend more than servant, Loyal, Truthful, Brave! Self less than Duty, even to the Grave.' Victoria, too, wanted to write a tribute to Brown in the form of a biography and had to be tactfully, and then forcefully, talked out of it. In 1884, she published a sequel to her *Leaves from the Journal of Our Life in the Highlands*, calling it *More Leaves from the Journal of Our Life...* etc. The queen dedicated it to the Highlanders and especially to 'my devoted personal attendant and faithful friend JOHN BROWN', thumbing her nose at those, and they were legion, who wanted to sweep the gruff highlander under the rug and forget him now that he was gone.

* * *

In March 1884, Prince Leopold went to stay at the Villa Nevada in the bright sun of Cannes. He often went to that much warmer and salubrious climate to escape the harsh winters of England. It was hoped that it would alleviate the joint pain from which, as a haemophiliac, he constantly suffered. At that time Helen, who was pregnant, was unable to accompany him. While there, he slipped and fell and injured his knee. It is not known if he simply lost his footing and fell, or if he had an epileptic fit which caused him to fall. Like so many bleeding episodes of haemophiliacs, it might have lasted a short time and resolved on its own, or it might have killed him. In this case it did the latter. He lingered through the afternoon of 26 March until the early hours of the 27th, when he died.

It was Bertie who went to collect his brother and bring him back to England. He wrote feelingly: 'I could not bear the thought of his returning home without a relative to look after him in death as they had done in life.'[14]

The queen was philosophical. Perhaps she finally understood that Leopold was a gift she would have to prematurely relinquish. She wrote to Vicky: 'his young life was a succession of trials and sufferings though he was so happy in his marriage. And there was such a restless longing for what he could not have; this seemed to increase rather than lessen.'[15] Did the queen, at last, understand Leopold? Did she at last have empathy for his situation? Maybe so, as she wrote in her journal:

My beloved Leopold, that bright, clever son, who had so many times recovered from such fearful illness, & from various small accidents, has been taken from us! To lose another dear child, far from me, & one who was so gifted, & such a help to me, is too dreadful! …. The poor dear Boy's life had been a very tried one, from early childhood![16]

He was her second child to die during her lifetime. The suddenness may have been shocking, but since finding out he was a haemophiliac, she no doubt knew and dreaded that this day would come all too soon for her son.

Helen gave birth some months after his death. The queen attended the birth at Claremont, where the Albanys lived and wrote the following:

I remained with dear Helen off & on, the whole time, till the Baby was born, a strong boy, who screamed very loudly, on coming into the world. … When dear Helen was reassured that the Baby was alive, & a boy, she exclaimed: 'Oh! my Leo, my Leo!', which cut me to the heart. She bore her suffering most bravely & is so thankful for God's mercy in having spared her & the child. … He is very small. When I returned to dear Helen, she said, 'Dear Mama, you will let the child be called Charles Edward, will you not, it was dear Leopold's greatest wish', which I knew. Of course I approved, though I should have preferred Leopold. But it will be amongst the names.[17]

Helen, who remained dedicated to her children for the rest of her life, died September 1922 of a heart attack. Her son, Charles Edward, through a series of unfortunate events, would succeed to the Coburg Duchy as Karl Eduard, and would later become a prominent Nazi.

* * *

More cheerful family matters came to the forefront in the 1880s. The Connaughts began their family. The queen noted that Margaret was born January 1882, with the remark: 'Louischen had been safely confined with a girl (always girls! my 18th grand-daughter!).'[18] No doubt she took comfort when 'Louischen' was delivered of a boy, Arthur, the following year and completed the family with Patricia in 1886.

At that point, Arthur was deployed to India and took command of the army at Meerut. He was subsequently promoted to Commander-in-Chief of the Army in the Bombay (Mumbai) Presidency and held that post for four years. Arthur and his wife were to stay on in India until 1890. The children lived there for several years but returned home while their parents stayed on.

Arthur was always his mother's fair-haired boy. What would she have thought if she knew that he, during his marriage to Princess Louise, conducted a discreet affair with Leonie, Lady Leslie (Winston Churchill's aunt) for a very long time? However, there was a difference between Arthur and his two older brothers. For Arthur and Lady Leslie, there was no scandal ever attached to this interesting relationship. Further, the duchess and her daughters knew about it and were close friends with Lady Leslie, corresponding with her and enjoying her companionship as much as did Arthur.

Prince Arthur became Governor General of Canada in 1911 and remained there until 1916. His wife died of influenza and bronchitis soon after the family's return from Canada in March 1917. Although several candidates were put forward, Arthur never remarried, and Lady Leslie remained his comfort. However, he did return to military life and maintained his commission until his death in 1942 at his home in Bagshot Park.

Family weddings were once again coming to the fore, now with the weddings of grandchildren and Victoria's last child, Beatrice. It may be from this time that the queen acquired the sobriquet 'Grandmama' of Europe, for many of these weddings would put her grandchildren on the thrones of Europe. Disraeli had called her the 'mother of many nations' and setting aside his usual hyperbole, in this instance it would prove to be true.

Vicky's daughter stole the march on all the grandchildren when she became the first to marry. Charlotte, the eldest daughter had proved to be an extremely difficult child. Vicky was highly critical of her which naturally drove her into her paternal grandparent's camp along with her brothers Wilhelm and Henry. Like her mother the queen, Vicky was disappointed that Charlotte was not a better student and easier child; undoubtedly, Charlotte sensed this, hence an ongoing estrangement from an early age. In addition, Charlotte was subject to depression and had myriad health problems that have led some historians to suspect that she was a victim of porphyria.

Charlotte became engaged at the age of 16 and married before her 18th birthday. Her groom was Bernhard, Hereditary Prince of Saxe-

Meiningen. As in many early marriages, it is likely Charlotte wanted to escape her parents. In the memoirs of her cousin, Queen Marie of Romania, the only positive descriptors used for the princess was that she was considered intelligent, sophisticated and very charming. Certainly, she seems to have preferred the cosmopolitan Berlin society to raising her own daughter and their relationship was ever contentious and difficult.

Charley was a leader in her very chic circle in Berlin and loved gossip and backbiting. Her sharp tongue and love of tittle-tattle would get her into a great deal of trouble not only with her family but with society at large. She was, according to her cousin Queen Marie, two-faced, self-serving, and malicious. At that point in her life, Marie had been very close to Charley and was disillusioned in a way that only a young person can be when she found that her idol had feet of clay. She was harsh in her depiction and wrote this and much more about her cousin. Apparently, there is no fury like a young person who is disenchanted. Charley is one of those historical characters that really need revision and rehabilitation, like American Presidents Ulysses S. Grant or Warren G. Harding. Hardly a flattering word was written about her. Perhaps that is how it must stay.

Vicky's son Wilhelm was next, and his marriage was of great significance since he was the heir presumptive of the German Empire and Kingdom of Prussia. His bride was Augusta Viktoria of Schleswig-Holstein, the daughter of Frederick VIII, Duke of Schleswig-Holstein, and Princess Adelaide of Hohenlohe-Langenburg, the daughter of Victoria's half-sister, Feodora. Chancellor von Bismarck disliked the choice since the Schleswig-Holsteins were dethroned by Prussia. In addition, Augusta Viktoria was not Willy's first choice. It was well-known in the family that Wilhelm was very much in love with his first cousin Ella, Alice's second daughter. He visited Darmstadt often while he was going to university at Heidelberg and proclaimed that he wanted her for his bride. He went so far as to propose to her, and she gently refused him since her affections lay elsewhere. Willy never spoke to her again.

He may not have spoken to or about her, but he wrote gently about her in his autobiography nearly fifty years later. He wrote about those halcyon days when they played lawn tennis and other games and how he went deer stalking with his uncle, the Grand Duke Ludwig, but did not mention in the memoir that he had proposed. Maybe all those years later, it was still too painful.[19]

'Dona' as she was called in the family was not one of Victoria's favourite granddaughter-in-laws. The queen had initially liked her, calling her 'gentle, amiable and sweet',[20] but her opinion soon changed. All who knew her considered her a 'hausfrau' type who produced six sons and a daughter for Wilhelm. It was thought that she and Willy had little to say to one another and that in his mind all she was good for was producing the children and caring for them.

Nonetheless, marry they did in 1881.

Dona never crossed her husband or took charge or tried to ameliorate his fraught relationships with his mother and British grandmother. She took Willy's part, not getting along with Vicky and wounding her whenever possible. She seemed to get particular pleasure in ignoring any of Vicky or Fritz's wishes and listened only to Wilhelm's Prussian grandparents. The queen was incensed about Dona's behaviour and railed against her treatment of her daughter, Vicky. She wrote that Dona was 'a poor, little, insignificant Princess raised entirely by your kindness to the position she is in, I have no words.'[21] The queen and Vicky's letters are littered with complaints about Dona, who was a fiercely loyal wife, but an unkind daughter-in-law.

Meanwhile, a horrific event occurred in Russia in March 1881 when Tsar Alexander II, the man with whom young Victoria had danced before her marriage, was assassinated. There had been four or five attempts in the past, but this one was successful. Naturally, Victoria's daughter-in-law, Marie of Edinburgh, quickly went to be with her brother the new tsar. Alexander II was most well known for having freed the serfs in Russia as well as other liberal reforms, but for many he didn't go far enough. The queen commented: 'in spite of his failings, he was a kind and amiable man, and had been a good ruler, wishing to do the best for his country.'[22]

When he was assassinated, his heir Alexander III naturally went the other way; he was extremely reactionary and countermanded some of his father's reforms. This, of course, made the queen terribly uneasy as the 1880s went on. She was worried that perhaps one of her Hessian granddaughters would marry a Russian. They had been raised with Marie and her brothers and knew them well. The queen foresaw only tragedy in such unions.

Unfortunately, she was right.

* * *

A more congenial and highly eventful wedding took place in April 1884. Alice's eldest daughter, Victoria was to be married to her cousin Prince Louis of Battenberg. Prince Louis, who was born in Graz, Austria, was the son of Prince Alexander of Hesse and by Rhine, and Julia, Countess, (and later Princess) of Battenberg. Alexander was the younger brother of Louis III, Grand Duke of Hesse and by Rhine and was therefore a first cousin of Victoria's father, Ludwig IV. There was some question of Alexander's paternity – although Ludwig II acknowledged Alexander as his son, it was generally thought that his actual father was a member of the court, August von Senarclens de Grancy.

Louis's mother, Julia von Hauke, was a Polish Countess, whom Prince Alexander met while he was visiting the court of his sister, Empress Maria Alexandrovna and Tsar Alexander II. They fell in love and married without permission and had to flee Russia because of the mésalliance. They finally settled in Darmstadt and Julia was granted the title of Countess of Battenberg, and later Princess of Battenberg.

The marriage was considered unequal and as a consequence, the children assumed their mother's title and were 'serene highnesses' instead of 'royal highnesses'. The couple had five children, four boys and a girl. The four young princes, Louis, Alexander, Henry, and Franz Joseph were considered the most handsome princes in Europe. Lest this be thought of as a shallow remark, Chancellor von Bismarck was the one who made this observation, and their looks would be their fortunes – at least in the marriage market. All four of these princes would play a major part in the queen's life.

Young Victoria Hesse in particular had already begun a long and fascinating correspondence with her grandmother that had evolved from 'bread and butter' thank-you notes when she was 8 years old, to the exchange of news, opinions and advice to the youngster. Young Victoria was a true intellectual, a voracious reader and a bit of a royal rebel. Ponsonby described her thus:

> The bride Victoria is bright, lively but full of strange ideas. She locks herself with her mother's books and papers and has imbibed Kant. Some say that she has shown her condemnation of princely titles by insisting on marrying a semi-Prince, going as low as she could in the scale of Princes without hurting susceptibilities.[23]

Louis and Victoria had planned to marry in March 1884, but the tragic death of Victoria's Uncle Leopold delayed the wedding for a month. Queen Victoria was particularly attached to this granddaughter as she was with all the Hessian children since their mother had died. She therefore made the somewhat surprising decision to attend the wedding. She felt the need to explain her decision to Vicky:

> It would be for many reasons be a painful and great effort; but it is merely as the poor dear children have no mother and have been so much for that very reason like my own that I ever thought of coming at all. But I look on it as a duty! For all such ceremonies are most painful to me.[24]

The queen arrived with her entourage on 17 April 1884. As she describes:

> At 9.10. we got to Darmstadt. Every thing was kept quite private, by my earnest request. Dear Louis [as she referred to Ludwig] (in plain clothes) his brother Henry (in uniform, as he commands the district) Ella & Irène (Victoria having hurt her leg) received us at the station, & Beatrice & I, drove at once with Louis to the Neues Palais, his charming house. Victoria (though still lame) Ernie (immensely tall) & sweet Alicky, who nearly upset me, when I thought of how darling Leopold had loved these nieces, received us at the door. Louis took me upstairs. I have got as sitting room, darling Alice's lovely one, left just as she had it, with all her things still lying about, which I recognized, & I am writing, lying on her own comfortable sofa. This sitting room opens into her bedroom, the sacred room, where she left this world … We breakfasted almost directly, with Louis, Victoria & Irène, & afterwards he brought in the Grand Duke Serge, who is very tall & gentlemanlike, but very thin, pale, & delicate looking. Then washed & dressed & laid down, feeling, very tired & sad.[25]

The visit to Darmstadt was of course a poignant reminder to the queen of the daughter she had lost. True to the spirit of her wish for the Hessians to think of her as their 'mama', Victoria made her wishes known with regard to the wedding arrangements. She instructed young Victoria (who did most of the work in reality) that she didn't want the guests to come more than five days before the date of the wedding which was 30 April. Daughter Vicky was permitted to come a day before the others in order to give *her* second daughter – also a Viktoria, known as 'Moretta' – a chance to be with Prince Louis's younger brother Alexander, known as 'Sandro' in the family. The two young people were secretly engaged at the time.

Another courting couple was Ella and her cousin Grand Duke Serge Alexandrovich of Russia. He was one of the younger sons of Maria Alexandrovna and Tsar Alexander II. The queen deplored this courtship not because she had anything against Serge, but because he was a Russian. Young Victoria had assured her grandmother that Ella would not marry a Russian and told her that the two young women hadn't even discussed it. The queen thus reassured thought it best to suggest as many other suitors as possible for her beautiful granddaughter. One such suitor was Grand Duke Frederick of Baden, but Ella rejected him to the queen's great distress.

The queen made her views about Russians known to Ella and continued to dance other suitors before her eyes. In the end, it seemed that Ella was going to marry Serge and the queen was helpless to change her mind. It wasn't that young Victoria had lied to her grandmother, and not even necessarily that she and Ella hadn't discussed it, but young Victoria was trying to mitigate the queen's disappointment.

Had Queen Victoria been adamantly against any of the marriages of her grandchildren, there would have been much more discussion instead of the queen wringing her hands in her journals. However, she knew, as the Hessian family knew, that the greatest wish of Alice and Ludwig was that their children never be pressured into marrying anyone they were set against. Though the queen hated the climate and politics of Russia she could set forth no real objections when Ella made up her mind, and the couple were engaged to be married.

One more couple were also courting during the days around Louis and Victoria's wedding. Beatrice, or 'Baby' as her mother persisted in calling her, though she was 28 years old and considered on the shelf, had fallen in love. The queen had done her best to keep young men away from Beatrice during her teens and twenties. Beatrice herself was shy and somewhat withdrawn, raised as she was in a house of constant mourning, and so no relationships or even friendships were ever solidly formed. Indeed, words like marriage and courtship were not supposed to be uttered in Beatrice's presence, and her 'crush' on the Prince Imperial, was lost in the past (if it had ever existed).

However, none of that mattered.

Like her mother, she 'beheld' Prince Henry of Battenberg, Louis's younger brother known as 'Liko', and that was it for her. Liko was, as the queen wrote in her journal, 'excessively goodlooking'[26] and Beatrice could not resist a handsome face any more than her mother could. However, during the wedding festivities, this went on without the knowledge of the queen.

Her attitude all along about the marriages of her daughters was that they were subjects of grief and even horror. It is curious, considering how happy Victoria had been in her marriage, but she expressed it many times. When she would find out about Beatrice's courtship and eventual engagement she wrote to Vicky:

> The pain it has caused me that my darling Beatrice should wish (which she never did till she had lost her dear brother) to marry, as I hate marriages especially of my daughters, but as I like Liko very much and as they are both so very much devoted to each other, and she remains always with me, I cannot refuse my consent.[27]

It seems she was deluding herself about Beatrice's not wanting to marry, and certainly not when an extremely handsome young man presented himself. But Victoria had a habit of seeing only what she wanted to see. Unquestionably, there was a selfishness about not wanting her daughters to marry, but it may have also been the uncertainty that each one faced when choosing a mate, and the agony each one might go through if that mate turned out to be nothing like they had expected. The vagaries of arranged marriages were only matched by the greater insecurity of falling in love and then being completely disillusioned. As the queen put it: 'One never knows how it will turn out.'[28]

Another incident that occurred on the very day of the wedding without the knowledge of the queen was the secret wedding of Alice's widower Ludwig to his mistress, Alexandrine de Kolemine. Madame de Kolemine had been Ludwig's mistress for quite a while and Ludwig's daughters knew and liked the lady. Why he would choose to marry her on the day of his eldest daughter's wedding is the stuff of which drawing room comedy is made. Days before, Ludwig had told young Victoria that he wanted to marry Alexandrine and that Victoria ought to be the one to tell her grandmother and see how she felt about the entire thing.

This, during the time of the preparations for the wedding that motherless Victoria was supervising, seemed spectacularly unfair. Obviously, Ludwig wasn't thinking straight. Somehow, young Victoria had the time to broach the subject with her grandmother. The queen, while understanding Ludwig's need for companionship, nevertheless didn't think that Madame de Kolemine was at all suitable. If he did choose to marry her, the queen went on, she couldn't be as close to him as before. In addition, she didn't like the idea of the younger unmarried girls, Irène and Alicky, being in her company. Remarriage to a suitable lady could of course be contemplated, but this choice, she felt, did him immense harm.

Young Victoria dutifully relayed her grandmother's comments. The result was that the Grand Duke was angry at his daughter. Young Victoria obviously couldn't dwell on that while trying to house and arrange meals for all the royalties who were going to attend the 'wedding of the decade' as it was called in the illustrated newspapers. On 30 April, Louis and Victoria were safely married and on their way to their honeymoon when it was revealed that Ludwig had also married on that day.

It seemed that previously, young Victoria was often enlisted to be the bearer of bad news to her grandmother. With Victoria unavailable, Lady Ely, the queen's stalwart lady of the bedchamber, was dispatched to relay the unfortunate news to Queen Victoria, everyone else not having the courage to do so. When she was apprised of events, the queen calmly said that the wedding would have to be annulled, the bride must be informed right away and sent Bertie, who was attending the festivities, to convey these sentiments to Ludwig. Though initially shocked at the objections (though it is difficult to understand why), he quickly acquiesced to the queen's wishes and Madame was bought off and quickly decamped back to Russia.

The Prussian contingent, who were incredibly snobbish, were instructed by Bismarck to leave immediately before they could be polluted by such behaviour, which they did. It was bad enough that young Victoria had married a man inferior to her on the royal scale, but that the Grand Duke should marry his completely unacceptable mistress – well the whole sorry escapade was outrageous, and the Prussians were not to be thus contaminated.

As young Victoria wrote: 'The episode was a nine days scandal in the whole of Europe, and a painful one for my father, alas.'[29]

* * *

More fall-out from the Hessian wedding was to come. After spending some 'unmarried' time at Osborne, or as the queen put it, while she was still herself, Ella and many members of the family were off to St Petersburg for her wedding to Grand Duke Serge Alexandrovich.

Serge was the youngest but one of the large family of six boys and one daughter of Alexander II of Russia. He was tall, slim, and according to his niece, Queen Marie of Romania, extremely handsome. He was also shy, reticent and awkward with people, which was interpreted as being unbending and cold. He had known Ella, as well as the rest of the Hessian family, since childhood. In fact, Alice once remarked to the queen that 7-year-old Serge had developed quite a passion for her eldest, Victoria, who was 7 months old at the time. They all played together for years and so Ella knew him well enough to know that much of what he displayed to the world was a façade.

Their engagement was announced in November 1883 to the queen's utter dismay. Ella had accepted Serge, then broken it off, and then accepted him again, so the queen thought – and told – young Victoria that she was changeable and '*unaccountable*; she told me how she hated the Russians, she refused Serge 3 weeks ago & now she takes him and forgets all'.[30] In exasperation, she wrote at the last, 'the less I say about it the better'.[31]

The queen was extremely uneasy about the engagement and thought her granddaughter would be unsafe there. One would only have to see what happened to his father to come to that conclusion and how restricted the current tsar was in his movements due to security measures. Ella, on the other hand, was convinced that she made the right choice, and tried to 'sell' the queen on Serge saying: 'I am so glad you will see Serge and hope he will make a favourable impression on you. All who know him like him and say he has such a true and noble character.'[32]

The queen had no intention of traveling to Russia for this wedding but wrote in her journal: 'Darling Ella's wedding day. May God bless, protect

& guide her! & may she be thoroughly happy!'³³ Hand it to her, she knew when to stand down.

The entire Hessian family went to the wedding, including all the children. It was then that 12-year-old Alicky became attached to her 17-year-old cousin, Nicholas, the tsarevich. As time went on, Ella and Serge's marriage proved childless, and rumours were everywhere about Serge's various perversions. Serge was a martinet who would constantly criticise Ella's clothes, her deportment, and the things she said and did. He treated her like a student who needed a firm hand and constant, but loving correction. Her countenance would remain serene, fervently desiring to please and all she would do is cast her eyes down meekly and say, in the French that the Hessians spoke to their Russian cousins: *'Mais Serge'*.³⁴

Ella continually denied that there were problems in her marriage and always told her grandmother how happy she was. The queen was not convinced. Her thought was that if people were that happy, they didn't have to constantly talk about it. Most of the rumours about Serge and the marriage were scandalous falsehoods, but Serge became the public face of Romanov oppression, and it was only a matter of time before he met his tragic fate.

Chapter Nine

Beatrice's Lohengrin

Prince Henry of Battenberg was tall, handsome, gorgeous in his skin-tight breeches, highly shined black boots and stiffly waxed moustache.

He was the youngest-but-one of the magnificent Battenberg family and was born in 1858 in Milan, where his father was stationed in the Austrian army. His Italian governess called him Enrico, which got shortened in some babyish mispronunciation to 'Liko'. Like so many princes, Liko served in the military as officer in the Prussian army. He also served as an Honorary Colonel of a regiment in Bulgaria where his older brother, Sandro, was the reigning prince.

Summer 1884 began a true struggle between the queen and her 'Baby'. Beatrice was determined to marry her handsome prince. Telling her mama in person was too difficult, so Beatrice took the easy way out and wrote her a letter revealing her feelings and explaining the matter. The queen decided that it was just a childish fancy and Beatrice would quickly get over it. Grand Duke Ludwig, who was spending time with the queen at Osborne as a reward for annulling his marriage to Madame de Kolemine, apparently reassured her that Liko was not looking at Beatrice that way. Besides, as the queen wrote to Vicky when Beatrice was just 16: '[Beatrice] is my constant companion and I hope and trust will never leave me while I live, I do not intend she should ever go out as her sister [Louise] did.'[1]

They were both wrong. Beatrice was determined to marry the man her brother Bertie called her 'Lohengrin' for his romantic looks, and her battle with her mother began in earnest. The situation was dire, and mother and daughter stopped speaking to one another. How could Beatrice leave her, the queen thought. Certainly, she had never expressed a desire to marry and now – well, this could not be permanent. Neither of the couple was deterred. The queen and Beatrice continued not speaking to one another and passing notes to one another during meals, and Liko visited his brother Louis, who was living nearby in England with his new bride young Victoria. It was a convenient meeting place for the secretly courting couple.

For six months, the queen would not discuss the issue. She thought 'Baby' was being monstrously selfish. However, by November 1884, she was slowly and reluctantly coming around. Both Bertie and Ludwig of Hesse told her her behaviour was nothing less than unkind. She very likely realised that she would have to give in and permit the marriage. Liko was invited for Christmas and asked for Beatrice's hand. Once the queen had settled that Liko would give up the Prussian army and the couple would always live with her with no residences of their own, she felt able to consent to the marriage.

To turn the knife a little into the snobs in Prussia, the queen granted Liko, who was only a serene highness, the designation of royal highness and made him a Knight of the Garter. And, because the queen disliked having 'courting couples' around her, there was emphatically to be no kissing, which she was sure Beatrice hated. Some thought these conditions were very hard on Liko, and interestingly, Liko's mother Princess Julia wondered what Beatrice saw in her son. He was no intellectual.

However, once the queen came around, she really came around. She wrote to Vicky:

> I am surprised at myself – considering the horror and dislike of the most violent kind I had for the idea of my precious Baby's marrying at all ... how I should have been so much reconciled to it now that it is settled. But it is really Liko himself who has so completely won my heart. He is so modest, so full of consideration for me and so is she, and both are quietly and really sensibly happy ... I hope and pray there may be no results! That would aggravate everything and besides make me terribly anxious.[2]

At any rate, there was great drama in Berlin, as the couple caused fury for Vicky's father-in-law, Kaiser Wilhelm I, and the entire Hohenzollern family. Liko was not considered to be of proper *geblüt* (blood or stock). The Empress Augusta, Wilhelm I's wife and a long-standing friend of the queen, wrote what Victoria called a very 'unamiable' letter about the engagement. Victoria was completely incensed. She remarked that many of the royal families of Europe had skeletons in their closets. Others could make of this remark what they wished.

Characteristically, the queen was much more upset about these slights than about her daughter's impending marriage. She hated the Prussian snobbery and gleefully quoted Lord Granville once again: 'If a Queen of England thinks a person good enough for her daughter what have other people got to say?'[3] Unfortunately, in the case of the Empress Augusta, an old friendship was ended.

As well, the match was looked down upon in Russia because of their issues with Prince Alexander Battenberg (as will be seen), and because Alexander III personally despised the Battenbergs collectively. They were tall, slim, and handsome, while he was bearish and homely.

Finally, the British public at large knew little to nothing about the Battenbergs, and for them here was yet another impecunious German coming to live off the British largesse.

The wedding would take place in July 1885 at Osborne. Young Victoria Battenberg wrote excitedly:

> Grandmama is full of plans for the wedding already. She wants it to take place here at Whippingham [Chapel] in July ... Aunty wants to have eight of her nieces as bridesmaids. The 3 Wales [Louise, Victoria, Maud], Irène and Alix [of Hesse] ... Aunt Helena's 2 [Helena Victoria and Marie Louise] & the eldest little Edinburghs [Marie and Ducky].[4]

* * *

Meanwhile, more of the nation's business was transacted with Gladstone during his second ministry. In November 1884, a further Reform Bill was passed in parliament. This widened the franchise even more to adult male house owners or renters and rural workers. The voter rolls were expanded by nearly 6 million voters. Historian Elizabeth Longford asserted that that was the last time the queen and Gladstone worked in any kind of harmony.

Just a few months later there would be a culmination of a foreign policy disaster that was nearly ten months and longer in the making – the Siege and Battle of Khartoum. It began several years before when the British established their dominance in Egypt in the short Anglo-Egyptian War of 1882. They had now seized control of Egypt and the canal, which made other European powers extremely uneasy. But defeating the revolt in Egypt just meant that the rebels moved down to the Sudan. That area was now dominated by the forces of the Mahdi, a sort of Islamic messianic figure, who wanted to drive the Egyptians, who he saw as apostates and puppets of the British, out of the country. His goal was to make the area a pure Islamic State.

General Charles George Gordon was sent to Khartoum in the Sudan in February 1884. His mission was supposed to be confined to reporting on an evacuation and complete withdrawal of forces from the Sudan, which the British government now thought the prudent thing to do. He made the unwise decision instead to try to eradicate the Mahdi-ist rebels. He successfully evacuated some civilians but kept army personnel there. Thus began the Siege of Khartoum, which lasted nearly a year. Eventually a relief expedition was sent out in January 1885, but it was too late. When the troops relieved the city they found that Gordon had been killed and the city had fallen to the Mahdi.

The queen was enormously upset, she blamed the government and specifically Gladstone, who, she said pointedly, had sent out the relief forces too late. He had always been called the GOM (Grand Old Man) now he was vilified as the 'Grand Old Spider' or the MOG (murderer of Gordon). More important, as January went into February, it still hadn't been established exactly what had happened to Gordon. By mid-February the truth was ascertained – he had been speared to death, and the queen minced no words when she wrote to Ponsonby:

> Mr Gladstone and the Government have – the Queen feels it dreadfully – Gordon's innocent, noble, heroic blood on their consciences. No one who reflects on how he was sent out, how he was refused, can deny it! It is awful … May they feel it, and may they be made to do so![5]

The queen wasn't the only one who was horrified by Gordon's fate. He was celebrated as a martyr and hero ever after and one of the last rugged individualists. She mourned all the more the anniversary of her dear Dizzy's death, considering whom she had to endure as prime minister, and noted in her journal: '19 April 1885. The anniversary of dear Lord Beaconsfield's death. Oh! Were he but still alive.'[6]

The Mahdi died in June of that year and the danger of invasion of Egypt by Islamic jihadists died with him.[7]

* * *

Closer to home another family crisis was to anger and exasperate the queen. This was the sad saga of her granddaughter and Vicky's daughter, Princess Viktoria (Moretta) and her engagement to Prince Louis Battenberg's brother, Sandro. This issue not only involved many members of the family, but also had political consequences.

Sandro had been elected Prince of Bulgaria under the terms of the Treaty of Berlin in 1878, ending the Russo-Turkish war. Bulgaria had previously belonged to the Ottoman Empire but was now an autonomous region. Tsar Alexander II had recommended his nephew, Prince Alexander Battenberg, to be reigning prince and he was unanimously elected by the Bulgarian Grand National Assembly in 1879. In 1881, he was invited to the Prussian court where he met and wooed the teenage Moretta, who was said to be an extremely charming young woman. She quickly became enamoured with the handsome prince and wanted to marry him; they became secretly engaged. She told her grandmother she was 'violently' in love with him and would marry no other.

The entire affair would last seven years, the warring factions being: Vicky and the queen who were for the marriage, and Chancellor Bismarck, Vicky's father-in-law, Kaiser Wilhelm I and young Willy, who were not. They felt that such a marriage might offend the now Tsar Alexander III, who thoroughly disliked his Battenberg cousin and who was furious that Sandro wanted to rule Bulgaria independent of Russian influence. In addition, the Prussians, who disliked the morganatic Battenbergs, thought such a marriage would blemish the Hohenzollerns.

Bismarck pushed for Sandro to break his engagement with Moretta, but Sandro was hesitant. First, he was lonely in Sofia, the capital of Bulgaria, without a wife or a real court. Second, he was anxious to free Bulgaria from Russian influence. He was in no mood to court favour from his cousin, the tsar, who had shown him nothing but contempt and, frankly, jealousy.

Eventually, under the constant pressure and contentiousness of both the tsar and Bismarck, he ended, as chivalrously as was possible, his engagement to Moretta. None of this helped him with the Russians or the Prussians. Ultimately, he was forced off the throne of Bulgaria and was replaced, ironically, by one of the Catholic Coburgs, Ferdinand of Saxe-Coburg and Kohári.

The queen was tremendously angry about how the situation played out. She wanted Sandro for her granddaughter and hated how the Russians had manipulated him, and how the Prussians had foiled the engagement plans. She was especially vocal about her grandson Willy, who was in the forefront of the opposition to the marriage. She wrote: 'As for Willie that very foolish, undutiful and – I must add – unfeeling boy I have no patience with, and I wish he could get a good 'skelping' [flogging] as the Scotch say and seriously a good setting down.'[8] She 'let it be known that she would refuse to see him if he insisted on visiting England.'[9]

The bitterness and anger over this sad situation would linger on. Sandro would eventually abdicate the throne of Bulgaria in 1886 and seek once again to marry Moretta, but it would not be permitted. He swallowed his disappointment and retired to private life in Darmstadt. At that point, Queen Victoria was persuaded that the marriage was no longer a good idea, and that it should not take place because of the friction it would cause between Russia and Prussia. Her son-in-law Fritz was ill, and it seemed that the subject was closed.

Sandro's ardour had also cooled by this time and Willy had sent him a letter saying, 'If you marry my sister I shall consider you the enemy of my family and my country.'[10] Things could not be plainer to the young man. At any rate, by that point Sandro had cut his losses and his affections were elsewhere. He took the name Count Hartenau, and married a beautiful opera singer called Johanna Loisinger.

Poor Moretta was much slower to get over the grief of a thwarted love. It also took her much longer to find a spouse. Many princes and even grand dukes were considered, but none panned out. Undoubtedly, Prince Adolph of Schaumburg-Lippe seemed like a consolation prize after the highly romantic Prince Sandro. Moretta certainly thought so, though she wrote in her memoirs it was a question of love at first sight, and then proceeded to try to convince the reader of that fact.[11]

Nevertheless, in 1890 she settled down fairly happily with the good and boring Adolph. And, indeed, it was observed that Moretta went from a rather plain girl to a graceful and good-looking woman. One of the queen's ladies said that the pair seemed quite devoted.[12] There were no children from this marriage and Adolph died in 1916. The princess, who was 61 years old at the time, went on a wild, desperate, romantic rampage and married again. He was thirty-five years her junior and a Russian émigré called Alexander Zoubkoff. Their marriage was an enormous scandal and her brother, of course, refused to come to their wedding or even speak to her. No other family members attended. Sadly, Zoubkoff was a scoundrel who bankrupted her and left her. Moretta contracted pneumonia and died alone in Bonn in 1929.

As for Sandro, his fate wasn't much better. After becoming Count Hartenau and marrying his opera singer in 1889, he took a commission in the Austrian Army. The couple had two children, Assen and Svetlana. He died in 1893 at the age of 36 of a ruptured appendix. Ironically, the Bulgarians clamoured for their first prince to come home to them. King Ferdinand agreed, and he was given a state funeral and buried in Sofia, in what is now called the Battenberg Mausoleum.

* * *

Happier family events also took place in this key year. Queen Victoria's granddaughter, young Victoria Battenberg, gave birth to her first child, Alice, on 25 February 1885. Alice was born in the Tapestry Room at Windsor, just as *her* mother, Victoria had been. And, as the queen had attended her daughter Alice on that day in 1863, she attended Victoria now. The queen commented: 'How strange, & indeed affecting, it was, to see her lying in the same room, & in the same bed, in which she herself was born.... L[ouis] is radiant.'[13] It was Queen Victoria's first great-grandchild born in Britain.

Alice was a beautiful child and would one day be called one of the most beautiful princesses in Europe, but she was also full of mischief. There is an incident that apparently happened when she was about 4 or 5. She'd been cleaned up and dressed in her finest clothes to see her great-grandmother, Victoria. She was instructed that she was to kiss the queen's hand, but when the crucial moment came, she refused. Queen

Victoria was affronted by this disobedience and scolded her saying: 'Naughty, Alice.' Whereupon, Alice retorted, 'Naughty, Grandmama.' She was quickly removed from Victoria's presence, and it is hoped that the queen had a good giggle when the child was safely away. Alice would later marry a Greek prince and be the mother of Prince Philip, the Duke of Edinburgh.

* * *

The months of that year flew by and of course, the event most dreaded by the queen – the wedding of Beatrice and Liko – was looming. In April Victoria wrote to Vicky:

> I count the months, weeks and days that she is still my own sweet, unspoiled, innocent Lily and child. That thought – that agonising thought which I always felt, and which I often wonder any mother can bear of giving up your own child, from whom all has been so carefully kept and guarded -- to a stranger to do unto her as he likes is to me the most torturing thought in the world while I feel no girl could go to the alter (and would probably refuse) if she knew all, there is something very dreadful in the thought of the sort of trap she is being led into.[14]

This is fascinating in view of the queen's successful marriage, but again, not only was she worried about the terrible uncertainty a bride might find, but also it must be emphasised that Victoria was against the idea of arranged marriages. It is probably why she was such an assiduous matchmaker and was so determined to find salubrious and happy marriages for her family. But, as Jane Austen wrote, happiness in marriage is a matter of chance, and no matter how compatible or how much in common a couple may have, there are no guarantees. Victoria would find this out to her great regret and sorrow.

There was a happy family gathering in April of that year in Darmstadt. Little Alice was christened. Queen Victoria made the journey, again because she undoubtedly felt it was her motherly duty.

In June of that year, there were more felicitous tidings for Victoria on the political side when Gladstone's government fell, and he handed in his resignation. The queen accepted with alacrity and sent for Lord Salisbury to form a new government. Before that happened, the queen extended to Gladstone the honour of an earldom, which Gladstone refused.

* * *

On 23 July 1885, Beatrice and Liko were married at the lovely chapel of St Mildred's, Whippingham, near Osborne House. Liko, who had an overfondness of uniforms, looked quite splendid, which was one of his talents. Or, as one author put it, he was 'vigorous in the pride of his young manhood'.[15] Beatrice, too, who had a tendency to plumpness, looked thinner and therefore quite delicate and lovely in her finery.

The weight loss was due to the abuse and insults directed towards Liko in the press by the British and continental papers. The reason, again, was because he was not 'equal' but much lower in the aristocratic order than Beatrice. In addition, the Prussians were also piling it on because it was beneath them to have Battenbergs as relatives by marriage.

The queen had dreaded the day, but nevertheless, wrote a long and detailed entry in her journal about the festivities. She stated that she could hardly realise that the event was taking place, though she slept well. As was often her custom before weddings of her children, Victoria and Beatrice breakfasted alone. Because it was a beautiful summer day, they did so outside under the trees. Beatrice dressed in her father's room while the queen looked on. She wore her mother's wedding veil with the customary sprays of orange blossoms, myrtle, and white heather decorating the simple ivory silk dress.

The guests that day were myriad members of the Russian, Scandinavian, and the many German family connections that the queen wryly dubbed, 'the royal mob'. Conspicuous by their absence were the Prussians. Though the engagement was technically at an end, poor Moretta of Prussia had to be kept away from Sandro at all costs. The queen decided that in order to avoid problems, her eldest daughter and her family would not be invited. With all that was going on, it was quite a relief.

The wedding ceremony was performed by the Archbishop of Canterbury, who had crossed from the mainland with many of the guests. It had been an extraordinarily rough crossing and a lot suffered extreme seasickness. It was noticed that the poor Archbishop was a little white in the face. However, the wedding party looked marvellous. The queen noted:

> Bridesmaids, 10 in number, all, Beatrice's nieces, stood awaiting us at the Gate [of the chapel]. The little ones looked so dear; Louise of Wales & Irène walked first after Beatrice, then Victoria of Wales, & Victoria of Schleswig Holstein, Maud of Wales & Alicky, Louise of Schleswig Holstein, & little Missy, & lastly Ducky & little Sandra. They were dressed in white, with bunches of red & white carnations on the front of the dress. ...
>
> Though I stood for the 9th time near a child & for the 5th time near a daughter, at the altar, I think I never felt more deeply than I did on this occasion, though full of confidence.[16]

After the ceremony, the couple and their guests travelled back to Osborne for the reception. There were toasts, photographs and at last Beatrice retired to put on her 'going away' outfit.

> The moment had come to take leave of my darling 'Baby', whom it cost me much to part with, even for such a short while. I felt utterly miserable when they left my room, & had not the heart to go down & see them drive away.[17]

Though the couple were only going away for a couple of days, the queen managed to look glum. In the evening, she had a large state dinner for the royalties and others who were present that day. Beatrice immediately wrote her mother that evening, saying they had safely arrived at Quarr Abbey, which was only six miles from Osborne. Quarr Abbey was a lovely mansion with extensive grounds, quiet and peaceful for the honeymooning couple, but near enough to come home right away if needed.

Meanwhile, back at Osborne:

> The illuminations were repeated, & were even more brilliant than last night, & the Yachts in Osborne Bay, were lit up & sent off rockets. The Band played on the Lower Terrace. ... The night was beautiful, & there was but little wind. I went out for a short while, & tried to

speak to people, but was so tired & felt so low, that it was an effort, & I escaped quietly to my room. My dear child was never out of my mind. God bless & protect her! —[18]

The queen and the Grand Duke Ludwig of Hesse and by Rhine, who had attended with his daughters and son, were no doubt consoling each other in their various losses, while the rest of the family continued celebrating. For Victoria, even the loss of a few days of her 'Baby' (which she insisted on continuing to call her) was too much to bear. 'Baby' would never be just 'herself' anymore and would have obligations to others instead of being solely dedicated to her mother.

There was a silver lining, however. As time went on, the wedding so dreaded by the queen actually gave her much happiness in the coming years. Naturally, she loved having a man about the house again, and Liko was charismatic as well as handsome. Give him credit, he seemed to know well how to deal with the queen, which he apparently did with a great deal of charm. She would begin to refer to Liko as the 'sunshine of our home'.

Most interestingly, Liko caused a bit of a revolution in the queen's household. Queen Victoria hated smoking and tobacco of any form. She was forced to designate one small and inconvenient room as a smoking room in her various homes, but she did it quite reluctantly. Her granddaughter, Victoria Battenberg, told a story which took place while they were staying at Balmoral. It was a time when the midges were most prominent in the highlands and the queen heard that the cigarette smoke kept them away. She asked Victoria, who was an avid smoker and would continue to be her entire life, for a cigarette. She tried one puff and frowned. It didn't help, but that is the only time anyone saw her try a cigarette. Ironically, the rest of the family smoked like chimneys.

Liko decided he would help in this situation and was able to persuade his mother-in-law that a larger more accessible room would be so much nicer. She acquiesced, and a larger room was designated. However, even with all his aforementioned charm, he couldn't get her to change the smoking hours, which were after eleven o'clock at night.[19]

Perhaps he wasn't a great intellectual, but Beatrice insisted that he was interested in everything and having a great deal of curiosity is no small thing. He loved to shoot, was a gadget man and loved the theatre. He would be among one of the first people to buy a car. Most important, the couple were extremely happy together. If Liko thought the terms under which he married Beatrice were a little confining, he was able to live under those terms for quite a while. After all, he was now the son-in-law of the queen and not some semi-royal who was scorned by the patronising Prussians.

Did he have much to do? Not really, he was made Governor of Carisbrooke Castle and the Captain-General and Governor of the Isle of Wight. In 1894, he was appointed to the Privy Council. None of these appointments had the effect, however, of giving the vigorous young prince any sort of occupation.

* * *

Around this time, the government was in turmoil and some historians have called this year of 1885–6 one of 'political chaos'. After the disaster in Sudan and the death of Gordon in 1885, Gladstone had resigned and Lord Salisbury of the Conservatives had become prime minister. He managed to stay in power under a minority government only until January 1886, when his government fell, and Gladstone came in once again. The queen had been desperate to ward off Gladstone, even to the point of opening parliament for the last time in 1886, but to no avail, the 'Grand Old Man' was back.

She railed against fate telling Ponsonby 'she has the gre[ate]est possible disinclination to take this half crazy & really in so many ways ridiculous old man – for the sake of the country'.[20]

Nevertheless, take him back, she was obliged to do. During Gladstone's third and very short ministry, the contentious issue that dominated British politics for the last part of the nineteenth century was the question of whether Ireland should rule itself under Great Britain, or should things stay as they were? The Conservatives were decidedly not for Home Rule for Ireland, and the queen even less so. She believed that the Irish should no more have their own parliament, than say, the Indians. She felt that they simply could not govern themselves. This was one of Gladstone's major issues and it was voted down; Gladstone's party was split over the issue and so, with the defeat of Irish Home Rule, once again Lord Salisbury was called in to form a new government in August of that year.

Robert Gascoyne-Cecil, Lord Salisbury, was prime minister for three terms during the reign of Queen Victoria. He was the first prime minister that was younger than the queen, but they too had a meeting of the minds, though, perhaps, not the heart. Lord Salisbury was the second son of the aristocratic Cecil family who had been serving the monarchy since Elizabeth I. He started his political life in the House of Commons and later, during Disraeli's ministry, served as Foreign Secretary. He was married to Georgina Alderson and had seven children. From all accounts, it was a happy marriage.

Initially, the two top Conservatives didn't get along. Salisbury was against the Reform Bill of 1867 that extended the voting franchise because he believed it was a cheap political manoeuvre. He had been with Disraeli at the Congress of Berlin in 1878, and was quite wary of the old man, but their success at the congress was enough to earn them both the Order of the Garter. In the beginning, Salisbury disliked Disraeli tremendously, but after a while, and probably with a great deal of finessing on Dizzy's part, he came to partner with, and later like and admire the other man.

Lord Salisbury was considered intelligent, witty, down to earth and extremely hard working. He wasn't interested in outdoor sports, contrary to many English gentlemen, but was considered exceptionally competitive when it was necessary. He believed strongly that monarchy created stability. More important, he understood how to get along with Queen Victoria. Theirs was a harmonious partnership between colleagues. He was not a father figure or a romantic figure, he was her friend. Salisbury did not flatter her like Disraeli, nor did he lecture and harangue her like Gladstone; instead, he gave the appearance that they were working together toward mutually agreed goals. Most important, she trusted him and was at ease with him.[21]

An interesting example of this was the issue of divorce. The queen disliked divorce and wanted no divorced women in court at any of her drawing rooms. Salisbury could see the unfairness of this and wrote a memorandum to her about the morality of not letting any divorced person be admitted to her presence, especially in the case of adultery, as it would be so much better for the integrity of the court. Of course, this couldn't be done as half the men would also not be able to appear. Salisbury had handled the queen just right – without force, flattery or even cajoling. She came to the conclusion herself and wrote in her journal:

Lady Blandford came by, I having allowed poor divorced ladies, who have had to divorce their husbands owing to cruelty, desertion, and misbehaviour, but are in no way to blame themselves, to appear at Court.[22]

To work with the queen, you had to understand the queen. Happily, Salisbury did. The queen thought she was rid of the hated old man Gladstone forever, but sadly for her, this would not be the case.

Part III

Jubilee

Chapter Ten

'…this never-to-be-forgotten day….'

Good news in the family came once again, when Arthur's wife 'Louischen' delivered her last child, Patricia. The queen hurried to Buckingham Palace where Arthur met her 'at the door & said all was doing well. He took me at once to see the baby, a dear, pretty little thing.'¹

However, rebellion came from quite an unexpected quarter. At the beginning of 1887, Irène of Hesse and by Rhine, Alice's third daughter, went against her grandmother and the establishment for perhaps the first and last time in her life. Though part of the 'three graces' with her elder sisters Victoria and Ella, Irène was a typical middle child. She was neither as beautiful nor as clever as her sisters. She was simply Irène, the Greek word for peace, and as such, took her place as the peacemaker and the 'pleaser'. However, just for once, she went on the offensive. She announced that she was engaged to her first cousin, Vicky's son, Prince Henry of Prussia (who, incidentally, was also going against the wishes of his family, as well, to marry Irène).

Vicky's third child Prince Albert Wilhelm Heinrich of Prussia, was born on 14 August 1862, at the Neues Palais, at Potsdam. Henry, like many in his family, pursued a naval career. He was a part of his brother's beloved navy and would eventually become Grand Admiral of the German Fleet. Though Henry was obviously not as repugnant as a Russian engagement, Queen Victoria was against the match since she didn't like him very much. She thought him dreadfully indulged by his grandfather, Wilhelm I, with no self-discipline. She considered him a heedless, non-intellectual, for whom his elder brother, the future Kaiser Wilhelm II, wrote speeches. She also felt that he had behaved badly during several family controversies. To be fair to Henry, perhaps he was just a more likeable and well-adjusted fellow who was easy-going. Nevertheless, the queen saw him as being bullied by his brother, and the only thing that he had evidently, up to that time, stood firm on, was his desire to marry Irène.

A more serious issue was the fact that Irène and Henry were first cousins on their mothers' side, as well as being closely related on their fathers', and the queen was always apprehensive about close cousins marrying – especially in view of what could be inherited by children of a closely related couple.

A more emotional issue was that the queen felt Henry did not treat his mother, Vicky, with respect. Vicky, conversely, was extremely pleased with the match since she liked Irène. It would be nice to have a quiet, biddable daughter-in-law, unlike the unkind Augusta Viktoria. Indeed, Irène always felt obliged to smooth over the family controversies and gave the impression of one who always stood in the middle, trying to explain her husband and her brother-in-law Willy to her grandmother the queen. It was not the most enviable of positions.

In the end, however, the deepest cut of all was that the queen learned about the engagement through the newspapers and had not been first informed as she ought to have been. The queen fumed in a letter to Irène's eldest sister, Victoria, from Osborne:

> It is impossible for me to tell you what a shock your letter gave me! Indeed I felt quite ill – for I am so deeply hurt at Irène's conduct towards me.... [S]he assured me again & again that she w[ou]ld never do that! How can I trust her again after such conduct?[2]

The queen was angry because she felt that no one told her anything. This was, of course, an extreme exaggeration, but being a pragmatist, she was quick to reconcile herself to matters as they lay. She remained hurt over what she considered Irène's dishonesty and felt that the girl would have an awkward position in the Prussian court. Indeed, the entire Hessian family, would, she was sure, be treated rudely in Berlin. However, she was firm that 'Henry must be brought round to a right view of things.'[3]

Irène came timidly to the defence once more as she tried to persuade her grandmother how 'open-hearted and true'[4] Henry was. Just a few days later she reassured her grandmother that they were indeed very happy and that, 'Harry [as Henry was called in the family] is really the good angel here & go between in all difficulties I have already seen & felt, & that I scarcely deserve him too.'[5] And, just a few days after that, Irène asked her grandmother to invite Henry to the upcoming Jubilee celebrations, taking place in June of 1887, which the Queen did. She would, she wrote, 'feel that you had quite forgiven me … I hope you are not angry with me for asking this?'[6] In the end, a more inoffensive marriage could not be found.

Irène and Henry lived a quiet life away from the contentions of the Prussian court. Irène proved her unobtrusive inner strength time and time again while dealing with Vicky and Willy, while raising her family in a private manner. Prince Henry remained in the Imperial Navy, leaving only in the aftermath of the Great War in 1919. Despite the queen's objections, they were a happy and compatible couple, sometimes called 'the very amiables'. One of their great sorrows would be that Irène was a carrier of haemophilia.

After this, the matchmaking queen was on the prowl for her last Hessian granddaughter, Alix. In Victoria's mind, she must not, in any circumstances go to Russia. She had Prince 'Eddy', Bertie's eldest, or the second son, George in her sights. But she made it clear that all must be done to prevent '<u>further</u> Russians or other people <u>coming</u> to snap her up'.[7]

However pragmatic she was in these matters, the queen sometimes gave over to feeling very sorry for herself. She wrote, 'I feel very deeply that my opinion and my advice are never listened to and that it is almost useless to give any.'[8]

* * *

Most unusual as well as exciting for Victoria was that in May 1887, just before the real festivities got underway, Buffalo Bill Cody and his Wild West Show were brought all the way from America and made remarkable headlines in London. When the queen read about it, she requested a private audience. On 11 May, the queen and her entourage sat in an arena and watched:

> … some 200 performers – cowboys, sharpshooters, musicians, American Indians as well as horses, bison, elk, mules and other cattle. When the show started, the first rider came in with an American flag and the queen rose and bowed – the first time royalty had done this since American Independence. Apparently when that was finished, Buffalo Bill approached the royal box, bowed, and proclaimed: 'Welcome, your majesty, to the Wild West of America.'[9]

* * *

Henry was not the only one invited to the Golden Jubilee celebrating Victoria's fifty years on the throne. Scores of other royalties and aristocrats from throughout the world were invited – kings, queens, crown princes and princesses as well as the odd maharajah and khedive.

The queen sat in the garden on the late afternoon of 20 June resting and writing in her journal after an exhilarating but tremendously exhausting day. She had terrible rheumatism which fatigued her, as well as severe backache. Nevertheless, she wrote a substantial entry: 'The day has come, & I am alone, though surrounded by many dear Children ... 50 years today since I came to the throne. God has mercifully sustained me through many great trials & sorrows.'[10]

She had dressed in her semi-mourning as she had been doing since the death of Albert and made very little concession to fashion or elegance on that day. She was cajoled by her children to wear something more festive than her accustomed bonnet and only eventually consented to attach some lace to it, making it a special bonnet, but she refused to wear a crown. She was the epitome of an older middle-class lady.

There were a few clouds on the horizon, however. Her beloved granddaughter Victoria Battenberg contracted typhoid and was seriously ill for a month before the Jubilee celebrations. It was feared that she would not be well enough to attend, but as it turned out, she was present, but her grandmother decreed for only for a few events and she was on no account to exhaust herself.

As well, in May 1887, Victoria's beloved son-in-law Fritz was diagnosed with several growths on his throat. This was a particularly bitter blow to the queen. Vicky and Fritz had waited so long to become emperor and empress of Germany; waited so long to be able to implement the liberal ideas that Albert had imbued, particularly in his eldest daughter, and now that future was in doubt. Several operations had already been performed on the unfortunate crown prince, and the German and British doctors were at odds with one another about the prognosis. Initially, they were confident that they had removed the diseased tissue. The family was aware, however, that he was in great pain and could no longer speak.

Connected to that cloud was the fact that the queen had reluctantly invited her Prussian grandson Willy to the celebrations. Vicky had specifically requested the invitation, and the queen could not refuse her.

Willy had assumed that he was invited and was prepared to represent his aged grandfather Kaiser Wilhelm I, as well as his seriously ill father. Fritz, to his son's surprise, felt well enough to attend and did so. Nevertheless, Willy showed up and was treated extremely coolly by the queen and other family members. He complained bitterly about this saying it was 'high time the old woman died. ... Well, England should look out when I have something to say about things',[11] he grumbled angrily when he got home, giving the impression that he hated his grandmother.

* * *

The queen drove from Windsor through to the decorated railroad station with Beatrice, Liko and some of her grandchildren on the morning of 20 June. The long processional would go from Paddington Station to Buckingham Palace. Victoria led off in an open landau, to be shown to the people, and the crowds were enormous. The enthusiasm of her subjects seemed to surprise her.

She had appeared only rarely in public since Albert's death and many of her subjects had never seen her. That day, as she rode through the streets and listened to the cheers, she was overwhelmed by their love and enthusiasm. After the processional there was a huge luncheon with all the assembled royalties, including, the queen noted, princes from Japan, Siam, Persia, and maharajahs by the handful from all parts of India in attendance. There was even the mountainous Queen of Hawaii, with the mellifluous name of Kapeolani, and her sister, Princess Liliuokalani.

That evening the queen had what she described as a family dinner attended by scores of people. The queen had scrupulously listed all the attendees at the state and family dinners and their seating arrangements in her journal. It was like a 'Who's Who' of all the crowned heads of Europe and elsewhere, truly a once in a century assemblage.

The Thanksgiving service the following day at Westminster Abbey, was even more impressive and emotional. It was a bright and sunny morning and Victoria travelled in a landau with Vicky and Alix facing her, once again to the loud and heartfelt cheers of the crowds. Following her were some thirty princes – her sons, her sons-in-law, (Fritz looking particularly heroic in his white uniform) some of her grandsons, and royalties from around the world. The crowds she noted, were again so enthusiastic and good humoured and the decorations as she drove through London, so beautiful with touching inscriptions. When the Queen arrived at the abbey, the Archbishop of Canterbury met her at the door. All, naturally, were in their places as Victoria made her way slowly to the altar, to the majestic strains of Handel.

The archbishop was wearing the velvet and gold robes that had been worn by the presiding Archbishop at the queen's coronation fifty years before. Victoria looked splendid in her Jubilee dress of black silk, so elegant and stiff that it rustled as she walked. On her head was her special bonnet with exquisite white lace woven with diamonds instead of the usual black.

She made her way slowly to the coronation chair and the *Te Deum* 'by my darling Albert' was played. The queen no doubt thought how could she truly enjoy this moment 'without my beloved Husband?' Then, as the music swelled, all her sons, daughters, sons-in-law, daughters-in-law, and several grandchildren, one by one, came up to the chair and curtsied to their mother and grandmother, and kissed her. When it was Vicky's turn, Victoria embraced her warmly, and for many more seconds than the others. Perhaps the queen was prescient; maybe she instinctively knew the troubles her eldest child would face in the coming years.

The service continued with more tributes, and as the finale the congregation all rose as one, and sang *God Save the Queen*. A moment that was overwhelmingly emotional. It was in describing this that the queen expressed her pride in her people and the genuine gratitude she felt for the patriotism, fervour, and honest emotion they had conveyed.

The complement returned to Buckingham Palace and the exhausted queen rested for a while. But even then, she spent the time opening telegrams so numerous that even Victoria, who wrote thousands of words a week, felt she could not answer them. They would have to be acknowledged through the newspapers.

Again, that evening there was a large dinner for all the royalties. The queen described her gown with a rose, thistle and shamrock embroidered in silver after England, Scotland, and Wales. Victoria was toasted by King Christian IX of Denmark, the father of Alix of Wales and her younger sister Dagmar, who was now Empress Marie Feodorovna of Russia and the wife of Alexander III. And it continued, 'after dinner the Indian Princes and Corps Diplomatique swam past her in a shimmering mist.'[12]

Following such a long day, the queen, who claimed to be half dead with fatigue, slipped away from the party, since there would be more to come. She missed the fireworks and the crowds singing *Rule Britannia* and *God Save the Queen* till the very early hours. She remarked in her journal that there was no disorder in the crowds, something of which she was very aware since there had been so many attempts on her life in the past.

The following day, 22 June, there were no further public spectacles, just presentations and the queen was grateful for no crowds or noise. There would be one more grand luncheon for the guests and afterward a large assortment of gifts and medals were given and received, as well as speeches made to the company and the household. All that over, Victoria with her children, Lenchen, Vicky and Affie, left the palace to go to Hyde Park and Constitution Hill where there were yet further presentations and gifts for the crowds who had assembled there. Thence on to Paddington Station where there were again crowds and cheering.

Finally, back to Windsor that evening there was a family dinner with Albert's brother, Ernst attending, as well as Alice's husband, Ludwig of Hesse. The boys from Eton School gathered in the quadrangle of the castle to sing to the queen. They regaled her with the *Eton Boat Song* and a Jubilee song especially composed for the occasion. The queen graciously went down to the quadrangle and 'she said in her clear, musical voice, "I thank you very much"'.[13]

After that, she at last retired after an exhausting and exciting couple of days. She wrote that they would 'ever remain indelibly impressed on my mind, with great gratitude, to … my devoted & loyal people. But how painfully do I miss the dear ones I have lost!'[14]

* * *

It was during this time that another man came into the queen's life. During the Jubilee year, she thought it would be a good idea to employ some Indian servants. Two suitable gentlemen were found and brought to Britain.

> My 2 Indian servants were there, & began to wait. The one, Mohamed Buksh, very dark, with a very smiling expression, has been a servant before with Gen: Dennehy, & also with the Rana of Dholpore, &

the other, much younger, called Abdul Karim, is much lighter, tall, & with a fine serious countenance. His father is a native doctor at Agra. They both kissed my feet.[15]

The queen stipulated that all the Indians should wear native costume and decided the colours of their shirts and sashes.

Abdul Karim was, as she wrote, from Agra. Karim was a clerk employed at the Central jail.[16] The superintendent of the jail, John Tyler, asked Karim if he would like to go to Britain as an Indian servant to the queen and Karim eagerly agreed. He was schooled in the manners, social customs of England, and etiquette of the court of Victoria and was paired along with Mohammed Buksh to serve their queen-empress.

There is little doubt that Queen Victoria took to exotic and interesting out-of-the-ordinary characters – people like Melbourne, Napoleon III and Disraeli, who went a little against the grain.[17] It would be this tendency that would compel her to embrace her Indian servants and eventually all things Indian – the food, actually learning to cook curries, the scents, the spices, the romanticism of it all to the languages. In particular, she began to rely on the tall handsome man whom she would call 'the *Munshi*' (teacher or clerk), Abdul Karim. His presence would eventually wreak havoc in the queen's household, but that would come a little later.

* * *

In the summer of 1887, after the Jubilee celebrations, the troubles of Victoria's beloved Vicky and her husband, Fritz, come back into centre stage. The doctors in Germany had diagnosed Fritz's throat issue as cancer of the throat. While in London for the Jubilee celebrations, Fritz went to a cancer specialist, Dr Morell Mackenzie, who operated on him yet again and removed the growth. Because it was a malignant cancer it appeared again. Nothing seemed to help – going to various spas to breathe fresh air and taking the waters produced no salubrious results. Fritz's throat continued to swell, he continued to be so hoarse he couldn't speak, and he constantly caught what the doctors assumed were colds.

In November of that year, the family had been advised to go to Italy for the warm climate and they chose San Remo for what they hoped might be a convalescence. At last, both the German and British doctors agreed on the cancer diagnosis. Willy went to visit his father at that time and confronted his mother who angrily lashed out at him. Willy told his mother he thought Dr Mackenzie was trying to feather his reputation by treating the Crown Prince, and that the succession should pass over the dying Fritz to himself. Vicky was enraged by this.

Willy, apparently not much bothered, returned to Berlin to await the news of his succession. In February 1888, Fritz had a tracheotomy. At that point, Fritz's father, Wilhelm I, was also mortally ill, dying on 9 March of that year at the age of 90. The queen was thrilled that her daughter was at last Empress Friedrich, but, certainly in back of her mind, the idea that Fritz couldn't live much longer had taken root. All Albert, Victoria, and Vicky's liberal dreams going up in smoke to the reality of the reactionary influence of Wilhelm I on his three eldest grandchildren, Willy, Henry and Charley. It was all so unjust.

That spring, the queen had vacationed in Italy and on the way back in April, she stopped at Charlottenburg, the palace in Berlin, to see her son-in-law and daughter. While there, she met with the 'Iron Chancellor' Bismarck with whom she noted that she had a very pleasant conversation. He, too, was unusually impressed with the nearly 70-year-old queen. And why not? Hadn't the queen a great deal of experience in foreign affairs and marvellous teachers like Melbourne, Disraeli and even Gladstone? It was then that the engagement between Sandro and Moretta was officially dropped and Victoria's last visit with Fritz who, they had to admit at last, was dying.

It was also interesting at this point that Lord Salisbury was advising the queen how to treat her grandson, Willy. He counselled her to be careful what she said to him as everything now would be weighed only to reflect credit on Willy. What he meant was 'William might be rude to you, ma'am, and then you might be rude to him.'[18] Naturally, Victoria wasn't going to be told how to treat her ill-behaved grandson.

Fritz made one more appearance before cancer claimed him. He attended the wedding of Irène and Henry at the chapel of the Charlottenburg Palace. According to Willy, his father, still so handsome in his uniform, stood with immense dignity through the service. On 15 June 1888, with a final bout of pneumonia, Fritz died. Victoria telegraphed to her recalcitrant grandson: 'I am broken hearted … Help and do all you can for your poor dear Mother … Grandmama V.R.I.'[19] And in her journal:

> The misfortune is so awful. My poor Child's whole future, gone, ruined, which they had prepared themselves for, for nearly 30 years! Heard poor Vicky was not ill but wretched.[20]

And, like a torrent, all of Willy's resentment against his mother and grandmother poured out in his unspeakable treatment of them and his three younger favoured sisters, Moretta, Sophie and Mossy. These resentments had been simmering since Willy was a very small boy with a withered arm. All the painful and unhelpful treatments he had endured had warped his feelings towards his mother and her surrogates, the younger sisters. Now that he was 'head of it all' as his grandmother put it, and being arrogant, self-important and egotistical, he would show them.

It would begin by him insisting that he always be treated as an imperial majesty when he visited family, which outraged the queen. She maintained that he would be treated just as he should be treated, no more and no less. If he wanted different treatment, she wrote to Lord Salisbury, he had better not come here!

Meanwhile, Willy marginalised his mother and younger sisters whenever possible so that they felt persecuted by his little meannesses and digs. Vicky knew her son and had taken precautions even before the death of Fritz. She sent sensitive papers, letters, including Fritz's diary of the last two years through the British embassy to England for safekeeping.

The queen considered Fritz's death an 'untold tragedy' and was worried about Willy's leaning toward Russia and making no mention of Britain in speeches.[21] She wrote him letters asking him to be kind to his mother but was disgusted in his going about to banquets and reviews so soon after the death of this father. That the queen was furious goes without saying. The slights of her daughter, of herself, of his younger sisters, his unending arrogance – Victoria doubtless again thought how he could use a good 'skelping'. Oddly, in his autobiography, written in 1926, he writes about the 'extreme kindness of Queen Victoria'.[22] Perhaps the intervening years gave him a more nuanced picture of his grandmother, but probably not.

* * *

The year of the Jubilee brought some good family news to the queen. Beatrice gave birth to her first daughter. Victoria Eugénie, named for her mother and for the ex-empress of France, was born 24 October 1887. It had been a difficult labour, but she pulled through and Liko, as the queen noted in her journal, called her Victoria's little Jubilee grandchild. Her nickname in the family was supposed to be 'Eua', an old Gallic name, but was subsequently misread and became 'Ena' in the family, and Ena she remained. She would, most remarkably, become the queen of Spain.

She joined her elder brother, Alexander, born in 1886 and would be the elder sister to Leopold born in 1889 and Maurice born in 1891. All of these children were born while Beatrice and Liko lived with the queen as they promised. Because of this, these children were closer to the queen than any of her others with the possible exception of the motherless Darmstadt grandchildren, who spent a great deal of time with Victoria. And these were the last grandchildren of Victoria and Albert. They numbered forty-two, and by this time were also numerous great-grandchildren.

Alexander was known as 'Drino' in the family. His grandmother wrote about him:

As a rule I like girls best but I did wish it should be a boy, to be like his dear father and Uncles, and as I thought it would be a pleasure to poor dear Sandro in all his trials and troubles.[23]

He would be the only son that would marry. His wife was Lady Irene Dennison, whom he married in 1917. They had one child, Lady Iris, who had an interesting career of her own in the old-fashioned sense of the word.

Leopold was, like his uncle, a sufferer of haemophilia and died in 1922 after a hip operation. Interestingly enough, despite his condition, he was able to join the army and served on the Isle of Wight Rifles and during the Great War, the King's Royal Rifle Corps, though his health was always precarious. The youngest Maurice, also served in the King's Royal Rifle Corps and died in action near Ypres, Belgium, in 1914. He was the first prince to die in the war.

There are many photographs with Beatrice, Liko, their children and the queen sitting around tables or outside under tents with Indian servants stoically standing by. They are having breakfast, having tea or luncheon *en famille*. Liko, handsome as ever, looks like he's enduring for his wife's sake and for the sake of the position he holds in the family. There is no hint of restlessness for him in this house of women and children, but it will come.

A birth of note in the family was Victoria Battenberg's second child, Louise, born in 1889. She was not born in England like her elder sister Alice, but in Darmstadt. She was the 'shrimp' of the family as her father Prince Louis called her, but she was destined to be the second wife of Crown Prince Gustaf Adolf of Sweden in 1923, and became queen of Sweden in 1950.

While grieving for her tragic son-in-law Fritz, life went on for Victoria. In August 1888 she had Abdul Karim appointed her *Munshi*, and he was called that ever after. He gave her lessons in Urdu, or what was called Hindustani at the time, and dried the signatures on her papers. She believed that he had been brought over as a servant by mistake. He was intelligent and told her that he had been a clerk and was an altogether different class than the other Indian servants that had come during the Jubilee year. 'No one was quicker than the Queen to appreciate a situation where human dignity seemed to be involved.'[24] He was different and must be treated so.

Towards the end of that year, Victoria became interested in the bloody and savage murders of 'Jack the Ripper'. These tragic serial murders took place in London's east end at Whitechapel, an area known for being extremely poor and underserved. Because of the poverty there was a large segment of women working as prostitutes and the area itself became a fascinating den of iniquity for the middle-class readers of the more exploitive journals.

She, like the other avid readers of these horrible tragedies, thought something ought to be done. She had consulted Lord Salisbury about it, and he had promised that the detecting would improve, more men would be deployed in the area and more of the areas would be lit. However, more murders occurred, and no such measures were taken. Victoria was aghast and wrote to her Home Secretary, Henry Matthews, on 13 November 1888 with myriad questions. They included: since the murderer's clothes had to be saturated with blood, why were they not found? How about sufficient surveillance at night? Were departing boats being checked for suspicious characters?[25]

A more personal connection came from this as there was some suggestion that 'Eddy', Albert Victor of Wales, Bertie's eldest son, may have had something to do with it. However, that suggestion is ridiculous on so many levels as to be completely absurd. Eddy could hardly have baffled Scotland Yard's best.

Chapter Eleven

'Mother of Europe'

The last decade of the nineteenth century was a period of great wonders. Hundreds of thousands of patents were issued at a furious rate and inventions were constant and ground-breaking. Electricity was lighting the streets and a process was devised to bring it to homes. The automobile had been invented by Karl Benz in 1886 and horseless carriages were beginning to be seen on the roads. The telephone was invented in 1876 and was demonstrated to Queen Victoria in 1878. By the end of the century there were hundreds of thousands of home telephones. The tabulating machine, the precursor of data processing, with punch cards was invented in 1891.

Pax Britannica – the period from the end of the Napoleonic age to the beginning of the Great War, saw Victoria's empire at its zenith, an empire on which, it was said, the sun never set. Britain was the great power of the world and the queen-empress was at its helm. But she was getting on, she was entering her eighth decade and her health was breaking down. Her sight was failing, she suffered from indigestion, rheumatism and sciatica, often walking with a stick, but was working as hard as ever.

This last twenty-year period was the apex of the queen's reign. In the 'dazzled imagination of her subjects the queen soared aloft toward the regions of divinity through a nimbus of purest glory.'[1] Dispensing with the hyperbole, she began to be seen as something other than human and fallible.

Victoria, however, went on as before. She spent much time writing to her children, grandchildren and family members, handing out advice, discussing intimate problems, proposing matches, and complaining as usual that she wasn't listened to. No red dispatch boxes escaped her, and she was far more involved in state business than perhaps even her most kindred of prime ministers would have liked. However, her authority was beginning to fade.[2]

Her beloved Lady Ely left her in April 1889. The queen had used her constantly as a messenger, a go-between, and when she wasn't talking to Ponsonby, a sort of private secretary, corresponding with various people. She remained with the queen until the death of her son, and her own declining health. She died in June 1890. The queen was truly saddened by the death of her close friend and someone upon whom she had long depended. 'No one can ever replace this dearest kindest friend', she lamented. 'She understood all my feelings and likings perhaps more than anyone else and was so gentle and sympathetic.'[3]

Happier times came that summer when Louise, Bertie's daughter, became the first one of her sisters to marry. Like her sisters, she was known mostly for being shy and retiring. Because her darling 'Motherdear' couldn't be bothered to find her a spouse and wished all her children to remain with her in perpetuity, Louise did it herself. She was a determined young woman and wanted to be free of her mother's smothering influence, and so she made what was considered at the time a controversial choice in Alexander Duff, 6th Earl and later 1st Duke of Fife (1849–1912). Controversial because he was a commoner, and a great friend of the Prince of Wales.[4] Strangely, the queen was happy with this engagement. She continued to hold in her heart a great romantic feeling for Scotland and the Scots. She wrote to Fife that,

> Dear Louise will, I am sure, be happy with you whom I have known and liked from your childhood. That my beloved grandchild should have her home in dear Scotland and in the dear Highlands is an additional satisfaction to me.[5]

On 27 July 1889, the couple married. They had two daughters: Alexandra (1891–1959) who went on to marry Prince Arthur of Connaught, her first cousin once removed; and Maud (1893–1945), who went on to marry Lord Carnegie, later the 11th Earl of Southesk.

Louise bloomed in Scotland away from London, enjoying hunting, music and finding her talents in painting and interior decorating. In addition, the ill-health that Louise had always suffered, along with her premature siblings, seem to improve away from the court, which makes one wonder about the pathology.

Louise was made Princess Royal in 1905 by decree of her father who was then king, and her daughters were thereafter Royal Highnesses.

While traveling to Egypt, the Fifes were shipwrecked off Cape Trafalgar. Once they reached land, they had a long and arduous trek before they were rescued. The duke contracted pleurisy and died in Aswan, Egypt, in 1912.[6] Louise lived on, but died at the relatively early age of 63 of a heart attack in 1931 at her home in London.

* * *

Bertie came in for criticism again as he served as a witness in the 'Tranby Croft scandal'. This new disgrace involved cheating at Baccarat at one of the innumerable house parties with which Bertie busied himself. The trial began on 1 June 1891 and tickets for the proceeding were sold. Though Bertie was not the defendant, he was nevertheless nervous in the witness box. The solicitor questioned him for about twenty or so minutes and then he was dismissed.

The queen stood steadfastly by her son during this time since she knew he wasn't the offender and there was little else she could do. However, Willy had no such inhibitions. He wrote a letter of reproof to his uncle saying, 'how unsuitable it was that a man of his position and age should gamble for substantial stakes'. It takes a special kind of nerve to write such things. The queen no doubt was horrified that her nephew was so 'impertinent', though not surprised.[7]

Though the Prince of Wales was finally allowed access to the red dispatch boxes, his life was already set in its patterns. He had been living a life of pleasure, mistresses, and gambling and seemed to be a self-fulfilling prophecy for his mother. She expected failure and dissipation from him, and sadly, she was never disappointed. As late as 1892, the queen (who always referred to herself in the third person when writing official letters) wrote to Ponsonby:

> The Queen wonders if this principle [of allowing the Prince of Wales to receive information about Cabinet proceedings] was ever adopted by Lord Salisbury.
>
> Would Sir Henry ask Lord Salisbury and ask Mr Gladstone to pause before pursuing this course regularly? She thinks it can only have been on very particular occasions.[8]

She didn't trust Bertie to be serious about anything and it was a pity. She would never know what a Master of Diplomacy Bertie would be when he at last became king. More of a shame was that he was king for such a relatively short time.

Married to a womaniser who had little to do for over sixty years except enjoy his own pleasures, Alix, the Princess of Wales continued to immerse herself in her pets and her now grown children. Some historians have called her infantilising of her children, even when they were adults, obsessive. Nevertheless, she was extremely popular with the public and a very active member of the royal family.

She was a 'fashion icon' for the time. Women imitated her dress, her collars, her chokers, and her hairstyles. Eventually, however, the illnesses she suffered from as a young woman caught up with her. She became profoundly deaf and limped from rheumatism, which was also imitated in society and called the 'Alexandra limp'. She would continue to maintain an incredibly youthful look due to her use of cosmetics, a sort of primitive acid skin peel and, of course, lots of retouching of photographs.

Victoria continued her love affair with beautiful and exotic India. In 1890, she decided to add what would be called the Durbar Room to her beloved Osborne. This was an occupation that absorbed the queen for several years. It was designed by John Lockwood Kipling (the father of Rudyard Kipling) and Bhai Ram Singh, a master carver and plasterer.

The room itself was designed in the elaborate Indian style all in alabaster with massive plaster carvings of peacocks, elephant gods and a lacy panelled ceiling. It was used as a state room for receptions and a banqueting hall. Scattered around the room were many items on display from both the Golden Jubilee in 1887 and the Diamond Jubilee in 1897. It had the distinction of being the first room in Osborne that was lighted by electricity. As beautiful as the queen felt the room was, others felt that it was incongruous with the Italianate architecture of Osborne.

She spent a great deal of time with the *Munshi* who began to think himself as good, if not better, than anyone in her household. While understandable, it was infuriating to the household. The queen was remarkably and unusually free of the social and racial prejudice for her time, but the same could not be said for the members of her household. The queen commissioned a portrait of the *Munshi* to be painted by Laurits

Tuxen, an extremely well-known painter of royal portraits and would later commission several more by other well-known artists.

No doubt this, as well as other favours and preferences stoked the flames of jealousy about Abdul Karim. Her servants, her attendants and her family alike all detested the man intensely. The queen was his constant defender, and put down any complaints by her staff or household to racism. In 1889, she elevated his title from a humble clerk to Hafiz Abdul Karim – a hafiz is someone who has memorised the entire Koran.

As time went on, like Brown, the *Munshi* became very proprietary about the queen, but unlike Brown, he had absolutely no defenders. Brown's defenders, which included Ponsonby and Disraeli, thought he at least had a good effect on the queen and was helpful. This was not the case with the *Munshi*. Brown had no pretentions of being an intellectual, while the *Munshi* quite possibly was being read in on Indian affairs which could well cause some problems with the queen's government. His presence began rumours once again that the queen was involved in what might have been considered an improper relationship with an inferior, or even that she was quite possibly mad.

* * *

But there are engagements of interest to look at before discussing the *Munshi* further. Several of the grandchildren were of an age to look for a spouse, and their grandmother continued to be an avid matchmaker.

Vicky's second to youngest daughter, Sophie had become acquainted with 'Tino', Crown Prince Constantine of Greece during the Jubilee celebrations in London. The couple were engaged in autumn 1888. They were married the following year in Athens, during what was considered the first major royal wedding in modern Greece. It united five of the great ruling houses at the time – Great Britain, Germany, Greece, Denmark and Russia.[9] The queen was happy about this marriage. Though Greece wasn't the most stable of thrones, it was an excellent marriage for a younger daughter who would someday be queen of Greece.

Willy, however, could never leave anything alone. After the birth of her first child, Sophie decided to adopt the Greek Orthodox faith. In 1890, Tino and Sophie were attending Moretta and Adolph's wedding in Germany and Sophie was prepared to tell her brother that she had made the decision to convert. Someone else had already informed him and as head of the Lutheran church he was highly incensed. Dona was delegated to discuss their anger about the conversion with Sophie and they argued. The empress, who was pregnant at the time, blamed Sophie for angering her so much that her labour started prematurely. The emperor told Sophie if she converted, she could not step foot in Germany again.

Sophie did it anyway and wrote a conciliatory letter to Willy explaining her reasons. However, Willy was having none of it. He bent only by saying the 'exile' would be for a period of three years. She famously telegraphed her mother saying 'Keeps to what he said in Berlin. ... Mad. Never mind.'[10] Willy tried to justify himself to the queen, writing that 'Sophie made an awful scene in which she behaved in a simply incredible manner.'[11] Victoria wasn't buying it. From her point of view, it was a case of Sophie simply not caring, and Willy being a tyrant and a bully and, as will be shown later, a complete hypocrite.

During that same wedding in Berlin in 1890, another engagement was in the offing. Lenchen's younger daughter Marie Louise was in attendance with her parents and older sister, Helena Victoria, and became enamoured with Aribert of Anhalt-Dessau.

Marie Louise was born in Cumberland Lodge in Windsor Great Park, 12 August 1872, just a few months younger than her cousin, Alix of Hesse. Marie Louise was an attractive young girl with cousins all over Europe, and the family also spent much time visiting various relatives. It was around this time, when Marie Louise and her family were staying at a hotel in Germany, that she caught the eye of Carmen Sylva, the pen name of Queen Elisabeth of Romania.

The queen thought it would be a wonderful idea if her nephew, Crown Prince Ferdinand of Romania, proposed to her. Nando, as he was called in the family, was the second son of Leopold, Prince of Hohenzollern-Sigmaringen (the Catholic side of the Hohenzollerns) and Infanta Antónia of Portugal. Nando's eldest brother, Wilhelm had no interest in the throne and renounced his rights so that young Ferdinand would be the heir of his childless uncle, the former Prince Karl of Hohenzollern-Sigmaringen, now King Carol I of Romania. At that point, Marie Louise had already met Aribert and was completely infatuated with him and so refused this suggestion. According to her memoir, Aribert was extremely handsome with a striking personality and a great deal of charm.

She married him in 1891. The marriage was promoted by Marie Louise's cousin, the Kaiser, whom she truly believed had done her a great kindness in helping it along. However, it was far from a match made in heaven. The couple were married for about ten years, during which time it was said that the groom could barely look at the bride and seemed to intensely dislike her. The state of her marriage, especially in the face of his obvious dislike, stressed Marie Louise so much that she was advised by her doctors to go on a long trip. She visited Canada in 1900 and while there she received a cable from her father-in-law commanding that she return to Anhalt; she also received a telegram from the queen on the same day asking her granddaughter to be sent home to her in Britain, which is what Marie Louise did.

After that the marriage was annulled, though Marie Louise always considered herself married to Aribert. The annulment was based on the facts that the princess had left and not returned, and that she had not produced a son. There were questions and speculations about whether the marriage was consummated (we will never know) and whether Aribert was bi- or homosexual. Rumour was that he had been caught with a man and the queen agreed to 'hush the matter up'.[12] Marie's Uncle Bertie was said to have remarked: 'Poor Louie, she came back just as she went', a somewhat snide implication that nothing of a physical nature took place. Obviously, the marriage was childless, and Aribert seemed to have no regrets at its termination, though that didn't stop his father from continuing to place the blame on poor Marie Louise.

Marie Louise was the only one of Lenchen's children who married. Her elder brother, Christian Victor died in 1900 at the age of 33 while serving during the Boer War. He was a great favourite of the queen's and there is a statue erected to him in Windsor. Her younger brother Albert never married, though he did have an illegitimate daughter in 1921, Valerie Marie zu Schleswig-Holstein, with an un-named, but 'high-born' lady.

Her sister Helena Victoria, or Thora in the family, had very much wanted to marry, but a suitable spouse was never found. Certainly, in contrast to Alix of Wales, Thora's mother had wanted that for her daughter. The 'Snipe' (which was rather a cruel commentary on her looks) was born at Frogmore House, Windsor, May 3, 1870. As mentioned, she and her family mostly resided very near or with Queen Victoria, Lenchen being one of the most useful of the queen's daughters. Her other useful daughter,

Princess Beatrice, whom the queen had counted on being her companion for the rest of her life, thwarted her mother's plans and married. Therefore, it was required that other daughters and granddaughters fill that role. Lenchen and her daughters were prime candidates since they were born, and lived, in Britain.

Interestingly, much later in her life, Helena Victoria was quite close to the Connaughts. Apparently, she was a favourite of her uncle, the Duke of Connaught and his family. When Crown Princess Margareta of Sweden tragically died in 1920, there was some talk of her widower, Crown Prince Gustaf Adolf, asking Helena Victoria to marry him. It seems a little odd, since she was much older than he. In all events, he soon turned his attentions to Lady Louise Mountbatten, a great-granddaughter of the queen and the younger daughter of Victoria Battenberg.

In 1917, along with other family members, Princess Helena Victoria gave up her German titles and surname. She was no longer of Schleswig-Holstein-Sonderburg-Augustenburg, instead she was simply HH Princess Helena Victoria. Eventually, she and Marie Louise lived together in London where they worked in myriad charitable endeavours and were avid patrons of the arts. The family took it all in good part, and the sisters used to joke that they were 'princesses of nowhere'.

Both sisters attended the wedding of their cousin Elizabeth and Lieutenant Philip Mountbatten RN (Victoria Battenberg's grandson).

* * *

More important to the queen and the succession to the throne was the marriage of the heir, Prince Albert Victor, Eddy. It was felt quite strongly that he needed a wife just as his father had needed one for stability, and in Eddy's case, for strong guidance. There was a great deal of speculation as to who would be suitable for him. Princess Victoria Mary of Teck, called 'May' in the family, was put forward in 1886. Others too were suggested: Princess Clementine of the Belgians and Princess Alexandra of Anhalt, but foreign-born brides were no more popular than foreign princes had been.[13] Eddy, too, was becoming a problem, with several scandals attached to his name as well as the 'Jack the Ripper' accusation. However, with all these issues, it was best that a bride was found for Eddy and that he settle down.

The problem was, which bride?

As mentioned, a foreign-born bride would have been an extremely unpopular choice at that point. However, one that might have worked was the youngest surviving daughter of his Aunt Alice: Alix of Hesse. Alicky was a beautiful young woman of nearly 18 and Eddy was 25. Eddy decided he was in love and proposed to her, but she declined. Alicky was already in love with Tsarevich Nicholas of Russia, the son of Alexander III, but Queen Victoria wanted this match desperately as she did not want another Hessian granddaughter going to Russia. Alicky told her grandmother that she would marry Eddy if forced to do so, but otherwise, only loved him as a cousin. The queen was extremely disappointed. How could Alicky turn down such a wonderful position in her mother's country? She wrote to her granddaughter Victoria Battenberg, 'Moreover, Eddie is not stupid, is very good, affectionate & a good looking young man.'[14] She left out that he was a good dancer, but sadly Eddy had little else to recommend him.

The prince, whose feelings failed to run deeply, mourned his loss of Alicky for a month and then fell in love again.[15] The lucky girl was Princess Hélène of Orléans, a daughter of the Count of Paris. The queen was adamantly against this love match since Hélène was a Catholic and even as the nineteenth century was closing, such matches were not permitted. Victoria warned him sternly that he would be left out of the succession if he continued in this vein. The young princess said she would convert to marry Eddy, but her father refused permission as did the pope.

Another princess in the running was Margaret of Prussia, Vicky's youngest daughter. The queen thought Mossy might do. She might not be conventionally pretty, but she was half-English and had a good figure. She came for a visit the following year in 1891 but made little romantic impression on her cousin.

The queen was not aware that Eddy was still enamoured with Hélène, evidently less fickle in this preference than with his cousin Alicky. He wrote about this to his younger brother George, how pretty she was and how much he liked her and truthfully, the letter sounds like it was written by a 15-year-old, not a man of nearly 27. At any rate, when it was clear that he couldn't marry Hélène, yet another possibility presented itself.

Princess 'May' of Teck, who had initially been rejected, was now being considered again. She was the daughter of the queen's first cousin,

Princess Mary Adelaide, Duchess of Teck, and Francis, Duke of Teck. May was an extremely well-rounded and well-travelled young woman. She had a knowledge of art and was fluent in German and French. Above all, she was a young woman of stability and good character – in some ways, Eddy's complete opposite. It was therefore thought that she would be an example for the prince, who was considered by his close relatives to be lethargic, and extremely unsophisticated. When people wrote about the prince, they constantly damned him with faint praise. The fact was, he could not be described as a bright, intelligent and forceful individual. To the contrary, Eddy was the despair of his parents and grandmother in his lack of interest in just about *everything*.

Eddy was told to propose to May who had been positively vetted by Victoria, and he dutifully did so. The couple were engaged in December 1891. Surely it was a question not only of May being accepted in the inner royal circles as her parents had not been,[16] but also her having a strong sense of duty and respect for the monarchy.[17] The queen knew that May was not in love with Eddy, but that didn't matter. May wrote in her diary that she was surprised by the proposal, but that hardly seems plausible.

A month after their engagement, Eddy caught a chill which turned into influenza. This flu was part of the pandemic of 1889–92 and called the 'Russian' or 'Asiatic' flu. Other family members had also caught the virus but had been able to throw it off. Eddy, however, was not so lucky. May and his mother Alix devotedly nursed him, but he succumbed on 14 January 1892, a little over a month before the wedding was scheduled. The heir was gone and the queen, the family and the nation were in shock.

> Whilst I was dressing Lenchen came in bringing the following heart rending telegram from poor dear Bertie: 'Our darling Eddy has been taken from us. We are broken hearted.' Words are too poor to express one's feelings of grief, horror & distress! Poor, poor Parents, poor May, to have her whole bright future to be merely a dream. Poor me, in my old age, to see this young promising life cut short! I, who loved him so dearly & to whom he was so devoted! God help us! This is an awful blow to the Country too! We are all greatly upset. — My 3 daughters breakfasted with me. Soon 100s of telegrams of condolence came pouring in. The feeling of grief immense. Had a telegram from Bertie, whom I had enquired after, saying they were

all fairly well, but very tired & exhausted. Just had a beautiful service, where our dear Boy is lying. Anxious to have last sad ceremony at Windsor. Pray do not think of coming. Weather to inclement to run risks.' — Heard also from Dr Laking that poor Bertie & Alix were bearing up wonderfully. Georgie better, all fairly well, including May Teck, for whom this is such a tragedy.[18]

As the queen noted, May took the entire thing quite bravely. The nation, too, got over its shock of losing the heir, and were presented with the second son: George, called Georgie in the family – a young man more engaged, energetic with no scandal attached to him. He was, as the queen wrote, 'so nice, sensible, and truly rightminded, and so anxious to improve himself'.[19]

Naturally, the new 27-year-old heir must find a bride for himself, or the queen must find one for him. Georgie had a decided preference for Princess Marie of Edinburgh, 'Missy', and had spent time on Malta with the family when Affie was his commander in the navy. Missy was 16 and quite young, though her mother, Marie, felt that princesses should be married off as young as possible before they got ideas of their own. Apparently, George decided to wait because she was so young, and though his father approved of the match, Marie had no wish for any of her daughters to marry in England.

Georgie may have had such scruples, but his Aunt Marie did not. Missy was introduced to Ferdinand of Romania and the couple became engaged in the summer of 1892. The queen was not pleased with this engagement and Affie was quite disappointed. Victoria wrote to Victoria Battenberg:

We have been much startled lately to hear of <u>Missy's Engagement</u> to <u>Ferdinand of Rumania</u>. He is nice I believe & the Parents are charming – but the Country is very insecure & the immorality of the Society at Bucharest <u>quite awful</u>.[20]

Missy was young and incredibly naïve – just 17 when the pair were married in January 1893. So, Missy was stuck with a shy German prince, who had little interest in her, who was to inherit a very new throne in the wilds of Romania. Their marriage was probably not ideal, but Missy, the quintessential egotist, made a perfect early twentieth-century queen of

Romania. Her memoir in three lush volumes, called *My Life* makes for absorbing reading. She was a gifted writer and used her talents wisely. She was not necessarily self-serving, but for her it was a question about how her dramatics would help the country she came to love passionately. This, she would declare, was the only way she loved.

She was a woman who lived in and up to her own fantasies with the exoticism of her Byzantine costumes and jewellery and her arcane ceremonies from long ago and far away. She also burned brightly and went out relatively quickly. This isn't to say that she didn't genuinely love her people and Romania, she did, performing as only she knew how. She was, no doubt, one of the first celebrity royals.

* * *

Victoria felt that May was too good a princess to give up and encouraged her grandson in her direction. May and Georgie had in fact comforted each other during this tragic time and, eventually, Georgie, waiting a respectful year after the death of his brother, proposed, and May, taking responsibility to its logical conclusion, consented.

Once again, appropriate for the marriage of an heir, the queen wrote pages and pages about it in her journal. She continued to be overwhelmed by the excitement and patriotism of her people and said the only comparable day she could describe was the Jubilee. May was brought in to see Victoria before they went to the Chapel.

> Mary [Adelaide, May's mother] … brought in May, who looked very sweet. Her dress was very simple. Of white satin with a silver design of roses, shamrocks, thistles & orange flowers, interwoven. On her head she had a small wreath of orange flowers, myrtle & white heather surmounted by the diamond necklace I gave her, which can also be worn as a diadem, & her Mother's wedding veil. —

The wedding itself took place at the Chapel Royal at St James's Palace. The queen was the first to arrive at the chapel, which was not intended, but she enjoyed watching all the different royalties and family members process into the chapel. Along with all her living children, King Christian IX and Queen Louise of Denmark, Alix's parents attended along with their grandson, the tsarevich Nicholas of Russia. The bridegroom followed and then came the bride with her

> 10 dear Bridesmaids: Victoria [of Wales], Maud [of Wales], Ducky [of Edinburgh], Sandra [of Edinburgh], Baby B[ee of Edinburgh], Thora [Helena Victoria of Schleswig Holstein], Daisy [Margaret of Connaught], Patsy [Patricia of Connaught], Alice Battenberg [Princess Victoria Battenberg's daughter] & Ena [of Battenberg, Beatrice's daughter], the 4 little ones looking very sweet.

For the queen, the occasion, as weddings always did, reminded her of weddings past.

> I could not but remember that I had stood, where May did, 53 years ago, & dear Vicky 35 years ago, that the dear ones who stood where Georgie did, were gone from us! May these dear Children's happiness last longer!

She had written those very words after Affie and Marie's wedding and sadly, that marriage was never very happy. The queen lived in hope.

As so many had done after them, Georgie, May, and the family showed themselves on the balcony of Buckingham Palace after the conclusion of the service. The queen noted that there was much cheering and enthusiasm. Afterward, there was the signing of the register, the wedding breakfast, and a break in the festivities for photographs. Then the assembled guests saw the couple go away for their honeymoon at Sandringham. At last, the queen did what she always did after a long and strenuous day:

> I went back to my room, feeling very tired, & I rested on the sofa. Went for a short while into the Garden.— All the family ... were dining with Bertie. Then were some very fine illuminations, & enormous crowds were out.[21]

After an odd beginning, Georgie and May were a very happy and compatible couple. The following year, May gave birth to a boy. Victoria was thankful and jubilant at the same time. '[R]eceived the joyful news that dear May had been safely delivered of a son, a fine strong child! What joy, what a blessing.'[22]

The new arrival was christened with a huge host of important names: Edward Albert Christian George Andrew Patrick David. The names in order were chosen for his late uncle 'Eddy', Albert for the Prince Consort, Christian for his great-grandfather Christian IX of Denmark, and the last names for the patron saints of England, Scotland, Ireland, and Wales. A huge load to carry no doubt and would have intimidated a stronger man than he. David, as he was called in the family, would later become Prince of Wales at Bertie's death, Edward VIII at Georgie's death, and finally the Duke of Windsor at his abdication and after his marriage to Wallis Simpson. But for that unique moment in June 1894, there were three heirs to Victoria's throne.

There was some sad family news after the July wedding of Georgie and May. Albert's older brother, Ernst II, the Duke of Saxe-Coburg and Gotha, died. Ernst had married Princess Alexandrine of Baden in May 1842 and their marriage remained childless probably as a result of Ernst's suffering with a venereal disease. Therefore, it was up to Victoria's son, Affie, to be the heir to the Duchy. Alexandrine was fiercely, even unaccountably, devoted to Ernst, calling him 'my treasure'. Ernst, on the other hand, had spent a great deal of time womanising and other such pleasures. Marie Mallet, one of Victoria's Maids-of-Honour wrote that he was 'an awful looking man, the Queen dislikes him particularly'.[23] Victoria ended up disliking him because he was always 'writing anonymous pamphlets against the Queen and the Empress Frederick',[24] which seemed extremely disloyal, especially since the duke was widely disliked and often caused a lot of disturbances in the family. When he died, Victoria was able to dredge up more positive memories of those early visits before her marriage, when both young men were so full of promise. She wrote:

> I was a good deal upset when it came. I thought of the happy past, so long ago, when he was so much with us, of his frequent visits formerly, — of so many many things, of dear Coburg, & that my child, our son was now the reigning Duke, a foreign sovereign!! My head was so full, I could think of nothing else, & of dear excellent Alexandrine who perfectly adored Ernest, though he was often very trying. May God support her & guide our dear Affie![25]

The following year, after Affie and his family were ensconced in Coburg, a large family gathering took place.

* * *

Grand Duke Ludwig IV of Hesse and by Rhine, Alice's husband, had died of heart disease and stroke a couple of months after the death of Eddy. Victoria was crushed by the death of this son-in-law, who visited England often and was like a son to her. Ernst Ludwig, or 'Ernie' as he was known in the family, succeeded his father in March 1892. The queen was in sympathy with this young man of 23 who had little instruction or experience in statecraft and was completely overwhelmed. Ernie was left in the duchy now with only his young sister Alix, who was also unprepared to take the reins of 'first lady' of Hesse. Because Victoria had always felt so motherly toward the Hessian family, she travelled to Darmstadt the following month to give Ernie a 'crash course' in governance.

As the summer came, there was much discussion between the queen and Ernie's sisters about a topic so dear to Victoria's heart: a match for the handsome young man. Naturally, the queen looked around. Initially it was thought that one of the Edinburgh sisters might do for him, but the queen hesitated and consulted with her physician, Sir William Jenner. The potential brides were first cousins, but Sir William felt that there would be no problems with such a union. They were healthy, lively and energetic girls and it was thought that they would strengthen any potential children of the marriage. The eldest girl, Missy, was now engaged and about to be married to Ferdinand of Romania.

The next Edinburgh sister was Victoria Melita, Ducky in the family, who at the point of consideration was 16 going on 17. Although most were aghast at the youth of these two princesses, their mother Marie, now Duchess of Saxe-Coburg and Gotha, was only too happy that they marry as young as was decent. The queen, in this case, decided that Ducky and Ernie were just right for one another. For one thing, they had the same birthday, for another, they enjoyed music and had, the queen thought, the same sense of humour.

It was destiny and the queen was happy to push the match. The only problem was that Ernie, who was young for his age and coddled by his sisters, was extremely slow in making up his mind to propose to the young lady. The queen lobbied long and hard for the match and enlisted family members to encourage him to come to the point, which he slowly did. Ernie proposed and Ducky accepted in January 1894.

The pair were lukewarm towards one another, but it was a marriage that their grandmother, Queen Victoria, had wanted badly, and so to please her, the two married. Ducky's mother was not entirely happy about the marriage as marriages between first cousins were not permitted in the Russian Orthodox Church; however, for once, she was overruled.

The large family gathering in Coburg took place in April 1894. Some have called it the largest 'gatherings of royalty ever seen in Europe'.[26] It was an event attended by a large segment of the queen's family that she named 'the royal mob'; it seems as though there were more of Victoria's descendants and other crowned heads assembled than ever before and there exists a very famous set of photographs that were made during the occasion. The Prussians, who viewed this as a fine marriage, the Romanovs, Bertie, the Connaughts, the Romanians and various other German royalties were present. The photographer was the Coburg court photographer, Professor Uhlenut. The photographs of these sittings were circulated all over Europe.

It was at this wedding that yet another drama was also taking place. At this time 20-year-old Alix of Hesse was trying desperately to decide if she could marry the Tsarevich Nicholas of Russia. Their love story and potential nuptials had actually been the subject of more interest than the tepid love story of Ernie and Ducky. The major issue for Alix was that she could not conceive changing her religion from Lutheran to Russian Orthodoxy. During the days before the wedding when so many were gathered in Coburg, Nicholas was enlisting family members to try to help her change her mind.

Victoria had been upset about this for some time. She wrote a long letter to Victoria Battenberg back in 1890 when Alix had refused Eddy. How, she wanted to know, could Alix do this? Didn't she know that his parents didn't want this? That a younger sister from a minor duchy would 'never answer'. Victoria was sure that Alix's sister Ella, Grand Duchess Serge, was conniving to get her to Russia, 'encouraging and even urging the Boy to do it'. Further, this must not be allowed to go on, Papa must put a stop to it.' Again, she was worried that the state of Russia was so bad that at 'any moment something dreadful might happen'. It wouldn't be a problem for Ella, but only could have tragic consequences for the wife of the 'Tronfolger' [heir to the throne].[27] She was not listened to, and Alix continued to be persuaded by family members.

As the wife of the tsarevich, it was imperative that she become Russian Orthodox, and she sincerely thought religion was more important than her feelings for Nicky. Ella, as well as Willy, eventually weakened her resolve. Ella told her that the religions were quite similar, and she had done it herself just a few years before, though she, as just a grand duchess, had not been required to do so. Willy assured her she could not afford to give up such a grand position. He urged her to reconsider because he thought that having Alix in Russia would bring their two countries closer together. He reminded her that it was her patriotic duty as a German Princess to do this.

Remember, this was the man who exiled his sister Sophie for changing her religion. The lack of introspection is staggering.

Alix gave in and the happy couple went to see the queen:

> Breakfasted alone with Beatrice. Soon after Ella came in, much agitated, to say that Alicky and Nicky were engaged, and begging they might come in. I was quite thunderstruck, as, though I knew Nicky much wished it, I thought Alicky was not sure of her mind. Saw them both. Alicky had tears in her eyes, but looked very bright and I kissed them both. Nicky said 'She is much too good for me.' I told him he must make the religious difficulties as easy as he could for her, which he promised to do. People generally seem pleased at the engagement, which as the drawback that Russia is so far away, the position a difficult one, as well as the question of religion. But, as her brother is married now, and they are really attached to one another, it is perhaps better so.[28]

The queen abhorred the idea of another one of her tender Hessian granddaughters going to Russia, but she knew when she was defeated.

The love between Alix and Nicky was real and passionate. Their marriage would be extraordinarily happy and produced a clutch of children, four girls and one boy. Tragically, Alix was a carrier of haemophilia and her son Alexei had it. Some felt the family's fate was predicated on Alix's obsession with healers and anyone who could obviate the pain of her child. Of course, there was more to it than just that. Their fate was sad and well-known – like millions of other families, they were savagely murdered during the Great War in 1918.

On the other hand, the marriage of Ducky and Ernie was just the opposite. Any affection between the two of them was lost during the seven years of their marriage. They had one child, a little girl called Elisabeth, and one baby boy that was still-born. However, that was not the root of their problems. Their marriage could not survive the fact that Ernie might have been homosexual or at least bisexual, nor, perhaps more important, that Ducky fell deeply in love with another of her first cousins, the Grand Duke Kyrill Vladimirovich of Russia.

The idea that they had some similarities did not trump the fact that their personalities were completely opposite; Ducky was passionate and robust, while Ernie was more of a languid and low-key character. The queen knew about the unhappiness of the couple, and it pained her greatly. However, she could not in all good conscience permit a divorce, so the couple had to bide their time.

At that point, Queen Victoria swore that she would never match another couple again.

Chapter Twelve

The *Munshi* and other Trials

Family matters aside, there were several issues with which the queen had to deal. Significantly, Gladstone was back in power in 1892. The Liberal party had been in disarray as a result of the defeat of the Irish Home Rule bill in 1886. Now, however, the general election of 1892 put the Liberal party back in as a minority government.

The queen had reluctantly accepted Lord Salisbury's resignation and had to send for Mr Gladstone, which she did, no doubt with great disinclination. When she received him at Osborne, she was shocked at his age; here was a man of 82, who hardly looked fit for the job. Together with the antipathy she had carried against the stalwart Liberal for so long, she continued to be determined to keep any audiences with him under twenty minutes if at all possible.

Gladstone reintroduced a Government of Ireland Bill in 1893, which would have provided Ireland with Home Rule. This time it passed the House of Commons but was defeated in the House of Lords. Because Gladstone's was a minority government, there was very little hope of getting the bill passed and once again, he felt it necessary to resign to the queen's no very great regret.

During his last audience at Windsor, they talked about the 'merits of rival oculists, royal thanks for his services, ... a gracious word on Mrs Gladstone, and not a single syllable about the close of a fourth premiership and of sixty years in English public life.'[1] However, that wasn't quite the last word. The queen wrote to Gladstone in March 1894 telling him that he was right to resign after so many years of arduous service and that she hoped that he would now enjoy peace and quiet. She wrote further that she would have offered him a peerage, but 'she knows he wld not accept it'.[2] Gladstone died in 1898 at the age of 88 of heart failure. He and his wife Catherine, who died in 1900, are buried at Westminster Abbey.

After Gladstone's retirement, Archibald Primrose, Lord Rosebery, became the leader of the Liberal party and became prime minister. He wasn't head of government very long, being forced to resign in 1895, and achieved little. Again, this was because of the issue of Irish Home Rule. Rosebery voiced agreement when some had talked about taking a vote in a general election about the act. Rosebery was against Home Rule and so was a segment of the Liberal party. The Conservatives easily came in with the help of disaffected members of the Liberal party.

Lord Rosebery is interesting for another reason. He had been a widower for some years following the death of his wife, Hannah de Rothschild, in 1890. One of Bertie's daughters, Victoria, known in the family as 'Toria', interested him, and it was said he wanted to marry her. It is unclear whether she didn't wish to marry him, or her parents would not countenance another marriage to a commoner. Later on, she was heard to say that she had wanted to marry him, and they could have been happy together. There were also whispers that Lord Rosebery had bisexual or homosexual tendencies. Toria, however, stayed with her parents and remained unmarried. Many of her relatives felt sorry for her, thinking that she was virtually nothing more than a 'glorified maid' to her mother. However, others felt that she had a strong sense of family and that she was indispensable to her parents.[3]

Finally, in 1895, Lord Salisbury returned as prime minister. His party this time had included those members of the Liberal party who were against Irish Home Rule and with these added members, Lord Salisbury was able to form a government. He would be prime minister for the remainder of the queen's lifetime.

* * *

The queen's household was in for more major upheaval in the person of the *Munshi*. Abdul Karim's duties had morphed from a servant who blotted the queen's signature to having an office of his own and people working under him. He became the queen's Indian secretary and as such was privy to dispatches and petitions to and from India. The household continued their dislike of him, feeling that he had been thrust upon them and they felt uncomfortable in his presence.

In 1892, at the queen's behest, the *Munshi*, who had been on leave in India, returned with his wife and family members including his mother-in-law and various other 'aunts', as others termed them. Karim was given a cottage in Osborne as well as in Windsor and Balmoral as the other favourite, Brown, had received before him. In addition, Sir James Reid was ordered by the queen to treat these ladies should they need treatment or become ill. Indeed, when it seemed that when Karim's wife could not conceive, the queen got involved and asked Sir James to find a female doctor that could examine her and consult on the problem.

In 1894, in order to stop the rumours that the *Munshi* was an upstart imposter, Victoria asked Ponsonby's son Frederick, who was returning to England from India, to investigate Karim's father. The young man went to the jail and found out that far from being a doctor or even the Surgeon General of the Indian Army (as the *Munshi* had claimed) he was an apothecary. When young Ponsonby returned to England and began his service with the queen as an equerry, she questioned him on his findings. She didn't believe him, told him he had obviously spoken to the wrong individual and was extremely displeased. '[I]t took several years before I was forgiven.'[4]

During the Coburg wedding of Ernie and Ducky, the *Munshi* declined to attend. Affie, now the Duke of Coburg, had let Ponsonby know that he would not let the *Munshi* attend the wedding with the queen's household. Instead, he must sit in the gallery with the servants. Karim refused this and a compromise was made that he would sit in the gallery, but no servants should be there. When Karim was escorted there, he recognised that there were servants there and he was enraged and stalked off. He complained to the queen later who 'cried'.[5]

Things became more serious when the Secretary of State for India, Lord George Hamilton, warned Victoria that he would no longer send secret dispatches to her if she showed them to Karim. It seems that information of a sensitive nature was leaking out in India, and it was known that the queen was giving the *Munshi* secret papers to read. Their basis for this supposition was Karim's association with a gentleman called Rafuiddin Ahmed, a political activist and a member of the Muslim Patriotic League. Most people felt that Karim was a tool of Ahmed's, and that he wasn't intelligent enough to be involved in any true subterfuge. Moreover, there wasn't concrete proof of that even after he was placed under surveillance when he went on leave to India. As much of a 'climber' as he was, another explanation was that he was loyal to the queen and would not betray her trust. However, that didn't stop the constant complaints and anger.

Eventually, Prince Louis Battenberg, Princess Victoria's husband, was asked to come and mediate the vexing matter. He looked at both sides, wanting initially to take his grandmother-in-law's side. But when he was shown the letter from Lord Hamilton, he had a completely different reaction. Prince Louis explained to the queen that showing Karim confidential papers would put the government in an awkward position. And if this was well known in India, the Hindus would resent Karim, a Muslim, being in such an elevated role.

It was Sir James Reid, who had become senior physician-in-ordinary at the retirement of Sir William Jenner, and Ponsonby who had the unenviable job of trying to solve this entire tumult. They were the ones to have to deal with the household and with the queen. And it seemed the more people complained about the *Munshi*, the more the queen was obdurate in his defence. Not only was the *Munshi* put in charge of the other Indian servants, but he was to take his meals with the household. Some have even said that she enjoyed these brawls created over Karim since at that point, in her mid-seventies, this was all the excitement she had. That she had a real affection for Karim shouldn't be overlooked, however.

As Melbourne was her father, Disraeli and Brown, her middle-aged romances, Salisbury her friend, the *Munshi* was her tall, handsome and affectionate son. She even signed notes from herself to him as 'your mother'. When examining it now, it seems like the stuff of schoolyards and the queen, infirm as she was, suffering from rheumatism and other maladies, must have been stressed beyond limits with the amount of bickering that took place.

Further, the *Munshi* had caused offense by arranging the publication of a photograph in the *Daily Graphic* where he is standing above the queen in what looks like a superior position. It appeared as though he was *her* teacher and guide. When Victoria found out about this, she was momentarily angry at him. However, as in all things, she forgave him quickly.

That mattered not, the household was in an uproar.

* * *

Once again other important family complications intruded on the warring household. In October 1894, Alix's soon-to-be father-in-law, Alexander

III of Russia, was dying of kidney disease and Alix was quickly sent for. She had been spending time with the queen – her last as a single woman. She had gone to Harrogate with her elder sister Victoria for cures for the sciatica in her back and legs. In addition, she was being tutored in Russian and in the Russian Orthodox religion. However, she was in no way being prepared for her role as tsarevna of Russia or later tsarina. She had to be hurried to Livadia, the tsar's summer palace in the Crimea, where the invalid was spending his last months.

Alix arrived in Simferopol where she was met by her fiancé Nicholas and his Uncle Serge, her sister Ella's husband. They hurried to the dying tsar's side and the waiting began. On 1 November, he breathed his last. Nicholas supposedly burst into tears and said, 'What am I going to do? I'm not prepared to be Tsar. I never wanted to become one.'[6] Unfortunately, he was right.

Certainly, Victoria had a very shrewd idea of how unprepared the couple were and how unsafe the throne was. Nevertheless, she wrote a letter to Nicholas expressing a deep desire that their two countries ought to coexist in friendship and how happy she was that Alix was with him during this awful time. The queen hoped for the best and understood that the young couple would desperately need her friendship. They were married several weeks after Alexander's death with Bertie, Georgie and Affie attending, as well as Alix's brother Ernie. The queen wrote, 'how impossible it seemed that gentle little simple Alix should be the great Empress of Russia!'[7] These words were not meant to be filled with irony, but from hindsight, they most certainly are.

* * *

It was at the beginning of 1895 that Sir Henry Ponsonby, the queen's loyal and devoted private secretary, suffered a stroke and had to give up his post. He had been feeling quite tired the previous year, and the queen noticed a change in his memory and his handwriting that seemed odd. That in itself irritated her as her vision was getting worse and worse. However, the queen sensed all was not right when he had attended her for what would be the last time: '[Sir Henry] looked at [Victoria] intently and remarked, "What a funny little woman you are." The Queen was supposed to have answered, "Sir Henry, you cannot be well", and rang the bell.'[8]

It was just after that that he had his stroke, lost his power of speech, and was paralysed. Reid was especially concerned during his illness and visited him three times a day. Many in the household would be sad to see this good humoured and tactful man retire. He had an instinctively good way of handling the queen and as a go-between, he often softened some of her more controversial missives. One friend wrote of him: 'No Sovereign has ever been more loyally, capably, and diligently served[.]'[9] Gladstone, in writing to his wife, Lady Ponsonby, praised 'his unrivalled tact, his wise reserve …, his admirable judgment[.]'[10] Ponsonby had seen his task as defending the queen from herself and in this he succeeded admirably.

The queen was terribly distressed and though she drove to his house for reports, she did not want to see him brought so low, it was too painful.[11] He died in November 1895 within three weeks of his seventieth birthday and was buried at St Mildred's, Whippingham, on the Isle of Wight. The queen wrote a letter to Lady Ponsonby saying she would miss him terribly and that he was universally beloved by all.

It was with Reid that the queen conferred about possible replacements for Ponsonby. As it had been all along, the doctor's duties far exceeded the medical. And with Ponsonby's stroke, Reid was the only male member of the household who had no compunction about approaching the queen about various matters. Therefore, at this point, '[h]is importance as a liaison between the Queen and the outside world was inestimable.'[12]

Eventually, the choice for Ponsonby's replacement fell on Sir Arthur Bigge, who would be not only her private secretary, but in 1913 would be private secretary to her grandson George V. Sir Arthur had been a friend of the Prince Imperial and was attached to the same unit when the prince was killed by the Zulus. He would be given a peerage and made 1st Baron Stamfordham in 1911.

* * *

Things between the *Munshi* and the household finally came to a head in 1897 when the queen was set to travel to Cimiez in the South of France. Victoria was writing in her journal as usual, noting that Lord Beaconsfield was dead sixteen years. Her *Munshi* was a common feature in the court circulars, and all was well. Sir James was treating Karim for gonorrhoea and had informed the queen. The *Munshi*, besides having many female dependants, was promiscuous.

When the household found out they revolted. They would refuse to eat at the same table with him in these circumstances and were they made to do so, they would, as a group, resign. They sent Woman of the Bedchamber Harriet Phipps to relay this message. When Victoria heard the 'demand' she became so enraged that she swept her arm over her desk and knocked everything on the floor.

There was no resignation and at last, the queen and her entourage journeyed to the Riviera, staying at the Hotel Excelsior Regina. Sir Arthur Bigge, as well as Lord Salisbury, had persuaded her for various reasons not to take the *Munshi* with her. She was made to see that perhaps the French would not understand the relationship. She agreed to this, but nevertheless, Karim showed up at the hotel during their stay. This wasn't the main difficulty, however, more problematic was that his friend Rafiuddin Ahmed also joined him. And again, questions were brought up about giving sensitive information to the *Munshi* of which a member of the Moslem Patriotic League might take advantage. He was evicted from the queen's hotel and was later followed by the police. But no disloyalty was ever proved against him.

Sir James, who nearly became ill being in the middle of all the *Munshi* controversy, confronted the queen once more about the situation. She was told that this was not only 'dangerous but potentially a huge embarrassment'.[13] Either Victoria was simply tired of battling the household in her defence of him, or she was convinced that having him so close might not be the best of ideas. By the end of the year there seemed to be an uneasy truce between the household and the *Munshi*. Indeed, the next spring holiday in 1898 was much more peaceful than the preceding year.

It was at this point, that Sir James and the household, seeing that the queen was getting more infirm, talked about making sure that all the queen's letters to the *Munshi* would never see the light of day. After her death, all the papers were burned in the presence of Bertie, Alix of Wales and Beatrice. Karim left Britain in 1900 to spend nearly a year in India and would only return a few months before the death of the queen. At this point, most people just found him dishonest, overbearing, sexually promiscuous and silly.[14] Marie Mallet, however, was more candid when she wrote, 'why the plague did not carry him off ... it might have done one good deed'.[15]

In all events, the *Munshi* and his family were sent back to Agra at Victoria's death and Karim died in 1909. On a visit to Agra in 1905, George, the Prince of Wales at that point, visited him and several other of the Indian servants of the queen. He wrote:

> In the evening we saw 'the Munshi'. He has not grown more beautiful and is getting fat. I must say he was more civil and humble and really pleased to see us. ... I am told he lives quite quietly here and gives no trouble at all. We also saw dear Grandmama's last four Indian servants who were with her up to her death[.][16]

Perhaps, in the end, the *Munshi* was also tired of all the havoc he – and it must be said, the queen – had created. Undoubtedly, it was – as the queen recognised – racism. But it was also something far more common: jealousy and envy of the favourite, just as with Brown and with so many of the favourites in history.

* * *

Happier news intervened in December 1895 when another boy was born to George and May. Even better was the fact that it mitigated the sad connotation of 14 December, the date that Albert died.

> This terrible anniversary returned for the 34th time. — When I went to my dressing room found telegrams from Georgie & Sir J. Williams, saying that dear May had been safely delivered of a son at 3 this morning. Georgie's first feeling was regret that this dear child should be born on such a sad day. I have a feeling it may be a blessing for the dear little Boy, & may be looked upon as a gift from God![17]

However, there would be more disruption in the queen's household. Liko, who had been the man of Victoria's house for nearly ten years, was at last getting restless. No doubt he was tired of ushering Victoria and Beatrice around, cutting ribbons at openings, and having honorary titles, such as the

Governor of the Isle of Wight, thrust upon him. So many years of sitting with the women and children under the awnings at Osborne, or indoors having tea, or stalking at Balmoral, was about as much as he could stand. Whenever he wanted to go somewhere on his own, as with a yachting trip to Corfu in 1889, there were tears, 'swollen eyes', and moping, from his wife.[18] The entire household came to dread such scenes.

He was still young, just 37, and had been a soldier before his marriage. He longed for action himself and just when this malaise was hitting him the hardest, the British War Office decided to organise what would be called the Second Ashanti Expedition; its destination: the Gold Coast, which is present-day Ghana. The group was formed in order to force compliance of African King Prempeh of Kumasi, who was raiding the Gold Coast for slaves and refused orders to stop. It was a war that lasted several months from December 1895 to February 1896.

Eventually, Liko was given permission to go with the expedition as military secretary to the commander-in-chief, Sir Francis Scott. Beatrice and Victoria reluctantly let him go. The queen felt the parting deeply and could think of little else. She and Beatrice feared the climate more than they feared any sort of battle, and Victoria had some sad premonitions. She was convinced that he would catch a tropical fever – and she was proven correct.

On 10 January 1896, the queen received a telegram that Liko had caught malaria. They had initially been told that the fever was slight and that he was recovering. He did not recover however, and died on 20 January just off the coast of Sierra Leone. He had been on his way home aboard the HMS *Blonde* when he died. The ship didn't have the right accommodations for a body and so improvised, fashioning a casket out of biscuit tins. The corpse was preserved in rum. Sadly, some people actually thought that was amusing. Ironically, the king surrendered without a fight the day that Liko died.

The queen reacted as though the loss was all her own – as she usually did in these cases. She felt she could not tell her daughter and had Arthur do it. She wrote:

What have we not all lost in beloved, noble Liko, who has died, in the wish to serve his country. He was our help the bright sunshine of our Home. My heart aches for my darling child, who is so resigned

& submissive. God in His mercy help us! ... My grief is great, & I am quite unnerved by the shock of this dreadful news.[19]

The prince was indeed the 'sunshine' of their household. The person who, with his charm and verve, brought life to an otherwise bleak house of women and children.

Unfortunately, there was controversy with his death. Louise, who had an extremely unsatisfactory marriage to Lord Lorne (the two agreed to living separate lives with the queen's permission), taunted Beatrice with the fact that Liko had confided in her and was more in sympathy with *her* than he was with his own wife. That she, Beatrice, in fact, meant 'nothing to him'.[20]

By some accounts, Louise was a spiteful troublemaker, and many were wary of her acid tongue. Marie Mallet wrote that she was 'fascinating but oh, so ill-natured. I positively dread talking to her, not a soul escapes.'[21] And further, 'never have I come across a more dangerous woman, to gain her end she would stick at nothing.'[22] Louise had been having extramarital affairs for some time, including her teacher and mentor Joseph Edgar Boehm as well as possibly the queen's private secretary, Sir Arthur Bigge. Although, it's not certain that the later accusation was true, these allegations made for a very unhappy few months. The sisters eventually reconciled.

* * *

One of the great coronations of the second half of the nineteenth century took place on 14 May 1896. Alix and Nicky were crowned at the Kremlin. The queen would not attend because she was physically unable, but even had she been healthy and mobile, her discomfort and anxiety about Russia did not abate. Victoria was uneasy about her family members going to the event: Bertie and Alix of Wales, Affie and Marie. She never stopped feeling that Russia was dangerous and that it would be particularly so in such a large gathering in which the crowd would number in the hundreds of thousands. The queen was keenly aware that all the security in the world might not suffice if anything untoward happened.

The queen wrote to Victoria Battenberg:

My blood runs cold when I think of her so young ... placed on that very unsafe throne, her dear life and above all her husband's constantly threatened and unable to see her but rarely. It is a great additional anxiety in my declining years![23]

The coronation itself was an extremely solemn occasion that was endured, standing up, by nearly 5,000 people, for nearly five hours. As inspirational as the ceremonies themselves were, there also took place a tragedy which set the tone for the rest of the reign of Nicholas and Alexandra. Some days later, while the festivities continued, a special feast for the common people was set up in a large spot just outside Moscow called Khodynka Field. There would be free meat and beer, as well as a souvenir mug of the coronation given to everyone who attended. The crowds had been gathering from the night before in order to partake of the crowned largesse. By daybreak, the throngs numbered in the thousands.

What happened next is a little bit murky. Some said rumours that there wouldn't be enough provoked the crush – and crush it was. Nearly 1,400 people were trampled to death and nearly that number again suffered injuries. When the crowned couple heard about it, they both broke down in tears. Sensibly, they wanted to cancel a ball taking place that evening, but Nicholas's uncles (including Serge, Ella's husband) talked them out of it. Because they attended, they were seen as heartless and uncaring. Many, including other members of the family and the court, were outraged that they attended these festivities. The image of Nero fiddling while Rome burned was mentioned. After making an appearance, they returned to the palace and Alix collapsed sobbing hysterically on a sofa. They were both in complete despair. But it was from then on that she was called by many of her subjects 'the German Bitch'.

The queen read about this tragedy with real dread. She was thinking about her Diamond Jubilee that was just over a year away. Certainly, Britain was not Russia, and the affection and loyalty that her subjects had shown during the Golden Jubilee was overwhelming to Victoria, but she was wise enough to know how fickle crowds could be.

* * *

What better to cheer up the frayed household than another wedding of one of the queen's many grandchildren? In this case, it was Bertie's youngest and favourite daughter Maud who, on her own and with absolutely no help from either of her parents got engaged to Prince Carl of Denmark, her first cousin. She was quite friendly with her cousin, the Tsarevich Nicholas, and there were some who might have hoped for a match in that direction. She was also quite taken with the very handsome Prince Francis of Teck, May's brother – a very feckless young man who was sought after by more than one young princess, but he wasn't interested. Though she was three years older than Carl (and according to some relatives, looked it), the couple had known each other since childhood. Carl was the son of her mother's brother Frederick VIII and his wife Louise of Sweden; it seems he was in love with his cousin and proposed in autumn 1895. The wedding took place July 1896 at Buckingham Palace.

Maud settled into a marriage in which it would seem she was adamant about certain prerequisites. She was insistent about visiting England whenever possible, not only because she missed her home country, but because she disliked the cold of her adopted one. Her father gifted her with Appleton House on the Sandringham estate. She and her husband had one child: Prince Alexander, in 1903, and it looked as though the family would have a quiet life.

It seemed Carl, who was a younger son and impecunious, would have no further prospects. However, all this changed in 1905 when Norway dissolved its union with Sweden. The Norwegian *Storting*, the governing body of that country, chose Carl to ascend to the Norwegian throne. He became King Haakon VII and Maud, surprisingly, became Queen of Norway. Doubtless, Maud's heritage was a strong motivator in the offer and the couple were crowned in 1906. Their young son became Olav, giving up the name of Alexander. Maud however, kept her name.

Maud adapted surprisingly well to her new country and the Norwegians were pleased with their new royal family. Maud was an extremely elegant woman with a wonderful dress-sense and wasp-thin waist that is constantly commented upon in photographs. She loved the wide variety of winter sports in which she could participate in Norway, and worked for charities and made public appearances when required. However, she shied away from unnecessary publicity.

She continued to be unwavering in her desire to visit England at least once a year,[24] and spent much of her later life there. She was the last surviving child of Bertie and Alix and was close friends with May. It was in London, during one of her frequent visits, that she died of heart failure. She, unlike her siblings, lived to the relatively old age of 69.

* * *

In October 1896, Alix and Nicky with their firstborn, Olga, visited the queen at Balmoral. 'Dear baby Olga, so big and beautiful', Victoria was reported to have said while the little one was on her knee in the pony cart.[25] Alix, for whom the queen courteously drew back as they both entered a drawing room, was astonished as the empress sailed by without a word of acknowledgment. The queen admonished her granddaughter and told her to be more amiable, but the reproof was not well received. Alix was now stiff, formal and withdrawn. It was the last time Victoria saw her granddaughter.

It was during this visit that the queen had a film made of many in her extended family and it was the first of its kind. The queen wrote: they 'were all photographed by Downey by the new cinematograph process, which makes moving pictures by winding off a reel of films'.[26] Like most of us, when confronted with cutting-edge technology, Victoria wanted some understanding of how the process worked. It is amusing to watch the film, which is available on YouTube.[27]

There are dogs, children jumping and running, adults looking awkward, one of Victoria's Indian servants and the queen in her pony cart milling 'round and round'. She looks like she's holding a dog, probably Turi, the Pomeranian whom she acquired in 1893. The rest of the group looks rather silly walking back and forth and up and down. Nicky is moving with a walking stick at which he is looking as he proceeds forward, as though he's trying to learn a particularly difficult dance move or measure the ground. He stops in the middle of the crowd and one of the ladies comes up to him and probably says something like, 'move, move!' Were it anyone else, we would say it was almost slapstick.

Apparently, there was a major premiere of this film the following month for the queen in her drawing room. She seemed thrilled with the results calling it a wonderful process. She wrote that the film represented 'people, their movements and actions, as if they were alive'.[28]

Throughout this visit, there was a large house party comprised not only of the queen, her Hessian granddaughter, Alix, Nicky and Olga, but many other family members anxious to see the imperial couple. One can only imagine the security at the castle during this time. Not only was the Russian Imperial Family a perennial target, but the queen herself was threatened by Irish American assassins. However, unpleasantness aside, the imperial couple were a 'hit' with the British press, and in particular, baby Olga was pronounced to be a darling, lovely, fat and intelligent baby who apparently learned to walk while she was in Scotland. The tabloids, with visions of a great royal match in the offing, were elated when they learned that this splendid feat was accomplished with the help of her cousin David, the future Edward VIII.[29]

With such illustrious visitors, the house party was extremely large. Mostly, it was the children and grandchildren of the queen who lived in England, though conspicuous by their absence were Princess Beatrice and her Battenberg children. Attending were the Connaughts, the Waleses with spouses and children, as well as Princess Helena Victoria of Schleswig-Holstein, always a favourite with her extended family, and often finding her way into these large group photographs.

Ironically, Nicky complained about the cold at Balmoral Castle, saying it was colder than Siberia. He felt the boredom that many felt up at the queen's highland retreat. He was taken out shooting all the time and was 'incapable of hitting anything'.[30]

After this autumnal visit, the queen and her court would go into full preparations for an unprecedented Diamond Jubilee.

Chapter Thirteen

'Our Hearts Thy Throne'

With a lot of the *Munshi* madness done, there were other happenings in the Riviera that spring of 1897. As she had done ten years before, Victoria wanted to rest up before the big festivities got under way in June of that year. With her in France were the Battenbergs, Princess Helena Victoria, and Grand Duke Peter Nicholaevich, who was there with his wife, the Grand Duchess Militza Nicholaevna, and her unmarried sister Princess Anna of Montenegro.

There was one more handsome Battenberg prince left to marry off, and though the queen had sworn off matchmaking, it is here that she perhaps lent a subtle hand. Prince Franz Joseph, the youngest of the Battenbergs, had been searching for a bride for some time. He had considered a young Consuelo Vanderbilt, who later became the Duchess of Marlborough, as a candidate, but she wasn't interested, calling him a dapper man of the world, an oily European with German princeling prejudices.[1] At any rate, she went on to an extremely unhappy marriage to the duke that her mother had first wished for her.

Franzjos, as he was called in the family, was luckier. That summer he caught the eye of Anna of Montenegro. They had become acquainted during dinners with Victoria and Beatrice and after several weeks, an engagement was announced. The queen was pleased with this engagement and wrote to Vicky:

> Franjos was engaged the night before last to the Princess Anna of Montenegro, a charming girl who is quite determined to marry him and is devoted to him. We are all most pleased as it is in every way a good match, being a near connection with Italy and also Russia.[2]

Things couldn't have been better in the queen's eyes. Not only was it a good match, but it was a love match. No doubt she felt a great deal of satisfaction about the entire affair, especially in view of the fact that there were already rumblings of trouble in the marriage of Ernie and Ducky.

The queen returned home rested and looking forward to the Diamond Jubilee celebrations, though she was clear that she did not want a big 'to-do' to commemorate sixty years on the throne. But as the time approached, she got caught up in the spirit and emotion of the moment. Her colonial secretary Joseph Chamberlain thought that this Jubilee should be a show of the power of a great empire, instead of all the crowned heads that had attended in 1887. Certainly, there were representatives from all the colonial possessions, but royalties from the continent, many connected to Victoria in some relation or other, also came. However, she decreed that no reigning sovereigns should attend because she was simply too old.

Once again services of Thanksgiving, processions and large state and family dinners were planned. They did not quite compete with the grandeur of the Golden Jubilee. For one thing, because of Victoria's near blindness, her stoutness and other infirmities, she could barely make it up the stairs of St Paul's, and for another, she was nervous. Crowds bothered her more than they had once done because of the disaster at Khodynka Field after the coronation of Nicky and Alix.

However, when the all-important day finally came, she not only rose to the occasion, but she rose above it. As usual, she breakfasted with her daughters, Lenchen and Beatrice. They started out to London midday on 21 June 1897. When they reached Paddington Station, they processed through London through streets and balconies of houses that were beautifully decorated with flags, flowers and bunting. The queen noted a mass of smiling faces and cheers that never ended. She wrote that, '[a]ll vied one with another to give me a heartfelt, loyal & affectionate welcome. I was deeply touched & gratified.'[3]

They reached the palace and welcomed the rest of the family and the masses of visiting royalties who presented the queen with various gifts and remembrances of the day. To receive her guests, she was dressed in black with a black crepe bonnet trimmed with egret feathers. Beside the family there were princes, ambassadors and envoys from all over the world, including the United States. A notable attendee was the ill-fated Archduke Franz Ferdinand of Austria-Hungary who was representing his uncle, Emperor Franz Joseph.

That evening there was a large state dinner and once again, the queen listed everyone in attendance in her journal. All those present wore every medal, decoration and sash that they could possibly find for the occasion. Even the queen, wearing a dress made in India, with the whole front embroidered in gold, was looking quite as grand as she could in her otherwise unfashionable silks and satins. She wore the inevitable widow's cap with diamonds and a diamond necklace. The celebrations went on until late and the noise could be heard from the streets. The queen was told that many people were sleeping in the parks.

The following day was the queen's 'never to be forgotten day'. The day was warm and sunny, and Victoria looked regal in her black silk. She was veiled in black net, dusted with diamonds, and had not abandoned her bonnet, even though once again her family had fruitlessly begged her to do so. Before the queen and her retinue left Buckingham Palace for the procession to St Paul's, she 'touched an electric button, by which I started a message which was telegraphed throughout the whole Empire. It was the following: "From my heart I thank my beloved people, may God bless them."'

The procession included, in the queen's landau, her daughter-in-law Alix of Wales and Lenchen. Vicky could not ride with her because an empress, even a dowager one could not ride with her back to the horses. She remarked that the denseness of the crowds was immense, but the order was wonderfully maintained. The carriage eventually made it to the steps of St Paul's where the queen had decided she would sit during the service. She knew she could never have made it up the stairs and was worried about having a service at all. The clergy assembled and Albert's *Te Deum* was played. At the finish of the service all joined in the singing of *God Save the Queen*.

After that, there was a long procession, nearly six miles, that wound from the South of London to Westminster Bridge and finally to the Houses of Parliament. During that long ride, Alix took the queen's hands in hers, pressing them to comfort her as she was overcome with emotion. 'No one ever I believe, has met with such an ovation as was given to me.... The crowds were quite indescribable & their enthusiasm truly marvellous & deeply touching.'[4] Spectators were sure that they saw tears in her eyes as the carriages slowly wound through the streets. The queen was continually surprised and touched at the devotion of her subjects. Maybe she was modest, or perhaps she remembered all too well the republican movement of the sixties and seventies.

That evening there was yet another elaborate dinner with the same guest list as the previous night. The queen was very tired, but nevertheless, tried to talk to as many people as possible. That night she wore yet another dress of black silk, trimmed with panels of grey satin veiled with black net and steel coloured embroidery. Her inevitable bonnet was trimmed with white flowers, white egret feathers and black lace; her jewellery was a brooch given to her by her household and her Jubilee necklace. A film was made of the procession and beacons were lit all over the country that evening.

The festivities continued unabated through the heat of the following days. The subsequent morning, the 23rd, she received members of the House of Lords, a gathering of the peers and the House of Commons. There were more crowds, this time driving in a carriage with Vicky, Beatrice and Arthur, and following them, a carriage with Bertie, Alix, Georgie, May and little David. The carriages reached Paddington Station and the queen and her family travelled back to Windsor where there were more crowds waiting to honour the occasion.

Victoria, with Beatrice, Vicky and Arthur, drove through Eton where she received addresses from the provost and the master, with all the boys lined up. Thence on through Windsor receiving dignitaries at various stops, through the road up the hill to the castle, lined, as she noted, with two or three thousand children from schools in the neighbourhood. She was utterly exhausted by the time they reached the castle, writing: 'It was nearly 8, when we arrived, & I felt exceedingly hot & tired. But I was much gratified by the great enthusiasm displayed everywhere.'[5]

* * *

But as the decade closed the queen was getting more and more infirm. She was plagued by cataracts in her eyes, she had trouble moving and walking because of her rheumatism and her girth, and life was becoming more difficult. That October, another family member from her girlhood was gone.

Princess Mary Adelaide, the queen's first cousin and the mother of Princess May, the Duchess of York, died at the age of 63. Mary Adelaide was the daughter of Prince Adolphus, the Duke of Cambridge, the tenth child and seventh son of George III and Queen Charlotte. (Remembering that Victoria's father, the Duke of Kent, was the fifth child and third son of the king and queen.) She had never been in line for the 'race for an heir', but she had been an extremely popular member of the royal family and may have been the first to be called 'the people's princess'. She was kind and well known for her impecuniousness and for her expensive tastes and extravagance, hence the family spent a great deal of time abroad living more cheaply. She was also well-known for her girth and was generally called 'Fat Mary'. However, she was also extremely charitable and spent a great deal of her life in philanthropy. Her biography is littered with letters asking for and receiving monies and favours for her particular causes.

During the Diamond Jubilee, she had gotten a particularly enthusiastic response from the crowds who had known about her generosity and had also been aware that she was recovering from a serious illness and operation. The recovery, however, did not last and after a second operation she died. The queen 'felt intensely the loss of her well-beloved cousin'.[6]

The queen's eyesight was getting progressively worse, and she was nearly blind. She would complain about the ink being too light and would exhort her private secretaries to write blacker. However, it would soon get to the point where her daughter Beatrice, who was always at her side, would have to read letters and inform the queen of all the events going on. Her assistant private secretary, Frederick Ponsonby, the son of Sir Henry, wrote to his mother: 'Imagine B[eatrice] trying to explain … our policy in the east … Apart from the hideous mistakes that occur … there is the danger of the Q's letting go almost entirely the control of things.'[7]

Later, Beatrice, who would be put in charge of her mother's journals and letters at her death, would be accused of a great historic vandalism. She would be the editor of Queen Victoria's journals and she would recopy much of them, censoring as she saw fit and destroying the originals. But at this time, it was obvious that a lot of the queen's household thought her unfit to be what appeared to be her mother's chief advisor.

Nevertheless, Victoria continued to enjoy many of the things in life. In particular, she continued to love music and in 1898, Pablo Casals would come to play for her as well as Liszt and Ignaz Paderewski. Interesting to note that Casals played for her and for President John Kennedy in 1961. A little earlier Pietro Mascagni came to Windsor to conduct *Cavalleria*

Rusticana. And she never failed to enjoy German lieder and Gilbert and Sullivan operettas.

In May of 1898, one of the queen's nemeses died. Gladstone had been prime minister for the last time from 1892–94, and for his health's sake, he should probably have abstained from the last ministry. He was 84 years old when he left office and quite infirm. He made his last speech in 1896, condemning the Armenian Holocaust perpetrated by the Turks. The queen and he had met in Cannes in 1896 and 'she shook hands with him for (to his recollection) the first time in the fifty years he had known her'.[8] Like the queen, the old man was losing his eyesight and in 1898, he was diagnosed with cancer. By April of that year, he was bedridden, and in May, he died.

The queen recorded:

Poor Mr Gladstone, who has been hopelessly ill for some time and had suffered severely, had passed away ... He was very clever and full of ideas for the bettering and advancement of the country, always most loyal to me personally, and ready to do anything for the Royal Family; but alas! I am sure involuntarily, he did at times a good deal of harm. He had a wonderful power of speaking and carrying the masses with him.[9]

One of her ladies observed that she put him in the same category as Bismarck, who had been so harsh with Vicky, and she couldn't resist that last dig.

Other changes were happening in the household as well. In 1897, Sir James Reid was created a baronet. He, according to his biographer, enjoyed his life as it was, and that the only woman in his life could be the queen. However, as time went on, perhaps he realised that he was entitled to more and in 1899 a wedding was afoot. Reid was 50 years old and not a great looker, but he had social status that he hadn't had in all those years of service and the wherewithal to support a wife should one present herself.

It appears that he met Sir Henry Ponsonby's niece, Susan Baring, who was having her first 'wait' as maid of honour to the queen. The two began to spend time together and in July 1899 the pair became engaged. The queen was quite annoyed about this. After all, though she enjoyed her married

'Our Hearts Thy Throne' 191

life and wanted to be with her spouse as much as possible, it hadn't seemed to occur to her that others might do so as well. She refused to let them announce the engagement until she got used to the idea, but she was furious; she told Susan's sister Elizabeth that she didn't 'expect to have my Maid-of-Honour snapped up before *my very nose*'.[10] She told Vicky that had she been younger, she would have let him go, but he was so necessary to her health at this time, she couldn't think of it. Victoria actually wrote out a detailed diktat about how the married people were to comport themselves when in her presence and residences, which the couple took in good humour.

The engagement was finally publicly announced at the end of August 1899 and the couple married in November of that year and eventually had a family of two daughters and two sons.

* * *

When one has such a large family, tragedies occur, it seems, on a regular basis. The queen's eightieth year was no exception. Young Affie, the son of Affie and Marie, and the heir to the Duchy of Saxe-Coburg and Gotha, Albert's beloved home, died. He had been an attractive, yet ineffectual and irresponsible young man. All the same, he must have had a great deal of charm. Even his critical Aunt Vicky had said that there was something 'taking' and appealing about him. He was ruined by his own fecklessness, a cruel tutor meant to 'Germanise' him, as well as a complete lack of parental support.

According to his sister's memoirs, Alfred was a sensitive boy filled with his own self-importance. He was a disappointment to his mother since he was not perfection itself, and so, as in many such cases, devoted himself to pleasure and proving his mother correct in her assessment of him. Yet, he was a weak-willed young man. He had been in the German military and went down a well-worn road of youthful dissipation out from which he never lifted himself. According to one of the queen's ladies, the state of his brain was the 'result of the terrible fast life he had led in Berlin from the time he was 17'.[11]

As a consequence, he contracted syphilis at the age of 24 and for reasons that are unclear he shot himself before his parent's Silver Anniversary celebration at Schloss Friedestein, in Gotha. One theory is that he had an argument with his mother.

The actual cause of his death is quite murky since he survived the gunshot. His sister Marie says in her memoir that her brother's health broke down, which could mean anything. Newspapers of the day said consumption or a tumour. There were rumours about an unsuitable marriage but there is no concrete evidence for that either.

Obviously, he needed somewhere to recover from such a serious wound, and, against doctor's advice, Marie Coburg sent her son to a sanatorium at Meran in the South Tyrol. Some thought the Duchess was just trying to get him out of the country before the guests arrived for the celebrations. He appears to have died as a result of the trip.

Queen Victoria was devastated. Not only had she lost a grandson, but also, the heir to her beloved Coburg was gone. Her son Affie was in a terrible state. He became extremely depressed and blamed Marie for the death. After that, he lived alone and drank heavily.[12]

One issue, however, couldn't be avoided. Now that the heir to the Dukedom of Saxe-Coburg and Gotha had died, it was essential to confirm the next heir. In reality, it should have been the next son – in this case, Arthur, Duke of Connaught. Arthur, however, had no wish to leave the military or become a German prince and neither did *his* son Arthur. It was also thought that it would be better to find a candidate who would be raised in Germany.

The Connaughts renounced their rights to the Coburg succession, and 'after a great deal of talk between my children about this vexed question of the succession',[13] it went to the next male in the family, Prince Leopold's son, Charles Edward. At the age of 15, Charles Edward became Karl Eduard and went to live in Coburg along with his mother and sister.[14]

* * *

In May of that year, the queen's birthday came around again. It was her 80th, but she felt she had lived so long, lost so many friends, relatives, children, and grandchildren, that there was no cause for celebrations. Vicky wrote a tribute to her:

> Eighty years of grace and honours – of usefulness and goodness – of trials and sorrow – with much happiness and many joys such as are given to few, though mingled with troubles and anxieties inseparable from a unique position as a sovereign and a mother.[15]

'Our Hearts Thy Throne'   193

Victoria always called it her 'poor old birthday', but in living that long she had surpassed her grandfather, George III, in being the longest reigning monarch in British history. She in turn would be surpassed by her great-great granddaughter Queen Elizabeth II.

* * *

Politics once again intruded forcefully in the queen's existence when the Second Boer War began in October 1899. Again, it was between the Boers of Transvaal and Orange Free State who declared war against the British. The British citizens of the area were called *Uitlanders* or foreigners, and it was thought they needed to be protected from the Boers. It didn't hurt that there were huge deposits of gold and diamonds in that area and people were coming from all over the world to prospect and get rich.

British troops were sent out from India and the cavalry from England. Paul Kruger, the President of the South African Republic sent out an ultimatum that all British troops must be cleared out. The Boers launched mostly successful attacks at the beginning of the war and put Ladysmith, Kimberley, and Mafeking under siege. By May 1900, however, the British were successful in relieving these sieges. By the last phase of the war, which lasted from 1900 to 1902, the British proceeded to annex the Transvaal and Orange Free state. An interesting side note to this is that future Prime Minister Winston Churchill, at the age of 26, was a reporter for the *Morning Post* in South Africa at this time. He was captured by the Boers but managed to escape. His escape made him famous.

Victoria, whose last years would be coloured by the war, did her best to be front and centre. She showed herself to, and was far more involved with, the public than she had been for a long time. The queen was on hand to see troops off, worked as assiduously as any other lady for the war effort, knitting and writing letters to families that had lost their sons. She visited the wounded, though as her health failed, she had to be wheeled around in a bath-chair.

The following month, her grandson the Kaiser visited. Willy had an extremely difficult relationship with his uncle, Bertie. He was provoking, and patronising to him, because he, Willy, was already an emperor, while Bertie was still the heir. This says a lot about the maturity level of the Kaiser, who at this point was over 40 years old. The impetuosity and imprudence that his grandmother continually accused him of was still there.

What is interesting is that in the last decade of the queen's reign, her relationship with Bertie improved tremendously. They found common ground in disliking the Kaiser, and both were 'fervent imperialists'.[16] His mother talked of him as being kind and affectionate, and now took pleasure in spending time alone with him. Ultimately, with all the water under the bridge, he loved her, but he also feared her.

For this visit, however, all controversial topics were avoided, and the visit went off without a hitch. One heart-breaking note was the discussions about the declining health of her beloved eldest daughter, Vicky. In 1898, Vicky had been in a riding accident and consequently the doctors found that the back pain she thought she had was actually inoperable breast cancer. It was later determined that it had spread to her spine. By the end of 1899, she was in agony and bedridden. The golden child of Victoria and Albert, who through her marriage was going to help achieve her father's goal of a liberal Europe united by still other marriages with the various royal families, was dying.

During his visit, Willy assured Victoria of his good will. He gave the strong impression that there was an understanding between Britain and Germany. However, it appears there wasn't, and that Willy was good at self-delusion as well as having a complete lack of self-awareness.

The following month was the so-called 'Black Week' of the Boer War. There was much bad news and some stunning defeats of the British army. A case of a great empire fighting against a home-grown militia. The British had been there before.

The tide would turn in May 1900. The queen noted a telegram came from the commanding officer, Major-General Robert Baden-Powell, later 1st Baron Baden-Powell, 'Happy to report Mafeking successfully relieved today.'[17] Not a lot of good news was coming out of South Africa at the time, so this was celebrated. As well, Victoria noted in her journal that it had been thirty-eight years since Albert's death.

She had been brought low with more bad news. The war would continue to make her unhappy but never completely doused her spirits. As ever, Victoria's fortitude and determination had nothing to do with her health, and she blocked out all probability of defeat. A quote, spoken when her minister from the Foreign Office, Arthur Balfour, visited her after a particularly bad patch of the war, illustrates this best. When Balfour attempted to commiserate with her, she replied, 'Please understand that there is no one depressed in this house; we are not interested in the possibilities of defeat; they do not exist.'

* * *

In April of that year, the queen decided not to go to Nice as had been her custom, but to visit Dublin for the first time since 1861. She and Albert had visited when young Bertie was there with his regiment; they had hoped to inspect his behaviour. Europe had not been kind about the British participation in the Boer War, so this seemed a long-awaited alternative.

She made the visit to thank Irish Commandos for their sterling effort in the Boer war. And, when the queen thanked someone, she did it in great style. She issued the following order:

> Her Majesty the Queen is pleased to order that in future, upon St Patrick's Day, all ranks in Her Majesty's Irish regiments shall wear, as a distinction, a sprig of shamrock in their head-dress, to commemorate the gallantry of her Irish soldiers during the recent battles in South Africa.[18]

This time she was accompanied by Lenchen and Beatrice. She noted enthusiastic cheering from the long drive from Kingston to Dublin. She was received in Dublin by Lord and Lady Cadogan as well as the Connaughts, the Duke being in command of the troops in Ireland. The party stayed in the viceregal lodge in Dublin and the queen showed herself to cheering crowds. Most special to Victoria was the children that gathered in the thousands for Children's Day in Phoenix Park. The sight of a benign little old lady with the sweetest smile imaginable delighted the throng of children whose cheers were deafening. As ever there were voices singing *God Save the Queen.*

There were more visits to various hospitals, reviews, a convent, and the Zoological Gardens. The queen especially liked the lions. She was apparently asleep a great deal of the time that they took long drives all over the city and outskirts and had to be prodded awake if there were crowds around.[19]

The queen celebrated her 81st birthday in Balmoral that year. She received congratulations and telegrams so numerous that six men and two 'telegraphists' had to help to answer them. Victoria wrote in her journal that day remarking about the pretty presents she received and that she dined with her household. She commented that after they drank to her health, she proposed that they drink to the health of the army in South Africa.

In June 1900, there was more war news from another part of the world. The so-called Boxer Rebellion had been going on since 1899. It was between various European Colonisers and Missionaries and a Chinese group called 'the righteous and harmonious fists', which the Europeans and Americans dubbed the Boxers. In June, the Peking (Beijing) Legations were put under siege for fifty-five days. The Boxers attacked and killed a large number of the foreigners; however, in August an eight-nation alliance was able to relief the siege. Unfortunately for the queen, it was difficult for her to get reliable news and so for several months, besides having the Boer War to worry about, she worried about her personnel in Peking.

In one journal entry she wrote, 'Very bad news ... All the foreigners, including 400 soldiers, women and children, who held out at British Legations, till ammunition and food exhausted, reported killed.'[20] Luckily this was not the case. She had occasion to write on 19 August that she had received 'most welcome news ... that the Allies had entered Pekin [sic], and found all well at the Legations'[21]

That June there was also cause to rejoice. One of the last great-grandchildren born in the queen's lifetime had arrived:

Heard on waking, that dear Victoria [Battenberg] had got a little boy, born at 6 this morning, & it was a great pleasure. — A showery morning & we breakfasted at Frogmore House in the Colonnade. Afterwards saw the pretty little Baby & also dear Victoria, just for a moment. She was very well.[22]

This little boy was Louis and Victoria Battenberg's last child and would be christened Prince Louis of Battenberg. There is a photograph of the queen with little 'Dickie' as he was called in the family. It is probably one of the last images taken of her. Victoria is holding the new baby, for whom she will serve as a godmother. She has become so infirm that she needs help cradling the child. The story is that there is a maid behind her helping her to hold the baby up.

The queen wrote that Prince Louis was a beautiful and large baby. When she was holding him at the christening, he was so active that he knocked off her spectacles. Victoria wasn't the least bit annoyed and is said to have laughed very much over that. He would later be known as Lord Mountbatten and still later, The Earl Mountbatten of Burma, the uncle of Prince Philip and the 'honorary grandfather' of King Charles.

During that summer, the queen had cause to worry not just about Vicky, but also about her son, Affie. After the death of young Affie, the duke's health deteriorated to a terrible decree. He was being treated for alcoholism by Dr Reid and was diagnosed with cancer of the tongue for which there was no cure at that time. By the end of July, the queen heard from her granddaughter Missy that her father's doctors did not 'think well of him'.[23] Victoria was of course extremely anxious and upset over these reports. On 30 July, he died an alcoholic, shattered at the death of his only son, alone and apparently loveless as Evelyn Waugh might have said.

The queen wrote:

Felt terribly shaken and broken and could not realise the dreadful fact.[24] ... My third grown-up child, besides three very dear sons-in-law. It is hard at eighty-one ... It is a horrible year, nothing but sadness and horrors of one kind or another.[25]

Apparently, the seriousness of Affie's illness was kept from Victoria and his sister Vicky until it was no longer possible. Neither mother nor daughter were able to travel to see him before his death.

His wife, the imperious Marie Alexandrovna died in October 1920. At that time, she was in exile in Zurich, Switzerland after the Great War, and the Russian Revolution. She had lost the lion's share of her fortune; all the monies having been held in trust in Russia. Her income from Britain was small and she became relatively penurious. She sold much of her jewellery in order to live. She was worn down by all the sad events of her life and death probably came to her as a friend. There was a malicious story that she became apoplectic when she received an envelope addressed to Frau Coburg, however this is just a story.

Bertie went to Affie's funeral in Coburg, and then took that opportunity to visit Vicky at her home in Friedrichshof. By this time, Vicky was so ill with spasms that she was screaming and groaning in excruciating pain.[26] Vicky's letters to her mother by this juncture were highly descriptive of the agonies she was going through:

> I have been suffering to such an extent ... I shall be prevented for some days from leaving my bed, and the attacks of spasm that seize me in the back, limbs and bones are so frequent that it is difficult to find a pause long enough to write in.[27]

Since Victoria's eyesight was so bad, either Beatrice or Lenchen was reading to her. Both women got to the point that they were not reading selections such as those above to their mother. Between the deaths, the wars, and her failing health, she was simply unfit to bear it any longer.

The Boer War continued and that autumn Victoria's grandson and Lenchen's son, Christian Victor, came down with enteric fever (closely related to typhoid) and malaria. He was in Pretoria, South Africa, at the time having been part of the relief of the Siege of Ladysmith in March of that year. He died in October at the age of 33 and is buried there: '[I]t seemed too dreadful and heart-breaking, this dear excellent, gallant boy, beloved by all, such a good, as well as a brave and capable officer, gone!'[28] This grief over her grandson added to her debilitation. Also in that terrible month, Victoria received her last letter from Vicky.

Victoria, who had loved food, was now losing interest. Her ladies noticed that her digestion 'after many years of hard labour'[29] was poor. Victoria was growing thinner and thinner and lost nearly half her body weight. At this point, Reid noticed that she was 'most depressed and cried much'.[30] The doctor and her household saw that there was cause for great concern over the deterioration of the queen's health. He felt it necessary to notify her family, who were in complete denial and believed that she would perk up as she had always done in the past.

Towards the end of December, Victoria and her household travelled to Osborne for Christmas. She continued to be extremely depressed and was by no means in a celebratory mood. The straw that broke the camel's

'Our Hearts Thy Throne' 199

back was the death of her companion of fifty years and her longest serving member of the household, Baroness Churchill. She had gone to bed on Christmas eve, and when her maid came to wake her for morning services, she was dead. '[T]he loss to me is not to be told.'[31]

One of her last journal entries gives a good picture of her state of mind and how the household had to handle her:

> Did not have a good night, was very restless, & every remedy that was tried failed in making me sleep. Then when I wished to get up, I feel asleep again, which was too provoking. — Went out with Lenchen & Beatrice about 1 & the former told me Sir J. Reid wished me to know that dear Jane Churchill had had one of her bad heart attacks in the night, & that he had telegraphed for her son, as he thought very seriously of her condition. I said 'You remember, I warned & asked her son whether it was safe for her to come as she was so ill at this very time last year.' — I felt anxious, & on coming home sent for Sir James, who said 'she is very ill', so I asked at once for another lady, to which he replied 'most decidedly'. Later, after I had some broth & rested a little, I took a short drive with Louischen & Thora [Helena Victoria], & we talked a great deal about dear Jane, as I was so distressed at her being so ill. Directly I returned, I again sent for Sir James, who said 'I was just coming to tell Y^r Majesty all was over.' She had died this morning early, in her sleep, & had just slept peacefully away. They had not dared tell me for fear of giving me a shock, so had prepared me gradually for the terrible news. I saw Harriet Phipps, who told me all about it. I naturally was much upset & very unhappy, as dear Jane was one of my most faithful & intimate friends.[32]

It is heart-rending to think that this would be her last Christmas and as she wrote, a 'terribly sad' one for her. The death of one of her closest friends in her present state was terribly disheartening. She wrote about her enormous loss. At this point she was dictating letters and journals instead of writing them herself as her eyesight worsened to blindness.

One of her last tasks in 1900 was providing a new executor in her private will. For that charge, she put in her grandson-in-law, who at that time was Assistant Director of the Naval Intelligence Division of the Royal Navy,

Prince Louis Battenberg. Victoria, who had always particularly favoured the Battenbergs, the snobbish Prussians even calling her a 'Battenberger', knew that she could rely on this, the eldest of the romantic Battenberg princes. She loved him, who after his marriage spent a great deal of time with the queen. She trusted him with her estate as well as being her naval aide-de-camp.

As 1901 came upon Victoria, she faced the year with much trepidation: 'Another year begun, and I am feeling so weak and unwell that I enter upon it sadly. The same sort of night as I have been having lately, but I did get rather more sleep and was up earlier.'[33]

By now the queen was not only suffering from rheumatism and blindness, but also acute indigestion and insomnia. She was doused with sleeping aids and plied with invalid foods. She had problems staying awake during the day, paying attention and her memory, which had been extraordinary, was going.

Her last audience took place on 14 January when Lord Roberts, who had been commander-in-chief in South Africa (where the war was still raging). She conferred the Order of the Garter on him, and they spoke a little about the war. By this time, the queen was suffering from mental confusion. Members of the household reported that she seemed not to know where she was. Several days later, her speech became indistinct, and it appeared to Reid that she might have had a stroke. She seemed apathetic and lethargic.

As the days went by, Victoria was slipping away. Beatrice and Helena, their mother's constant attendants, continued to be blind to anything but a full recovery, and Sir James was getting more and more concerned. As Louise joined the party at Osborne, the dynamics of the sisters played havoc on Sir James' nerves. Though he liked Louise the best, 'men usually did',[34] he was worried about her disruptiveness. And, as in all serious illness, sometimes the patient would improve, giving false hopes, only to have those hopes dashed when they once again began to fail. The queen's illness was this way.

By the eighteenth of the month, family members were being summoned to Osborne. Prince Arthur, who had been in Berlin at the time, was telegraphed and Willy decided, uninvited, to accompany him back to the Isle of Wight. The queen had stated that she abhorred the idea of having one's relations 'swarming around like a cloud of starving vultures. "That I shall insist is never the case if I am dying. It is awful."'[35]

Nevertheless, they came; welcome ones like her daughters: Lenchen, Louise, Beatrice, and her little Pomeranian dog, Turi, and even the unwelcome ones – and Willy was certainly that. The Kaiser had forced his way to her bedside and spent the last several hours of the queen's life with his good arm around her holding her up on one side while Sir James was on the other. It appears that Willy behaved himself. According to Ponsonby, he had comported himself in a most dignified manner. He said to the Princess of Wales: 'My first wish is not to be in the light, and I will return to London if you wish. I should like to see Grandmamma before she dies, but if that is impossible I shall quite understand.'[36]

Though it seems entirely out of character, in the end, it is doubtful '[the queen] recognised him; she seems to have mistaken him for his father.'[37] Sometime during that last afternoon, she said to Reid, 'Sir James, I'm very ill.' He held her hand and reassured her with 'Your Majesty will soon be better.'[38] With her children about her, the queen requested that Bertie give her a last kiss. She smiled and 'she murmured "Bertie"'.[39]

She died at 6.30 that evening and *the King* closed her eyes.

Chapter Fourteen

'...a long, full and beautiful life.'[1]

The local police surrounded Osborne at the queen's death. No one was allowed in or out as the formalities were arranged. At last, as is the custom, a small notice was put out on the gate announcing that 'Her Majesty the Queen breathed her last at 6.30 P.M., surrounded by her children and grandchildren.'[2], and very soon, the entire world knew.

As a last kindness to the queen, Bertie allowed her still beloved *Munshi* to pay his last respects. He was permitted a few moments alone with her, standing solemnly and putting his hand on his heart. Soon, he and his family left Osborne and England to return to Agra.

Then, Bertie, Willy, Arthur and Arthur's son (also Arthur), lifted her into her coffin, her wedding veil covered her face, her wedding dress placed over her body and over the dress – the Union flag.

* * *

She wanted a white funeral because her mourning was at last, she said, over; she was now reunited with Albert. As in every other death in her life, Victoria had long been preoccupied with the rituals of her own. Dr Reid and some of her ladies, without any of the family present were instructed to put various items and keepsakes into her coffin with her. They had been enumerated by a letter that the queen had written in 1897. Among them were some of her favourite jewels, photographs of Albert, the children and John Brown, and Prince Albert's dressing gown which had been embroidered by Alice. She had John Brown's mother's wedding ring put on her left hand and

> respecting the feelings of her family, [Reid] put the photograph of John Brown and a lock of his hair, inside a small case ... in Her Majesty's left hand, discreetly wrapping them in tissue paper and

covering them with Queen Alexandra's flowers. 'And my duties were over with the Queen after twenty years' service!'[3]

In addition, she had requested a military funeral. She disliked what she thought of as the flamboyance of a royal funeral and the comparatively restrained dignity of a military funeral appealed to her. In addition, the country was at war. Victoria Battenberg wrote: 'Grandmama was always very proud of being a soldier's daughter.'[4] There was, however, some confusion as no one had buried a monarch in recent memory and the last military funeral had been the Duke of Wellington's nearly fifty years before.

While her household and others were trying to figure the logistics of an unprecedented and complicated ceremonial occasion, Victoria's subjects were in a state of shock, and many could not realise what had happened. They had not been prepared for the death, and most probably hadn't known she was failing. Her death was such a seminal and explosive event; so completely shattering, that for many the world had changed beyond recognition. The *New York Times* called it: 'The greatest even in the memory of this generation, almost the most stupendous change in existing conditions in England that could be imagined.'[5]

The only public death in recent memory that comes close is the feelings people expressed after the death of Franklin Roosevelt in 1945. After twelve years in office, many in the United States could not remember another president by his death. But that seems little in the face of over sixty years on the throne.

So many felt the need to express the disbelief and utter loss they felt at such a profound death. She who represented an entire generation; indeed, an entire world, was now gone. The word had quickly spread that day and people gathered in groups singing *God Save the Queen*. There was an almost unnatural quiet as the news was quickly transmitted throughout the world and newspapers described a deep gloom hanging over London. All theatres and amusements were closed as people gathered in the streets, simply wanting to be together on such a historic day.

In Washington DC, in an exceptional move, President William McKinley felt that no one would object if the flags were lowered at half-mast. This was the first time that American flags had been lowered at the death of a British monarch. It was done on the day of Queen Victoria's death and then again on the day of her funeral.[6] The mourning and incredulity were felt all through the English-speaking world and beyond.

For her large extended family, the matriarch, and the centre around whom they all revolved, was gone. Though there were many of the children and grandchildren at the deathbed, her golden child, Vicky, the Princess Royal could not be there.

Vicky's daughter-in-law Irène wrote from her deathbed, 'Poor Aunt Vicky ... lies there & cries her heart out not to be able to see beloved Grandmama's face one last time.'[7] Vicky herself wrote, 'the best of mothers and the greatest of Queens, our centre and help and support—all seems a blank, a terrible awful dream. Realise it one cannot.'

Her granddaughter, Alix, now Empress Alexandra of Russia wrote: 'I cannot believe she is really gone, that we shall never see her any more ... Since one can remember, she was in our life, and a dearer kinder being never was.'[8]

Victoria Battenberg, her eldest Hessian granddaughter, was one of the people who sincerely understood Victoria as a queen and as a human being. She and her family had lived in England for most of her marriage and she was the one in closest touch with the queen. She once remarked how at one point they were practically next door to Buckingham Palace, and she could walk there and enter a side door to visit her grandmother. She wrote that she was hardly a Victorian as 'we think about it', and that her death was a 'great personal loss'.[9] As it was to most of her family as she was truly loved.

Her household, too, was bereft.

Arthur Ponsonby, the son of Sir Henry, wrote that she did not belong to any 'conceivable category of monarchs or of women'. He further added 'There might be princesses and duchesses, there might be women distinguished in many spheres, there might be queen this, that or the other in history, but for over sixty years she was simply without prefix or suffix "The Queen."'[10]

* * *

The date of the funeral was fixed.

On 1 February 1901, the coffin was brought from Osborne on the Isle of Wight and the following day it wound its sad way through London.

The silence throughout the grieving city was eerie. The procession took hours with Bertie, Arthur, and Willy riding on horseback behind the coffin. Behind them were monarchs, other royalties, and relatives. The procession eventually arrived at Paddington Station where the coffin would be taken to Windsor. When the coffin arrived at Windsor, the horses that were to pull the carriage became restive and broke their traces. Prince Louis of Battenberg suggested that a naval escort should pull the carriage to the chapel and the Prince of Wales agreed.

The flag-draped coffin took a much smaller journey to the Albert Memorial Chapel, where it stayed until 4 February when it was then taken to Frogmore. There, with only her family, the royalties and her household, Victoria would be laid at last, next to her dearest Albert, in eternal rest.

* * *

Bertie became king the moment Victoria breathed her last. He, too, became the representative of an entire age, taking the name Edward VII, instead of Albert, which his mother would have preferred. His rationale being that there was only one Albert, but it was, perhaps, his final act of rebellion against his parents. Nonetheless, though his reign was brief, he made a good king. He died 6 May 1910 of complications of bronchitis and heart disease. There are so many reasons why his short reign was a shame. Possibly, the most important was that he might have been able to rein in his impetuous nephew, Kaiser Wilhelm, in 1914; however, it was not to be. He was 68.

His long-suffering wife Alix lived to an old age, making an effort to the last, to preserve her beauty. She died in November 1925 of a heart attack. She was 80.

Vicky languished into the summer of 1901 and died of the cancer that had been consuming her on 5 August 1901. She was 60.

Lenchen continued her charitable works after the death of her mother. Prince Christian died in 1917. Because of the Great War, Lenchen and several other members of the royal family gave up their German names in 1917. Lenchen's daughters were princesses without any designation. Lenchen lived on to 1923 and died at her residence at Schomberg House. She was 77.

Princess Louise seemed reconciled and closer to her husband and more devoted during and after her mother's death. Lord Lorne, who became the Duke of Argyll, died in 1914. Louise lived in Kensington Palace with others in the family, one of whom called the palace the 'Aunt Heap'. Louise also continued to live life on her terms, much more of an individual, and even a rebel than her sisters. She lived to see her nephew King George V (George) have his Silver Jubilee in 1935 and died in 1939 at the palace, aged of 91.

And Beatrice, her mother's shy and devoted Baby, went on to be the dubious editor of her mother's legacy as she transcribed and edited her expansive journals. Her task was to destroy anything liable to 'affect any of the family painfully'.[11] It was an immense job since Victoria wrote from 1831 to just a few days before her death – seventy years later. Victoria had filled 122 volumes of journals as well as countless private letters and papers. It took Beatrice thirty years to accomplish this monumental task, and as she transcribed and edited the contents in 111 copybooks, she destroyed the originals. As mentioned, royal historians considered it a great historical malfeasance, and many complained that she was ill-suited to be entrusted with such a profound undertaking.

Her nephew George V tried to stop this destruction, but, unfortunately, to no avail. Beatrice's copybooks are now housed in the Royal Archives at Windsor. Beatrice died in 1944 at Brantridge Park, the home of Princess Alice, Countess of Athlone, Leopold's daughter, and Beatrice's niece. She was 87 years old and the last of the children to die.

* * *

Victoria's beloved granddaughter, Victoria Battenberg, lived to extreme old age. Like the Tecks and the Saxe-Coburg-Gothas, Victoria's family gave up their German styles and titles in 1917. They adopted the surname of Mountbatten and Louis became the First Marquess of Milford Haven. Louis died in 1921, just before their youngest son, Lord Louis, married Edwina Ashley. Young Louis made a career in the Royal Navy and after World War Two, became the last Viceroy of India, and The Earl Mountbatten of Burma, a title that he passed on to his daughter.

Alice, the eldest daughter of Victoria, the now Dowager Marchioness of Milford Haven, married Prince Andrew of Greece and through this marriage, Victoria became the grandmother of Prince Philip of Greece who also joined the Royal Navy. After the conclusion of World War Two, the prince married his third cousin, the Princess Elizabeth of Great Britain and Northern Ireland, and became the Duke of Edinburgh. Victoria Milford Haven died in 1950 at the age of 87. Princess Elizabeth became Queen Elizabeth II and surpassed her great-great-grandmother as the longest reigning monarch in British history.

As to Alice, Countess of Athlone, she was the last of Queen Victoria's grandchildren to die. She was born in 1883, the eldest of two children of the Duke and Duchess of Albany, and like so many of Queen Victoria's grandchildren, especially the latter group, she was born at Windsor castle.

Though the Albanys had been residing in Coburg when Karl Eduard became the duke in 1900, they often visited the queen. In fact, Alice and her mother frequently stayed for prolonged periods at their house in Claremont and naturally, they were well acquainted with their vast British family connection.

In 1903, during a stay at Claremont, Princess Alice describes in her lively memoir *For My Grandchildren*, a great deal of visiting back and forth between various family members including the Connaughts and the Tecks in particular. It was then that the Princess became better acquainted with her cousin, Prince Alexander of Teck, the youngest brother of Princess May, the Princess of Wales, who was later Queen Mary of Great Britain.

The couple became engaged and were married on 10 February 1904. In due course, they had three children, May, Rupert and Maurice. Sadly, of the three, May was the only one to marry and have children. Maurice died in infancy and Rupert died at the age of 20 in a car accident. He was a sufferer of haemophilia and the cause of death was an intracranial bleed.

Like other members of the British Royal Family, the Tecks gave up their German names and titles in 1917. They became the Cambridges and Prince Alexander became the Earl of Athlone and Princess Alice, the Countess of Athlone. Apparently, Prince Alexander was 'furious' over this, thinking 'that kind of camouflage stupid and petty'.[12]

Alice died in 1981 at the age of 97. She 'lived through six reigns and attended four coronations. She rode in the carriage processions for Queen Victoria's Diamond Jubilee in 1897 and in the Silver Jubilee procession of Queen Elizabeth in 1977.'[13]

Afterword

Queen Victoria has over 1,300 descendants. Her children and grandchildren have sat on thrones throughout Europe forging those interweaving family ties that Prince Albert envisioned, but without, alas, the liberal political influence of which he fervently hoped. Her progenies continue to this day to reign in Sweden, Norway, Denmark and Spain; however, the most prominent of her line are her great-great-grandchildren, the late queen and her consort, Prince Philip.

I have always thought that the late queen's diligence came from Victoria. Though it was true enough that Queen Victoria disappeared from public view in her deep mourning, she, herself, would have never seen it as negligence. That diligence was passed down to grandson George V who took the example, along with his own strong sense of duty and evolved into a modern king. He in turn passed it on to his second son Albert, who ascended to the throne after his older brother Edward VIII abdicated to marry 'the woman he loved', Wallis Simpson.

Albert became George VI who scrupulously did his duty though it ruined his health. He was the paradigm for his daughter, Elizabeth, who sat on the throne from 1952–2022. She, like the preceding queen regnant, never abdicated as it would have been a dereliction of duty.

Elizabeth followed a woman, born in Georgian England, who herself became the name of an age; particularly in the second part of her life, she wasn't just the clichéd 'Widow of Windsor' or a straight-laced Victorian. As a reigning queen, she was steadfast in her love for her people, even when she hid from them. She was continually surprised and sincerely touched by their devotion. She was a woman who had a great susceptibility to a handsome face throughout her life and was loyal to the men in whom she put her trust, and never wavered. If she loved, platonically or otherwise, she never faltered and was ever faithful.

This shy little woman with the sweet smile; this Queen Victoria, who is infinitely fascinating. She was capricious, intelligent, interfering, emotional, contradictory, yet solid as the Rock of Gibraltar. She had a sense of proportion, a lack of prejudice and, unfortunately for some of her family, a prescience that she, herself, would have abhorred. Above all, she had strength, dignity, and a sense of herself that was unusual for women of the time. She can be seen as a transitional figure from the dissipated Georgians to a monarchy more 'middle-class' and in tune with the modern age.

Notes

Abbreviations
BA – Broadlands Archives
QV or V – Queen Victoria
QVJ – Queen Victoria's Journal
RA – Royal Archives
VMH – Victoria Battenberg later Victoria Milford Haven

Introduction
1. Florence Becker, Lennon, *The Life of Lewis Carroll*, page 27.
2. A.N. Wilson, *Victoria*, p.552.

Part I: Beginnings

Chapter One: The Race for an Heir
1. There were Catholic Stuart Princes from Mary and Anne's half-brother, but they were ineligible.
2. The Countess of Darlington and the Duchess of Kendal.
3. Elizabeth Longford, *Born to Succeed*, p.327.
4. Lytton Strachey, *Queen Victoria*, p.12.
5. Arturo Beéche, *The Coburgs of Europe*, p.35.
6. Roger Fulford, *The Wicked Uncles*, p.113.
7. Strachey, p.14.
8. The next brother, Ernst Augustus, married Princess Frederika of Mecklenburg Strelitz and became King of Hanover. Prince Augustus Frederick, Duke of Sussex who married unequally twice, and lastly Prince Adolphus, Duke of Cambridge, who married Princess Augusta of Hesse-Kassel.
9. Beéche, p.41.
10. Stanley Weintraub, *Victoria*, p.40.
11. A.N. Wilson, p.36.
12. *New York Times*, 1 December 2016.
13. Christopher Hibbert, *Queen Victoria*, p.7.
14. Wilson, p.41.
15. Lynne Vallone, *Becoming Victoria* p.9.
16. An interesting side note to Karl was that as an adult, in 1842, he joined with twenty-one noblemen and formed an association with the express purpose of purchasing land in the Republic of Texas (as it was at the time, it became part of the United States in 1845) for German immigration. There is a town of Leiningen in Llano County in Texas because of this. In addition, despite his youthful desire for money – the reason that historians think he allied with Conroy – he was considered a liberal and progressive thinker. www.tshaonline.org/handbook/entries/leiningen-carl-friedrich-wilhelm-emich-iii-prince-of

17. Hibbert, *QV*, p.17.
18. Victoria began writing in her diary in 1832 and the entries went on until a few weeks before her death in 1901.
19. David Cecil, p.315.
20. Richard Hough, p.22.
21. Hibbert, *QV* p.11.
22. This house had been given to Princess Charlotte and Prince Leopold upon their marriage. After Charlotte died, Leopold was maintained by an allowance from Parliament and kept the house.
23. This was an agreement between the great powers of the day: Great Britain, France, and Russia.
24. Hibbert, *QV* p.4-5.
25. Fulford, *Wicked* p.125.
26. One of them being Elizabeth.
27. Fulford, *Wicked*, p.145.
28. John Van der Kiste, Charles Grenville diaries quoted in *George III's Children*, p.167.
29. Viscount Esher, (ed.) *The Girlhood of Queen Victoria*, vol.1, p.194.
30. Woodham-Smith, p.138. Since she was a woman, she could not succeed to the Hanoverian throne. The 123-year link between the kingdoms was over. RA VIC/MAIN/QVJ (W) Timeline. Retrieved 16 October 2021.

Chapter Two: 'I beheld Albert....'
1. Edith Sitwell, p.58.
2. On the second day of her reign, she dropped 'Alexandrina' from her name. Esher, vol. 1, p.183.
3. Cecil, p.308.
4. www.gov.uk/government/history/past-prime-ministers/william-lamb-2nd-viscount-melbourne
5. Cecil, p.318.
6. She complained about her weight, which was about 125 lbs. Even for those days when body fat indices were unknown, she knew that at about 4'9", she was overweight.
7. RA VIC/MAIN/QVJ (W) 28 June 1838 (Lord Esher's typescripts). Retrieved 16 October 2021.
8. Usually referred to as ipecac, from a plant in Brazil.
9. Longford, p.95.
10. Hubbard, p.27.
11. Woodham-Smith, p. 165.
12. Auchincloss, p.29.
13. Longford, p.102.
13. Woodham-Smith, p.169-70.
14. Longford, p.109.
15. Esher, vol. 1, p.186.
16. Weintraub, p.89.
17. RA Y34/51, Princess Feodora to Princess Victoria, 16 April 1836 quoted in Woodham-Smith, p.119.
18. His father was the brother of Caroline of Brunswick, George IV's hated wife.
19. Richard Hough, *Victoria and Albert*, p.54.
20. Weintraub, *Uncrowned King*, p.51.
21. *Ibid.*, p.72.
22. Worsley, p.123.

23. *Queen Victoria's Journal* 14–15 October 1839 quoted in Woodham-Smith p.184.
24. And did so for her Golden Jubilee.
25. Hough, p.68.
26. RA VIC/MAIN/Z/491, of. 2v (January 1862): RA QVJ/1840: 11 February quoted in Lucy Worsley, p.148.

Chapter Three: '…only the husband….'
1. Auchincloss, p.38.
2. *Ibid.*, p.51.
3. Hough, *Victoria and Albert*, p.70.
4. RA QVJ/1840: 24 April, quoted in Worsley, p.151.
5. Weintraub, *Victoria*, p.106-7.
6. Woodham-Smith, p.216-7.
7. Weintraub, *Uncrowned King*, p.104.
8. *Ibid.*, p.108.
9. Woodham-Smith, p.223.
10. RA VIC/MAIN/QVJ (W) Queen Victoria and her Prime Ministers, by Lawrence Goldman. Retrieved 16 October 2021.
11. Sitwell, p.160.
12. www.english-heritage.org.uk/visit/places/osborne/history-and-stories/description/
13. Hough, *Victoria and Albert* p.108.
14. *William II, Ex-Emperor of Germany*, My Early Life, p.144.
15. Mallet, p.xviii.
16. Weintraub, *Uncrowned King*, p.187.
17. https://en.wikipedia.org/wiki/Albert,_Prince_Consort#Consort_of_the_Queen
18. Hough, *Victoria and Albert*, p.117.
19. Buchanan, p.5.
20. Hough, *Victoria and Albert*, p.144.
21. Hannah Pakula, *Uncommon* p.48.
22. Van der Kiste, *Dearest Vicky*, Victoria to 'a friend', 20 March 1856, p.29.
23. Brook-Shepherd, p.33-34.
24. The cable was laid in 1858.
25. Brook-Shepherd, p.36.
26. A complex set of diplomatic and other issues arising in the nineteenth century from the relations of two duchies, Schleswig and Holstein, to the Danish crown, to the German Confederation, and to each other. Lord Palmerston joked that only three people understood the particulars, Prince Albert who is dead, a German Professor who has gone mad, and he, Palmerston, who has forgotten all about it. https://en.wikipedia.org/wiki/Schleswig-Holstein_Question

Part II: Widowhood

Introduction
1. Arnstein, p.111.

Chapter Four: 'My dreadful & overwhelming calamity….'
1. RA VIC/MAIN/QVJ (W) 1 January 1862 (Princess Beatrice's copies). Retrieved 18 October 2021.
2. E.E.P. Tisdall, *Queen Victoria's Mr Brown*, QV to King Leopold 21 December 1861, p.61

3. The foundation was laid just a few months after the prince's death and the prince was moved there 18 December 1862.
4. Weintraub, *Victoria*, p.306.
5. George Buckle, *The Letters of Queen Victoria: Second Series 1862-1878*, vol. 1, p.12.
6. RA VIC/MAIN/QVJ (W) 1 July 1862 (Princess Beatrice's copies). Retrieved 19 October 2021.
7. RA VIC/MAIN/QVJ (W) 8 March 1858 (Princess Beatrice's copies). Retrieved 19 October 2021.
8. Frederick Ponsonby, (ed.) *Letters of the Empress Frederick*, p.469.
9. RA VIC/MAIN/QVJ (W) 22 July 1862 (Princess Beatrice's copies). Retrieved 19 October 2021.
10. Michaela Reid, *Ask Sir James*, p.43.
11. Arthur Ponsonby, p.57.
12. David Duff, *The Shy Princess*, p.38.
13. Longford, p.314.
14. RA VIC/MAIN/QVJ (W) 30 September 1861 (Princess Beatrice's copies). Retrieved 20 October 2021.
15. RA VIC/MAIN/QVJ (W) 3 September 1862 (Princess Beatrice's copies). Retrieved 20 October 2021.
16. Georgina Battiscombe, *Queen Alexandra*, p.54.
17. Tisdall, p.96.
18. Jerrold, p.100.
19. RA VIC/MAIN/QVJ (W) 28 May 1862 (Princess Beatrice's copies). Retrieved 24 October 2021.
20. Jerrold, p.173
21. Giles St. Aubyn, p. 359.
22. Julia Baird, p.360-1.
23. Jerrold, p.89-90.
24. Buckle, *The Letters of Queen Victoria: Second Series 1862-1878*, vol. 1, p.268.
25. E.F. Benson, *Queen Victoria's Daughters*, p.114.
26. Jerrold M. Packard, *V's Daughters*, p.111.
27. 21 August 1865 (Princess Beatrice's copies). Retrieved 25 October 2021.
28. Noel, pp.118-20.
29. QVJ's quoted in Packard, p.115.
30. King, p.57.
31. Reid, p.106.
32. Tisdall, p.124.

Chapter Five: '…we, authors, ma'am….'
1. Auchincloss, p. 89.
2. Buckle, *The Letters of Queen Victoria: Second Series 1862–1878*, vol. 1, p.391.
3. www.dailymail.co.uk/news/article-10018695/Queen-Victoria-nagging-wife-Prince-Alberts-revealing-letters-tell-selfish-Queen.html
4. Letter from QV to Mr Theodore Martin, later Sir Theodore Martin, a biographer of Prince Albert 16 January 1868 quoted in Buckle, *Op.cit*, p.490.
5. https://www.c-span.org/video/?54339-1/disraeli-biography
6. Theo Aronson, *Victoria and Disraeli*, p.109.
7. Auchincloss, p.87.
8. Pearson, p.195.
9. Sitwell, p.257.

10. VMH, p.129.
11. Aronson, *Disraeli*, p.107.
12. RA VIC/MAIN/QVJ (W) 7 December 1868 (Princess Beatrice's copies). Retrieved 2 November 2021.
13. Regarding the privy purse, it is interesting to note that upper and middle-class Victorians saw themselves as the benefactors of the poor. In this way, charitable causes took up a smattering of their income and the queen and her children were no different. We can see the patronages that are spread among the working royals today had their start during this time. The queen herself gave more than 10 per cent of her annual privy purse to charity. Arnstein, p.175.
14. Letter to Crown Princess Friedrich, 9 April 1870 quoted in *Queen Victoria in her Letters and Journals*, Christopher Hibbert, p.219.
15. A. Ponsonby, p.407.
16. Jerrold, p. 85.
17. A. Ponsonby, p.407.
18. Auchincloss, p.104-5.
19. An interesting connection was that Ponsonby's aunt was Lady Caroline Lamb, Lord Melbourne's wife.
20. Jerrold, p.107.
21. Auchincloss, p.139.
22. Letter from Victoria to Vicky, quoted in Hubbard, p.223.
23. Auchincloss, p.113.
24. Hubbard, p.223.
25. Queen to Vicky quoted in Roger Fulford, (ed.), *Your Dear Letter: Private Correspondence of Queen Victoria and the Crown Princess of Prussia 1865-1871* p.201
26. Stanley Weintraub, *Edward the Caresser*, p.166.
27. Aronson, Theo, *The King in Love*, p.18.
28. Weintraub, *Edward*, p.167.
29. Battiscombe, p.86.
30. RA VIC/MAIN/QVJ (W) 19 July 1870 (Princess Beatrice's copies). Retrieved 4 November 2021.
31. *Ibid.*
32. RA/VIC/MAIN/QVJ (W) 12 September 1870 (Princess Beatrice's copies). Retrieved 8 November 2021.

Chapter Six: Family Matters
1. Auchincloss, p.152.
2. Hawksley, p.124-5.
3. Dimond, p.130.
4. The Prussians were snobs and complained about several of the matches of Victoria's children and grandchildren. They were not 'of the blood'.
5. Longford, p.385.
6. RA VIC/MAIN/QVJ (W) 10 December 1871 (Princess Beatrice's copies). Retrieved 4 November 2021.
7. St. Aubyn, p. 388.
8. RA VIC/MAIN/QVJ (W) 27 February 1872 (Princess Beatrice's copies). Retrieved 4 November 2021.
9. *Ibid.*
10. A. Ponsonby, p.100-1.
11. Letter from QV to Vicky dated 8 May 1872, Hibbert, *QV in Her Letters...*, p.228.

12. RA VIC/MAIN/QVJ (W) September 23, 1872. (Princess Beatrice's copies). Retrieved 4 November 2021.
13. Aronson, *Disraeli*, p.121.
14. Buckle, *The Letters of Queen Victoria: Second Series 1862-1878*, vol. 2, p.260.
15. Van der Kiste, *Dearest Affie*, p.41.
16. Letter from QV to Vicky dated 2 August 1873, Hibbert, *QV in Her Letters…*, p.233.
17. Marie Erbach-Schönberg, (Princess of Battenberg) *Reminiscences*, p.110.
18. Mandache, p.6.
19. RA VIC/MAIN/QVJ 23 (W) January 1874 (Princess Beatrice's copies). Retrieved 12 November 2021.
20. RA VIC/MAIN/QVJ (W) 25 November 1876 (Princess Beatrice's copies). Retrieved 5 November 2021.

Chapter Seven: '…we, authors, ma'am' redux.
1. Aronson, *Disraeli*, p.129.
2. https://en.wikipedia.org/wiki/Suez_Canal#cite_note-1
3. Aronson, *Disraeli*, p.143.
4. Arnstein, p.141.
5. An Indian imperial style mass assembly to mark the accession of an emperor or empress.
6. Synge, p.135.
7. Aronson, *Disraeli*, p.170.
8. Buckle, *The Letters of Queen Victoria: Second Series 1862–1878*, vol. 2, p.646.
9. RA VIC/MAIN/QVJ (W) 14 December 1878 (Princess Beatrice's copies). Retrieved 5 November 2021.
10. Aronson, *Queen Victoria and the Bonapartes*, p.163-66.
11. Hibbert, *Queen Victoria*, p.399.
12. RA VIC/MAIN/QVJ (W) 13 March 1879 (Princess Beatrice's copies). Retrieved 12 November 2021.
13. RA VIC/MAIN/QVJ (W) 13 May 1879 (Princess Beatrice's copies). Retrieved 12 November 2021.
14. Arnstein, p.161.
15. Longford, p.437.
16. RA VIC/MAIN/QVJ (W) 19 April 1881 (Princess Beatrice's copies). Retrieved 5 November 2021.
17. Lee, p.466.
18. Aronson, *Disraeli*, p.194.
19. Guedalla, p.7.

Chapter Eight: '…the queen's stallion….'
1. Packard, *V's Daughters*, p.208.
2. Zeepvat, p.74.
3. QV to Vicky 23 November 1881, *Beloved Mama*, p.111.
4. Buckle, *The Letters of Queen Victoria: Second Series 1879–1885*, vol. 3, p.249.
5. QV to Vicky 29 April 1882, *Beloved Mama*, p.118.
6. RA VIC/MAIN/QVJ (W) 27 April 1882 (Princess Beatrice's copies). Retrieved 6 November 2021.
7. Zeepvat, p.181.
8. Reid, p.31.
9. Hubbard, p.210.

10. RA VIC/MAIN/QVJ (W) 29 March 1883 (Princess Beatrice's copies). Retrieved 6 November 2021.
11. Hibbert, *QV*, p.441.
12. Hubbard, p.271.
13. The Queen to Hugh Brown after John Brown's death. Auchincloss, p.154.
14. Bolitho, p.255.
15. QV to Vicky 29 March 1884, *Beloved Mama*, p.162.
16. RA VIC/MAIN/QVJ (W) 28 March 1884 (Princess Beatrice's copies). Retrieved 6 November 2021.
17. RA VIC/MAIN/QVJ (W) 19 July 1884 (Princess Beatrice's copies). Retrieved 6 November 2021.
18. RA VIC/MAIN/QVJ (W) 15 January 1882 (Princess Beatrice's copies). Retrieved 6 November 2021.
19. William II, Ex-Emperor of Germany, *My Early Life*, p.137.
20. E.F. Benson, *The Kaiser and English Relations*, p.36.
21. Letter from QV to Vicky dated 10 January 1885, Hibbert, *QV in Her Letters...*, p.288.
22. Buckle, *The Letters of Queen Victoria: Second Series 1879-1885*, vol. 3, p.202.
23. Packard, *V's Daughters*, p.165.
24. *Beloved Mama*, p.148.
25. RA VIC/MAIN/QVJ (W) 17 April 1884 (Princess Beatrice's copies). Retrieved 9 November 2021.
26. RA VIC/MAIN/QVJ (W) 26 April 1884 (Princess Beatrice's copies). Retrieved 6 November 2021.
27. QV to Vicky 30 December 1884, *Beloved Mama*, p.176.
28. Longford, p.511.
29. Miller, *The Four Graces*, p.46.
30. Hough, *Advice*, 556-7.
31. QV to Vicky 5 December 1883, *Beloved Mama*, p.153.
32. Ella to QV 15 March 1884, Lubov Millar, *Grand Duchess Elizabeth of Russia*, p.23.
33. RA VIC/MAIN/QVJ 15 June 1884 (Princess Beatrice's copies). Retrieved 6 November 2021.
34. Marie, *The Story of My Life*, vol.1, p.94.

Chapter Nine: Beatrice's Lohengrin
1. QV to Vicky 20 October 1873, Hibbert, *QV in Her Letters*, p.234.
2. *Ibid.*, p.287.
3. Longford, p.479.
4. VMH to Ernst Ludwig, 3 January 1885, Miller, p.53.
5. Hibbert, *QV in Her Letters*, p.290.
6. *Ibid.*, p.291.
7. Wilson, p.447.
8. QV to Vicky 13 February 1885, *Beloved Mama*, p.183.
9. St. Aubyn, p.466.
10. A. Ponsonby, p.294.
11. Victoria, Princess of Prussia, *My Memoirs*, p.112.
12. Mallet, p.139.
13. RA VIC/MAIN/QVJ (W) 25 February 1885 (Princess Beatrice's copies). Retrieved 6 November 2021.
14. QV to Vicky 15 April 1885, *Beloved Mama*, p.186.
15. Sara, p.49.

16. VIC/MAIN/QVJ (W) 23 July 1885 (Princess Beatrice's copies). Retrieved 7 November 2021.
17. *Ibid.*
18. *Ibid.*
19. Packard, *V's Daughters*, p.234-5.
20. Stanley Weintraub, *Victoria*, p.478.
21. Auchincloss, p.191.
22. 10 May 1887, *QVJ*, Nevill, p.120.

Part III: Jubilee

Chapter Ten: '…this never-to-be-forgotten day….'
1. RA VIC/MAIN/QVJ (W) 17 March 1886 (Princess Beatrice's copies). Retrieved 12 November 2021.
2. QV to VMH, Osborne, 2 February 1887, BA S 372.
3. Richard Hough, *Advice*, p.88.
4. Princess Irène to QV 19 March 1887 RA VIC/MAIN/Z/89/10.
5. Princess Irène to QV 24 March 1887 RA VIC/MAIN/Z/89/11.
6. Princess Irène to QV 6 April 1887, RA VIC/MAIN/Z/89/13.
7. QV to VMH 2 January 1888 Miller, p.64.
8. Hibbert, *QV in Her Letters*, QV to VMH 2 March 1887, p.301.
9. www.codyyellowstone.org/blog/that-time-buffalo-bill-rode-for-royalty/
10. RA VIC/MAIN/QVJ (W) 20 June 1887 (Princess Beatrice's copies). Retrieved 6 November 2021.
11. Hibbert, *QV*, p.382-3.
12. Longford, p.501.
13. *Ibid.*, pp.501-2.
14. All quotes not otherwise cited about Jubilee from RA VIC/MAIN/QVJ (W) 20 June 1887 (Princess Beatrice's copies). Retrieved 6 November 2021.
15. RA VIC/MAIN/QVJ (W) 23 June 1887 (Princess Beatrice's copies). Retrieved 6 November 2021.
16. Basu, p.37.
17. St. Aubyn, p.300.
18. E.F. Benson, *The Kaiser and English Relations*, p.55.
19. Longford, p.506.
20. RA VIC/MAIN/QVJ (W) 15 June 1888 (Princess Beatrice's copies). Retrieved 12 November 2021.
21. Hibbert, QVJ 26 June 1888, *QV in Her Letters*, p.312.
22. William II, Ex-Emperor of Germany, *My Early Life*, p.145.
23. Hibbert, QV to VMH, 23 November 1886, *QV in Her Letters*, p.300.
24. Longford, p.508.
25. Buckle, *The Letters of Queen Victoria: Series Three 1886–1901*, vol. 1, p.449.

Chapter Eleven: 'Mother of Europe'
1. Strachey, p.197.
2. Weintraub, *Victoria*, p.514.
3. Buckle, *The Letters of Queen Victoria: Series Three 1886–1901*, vol. 1, p.614.
4. …which was never a good recommendation as far as their grandmother, Queen Victoria was concerned.
5. Buckle, *The Letters of Queen Victoria: Series Three 1886–1901*, vol. 1, p.506.

6. Charlotte Zeepvat, *Queen Victoria's Family: A Century of Photographs*, p.144.
7. E.F. Benson, *The Kaiser and English Relations*, p.83.
8. Hibbert, QV to Sir Henry 9 November 1892, *QV in Her Letters* p.324.
9. Van der Kiste, *Kings of Hellenes*, p.48.
10. *Ibid.*, p.52.
11. Wilson, p. 549.
12. St. Aubyn, p.582.
13. Roff-Lawrence, *Becoming Queen Mary*, Chapter Six.
14. Cadbury, p.110.
15. Pope-Hennessy, p.196.
16. …their marriage had been morganatic and their spendthrift ways had been a scandal.
17. Cadbury, p.155.
18. RA VIC/MAIN/QVJ (W) 14 January 1892 (Princess Beatrice's copies). Retrieved 12 November 2021.
19. Victoria to Vicky St. Aubyn, p.567.
20. QV to VMH Balmoral 2 June 1892 BA S 405.
21. All wedding quotes not otherwise cited from RA VIC/MAIN/QVJ (W) 6 July 1893 (Princess Beatrice's copies). Retrieved 7 November 2021.
22. VIC/MAIN/QVJ (W) 23 June 1894 (Princess Beatrice's copies). Retrieved 12 November 2021.
23. Mallet, p.53.
24. https://web.archive.org/web/20050904174352/http://www.picrare.com/Royalty_Digest/RDArticles/6RDArticles6QVandUncleE.htm
25. RA VIC/MAIN/QVJ (W) 22 August 1893 (Princess Beatrice's copies). Retrieved 7 November 1893.
26. St. Aubyn, p.573.
27. Hibbert, QV to VMH 29 December 1890, *QV in Her Letters*, p.318.
28. Buckle, *The Letters of Queen Victoria: Series Three 1886-1901*, vol. 2, pp.394-5.

Chapter Twelve: The Munshi and other Trials

1 Guedalla, p.150.
2 Guedalla, p.777.
3. https://www-oxforddnb-com.lib.pepperdine.edu/view/10.1093/ref:odnb/9780198614128.001.0001/odnb-9780198614128-e-36655?rskey=sYxmkU&result=1
4. F. Ponsonby, *Recollections*, p.32.
5. Basu, p.177.
6. Alexander, Grand Duke of Russia, *Once A Grand Duke*, p.169.
7. Buckle, *The Letters of Queen Victoria: Series Three 1886-1901*, vol. 2, p.454.
8. Wilson, p.523.
9. A. Ponsonby, p.404.
10. *Ibid.*, p.405.
11. Hubbard, p.310.
12. Reid, p.163.
13. Taylor, p.253.
14. Dennison, *QV,* p.148.
15. Mallet, p.216.
16. Basu, pp.290-91.
17. RA VIC/MAIN/QVJ (W) 14 December 1895 (Princess Beatrice's copies). Retrieved 7 November 2021.
18. Mallet, p.34.

19. RA VIC/MAIN/QVJ (W) 22 January 1896 (Princess Beatrice's copies). Retrieved 7 November 2021.
20. St. Aubyn, p.589.
21. Marie Mallet in St. Aubyn, p. 583.
22. Mallet, p.50.
23. Hibbert, QV to VMH 21 October 1894, *QV in Her Letters*, p.329.
24. Certainly Norway was even colder than Denmark.
25. Buchanan, p.207.
26. QVJ, 3 October 1896 accessed at http://www.queenvictoriasjournals.org.
27. https://youtu.be/E10c50DNhHY -- The Film
28. http://www.victorian-cinema.net/victoria
29. Helen Rappaport, *Four Sisters*, pp.39-40.
30. St. Aubyn, p.577.

Chapter Thirteen: 'Our Hearts Thy Throne'
1. Balsan, p.28.
2. Ramm, QV to Vicky 31 March 1897, pp.201-2.
3. RA VIC/MAIN/QVJ (W) 21 June 1897 (Princess Beatrice's copies). Retrieved 7 November 2021.
4. All quotes about the Jubilee not otherwise cited from RA VIC/MAIN/QVJ (W) 22 June 1897 (Princess Beatrice's copies). Retrieved 7 November 2021.
5. RA VIC/MAIN/QVJ (W) 23 June 1897 (Princess Beatrice's copies). Retrieved 7 November 2021.
6. Kinloch, vol. 2, p.313.
7. Hibbert, *QV*, p.465.
8. In H.C.G and M.R.D. Matthew, *Gladstone 1875-1896* quoted in https://en.wikipedia.org/wiki/William_Ewart_Gladstone#cite_note-173.
9. Hibbert, *QV in Her Letters*, p.337.
10. Reid, p.188.
11. Mallet, p.158.
12. Beéche, pp.82-85.
13. Buckle, *The Letters of Queen Victoria: Series Three 1886-1901*, vol. 3, p.348.
14. Robert Golden and Arturo Beéche, *Albany*, pp.102-3.
15. Frederick Ponsonby, (ed.), *Letters of Empress Frederick*, p.461.
16. St. Aubyn, p.560.
17. Duff, *Travels*, p.362.
18. *Ibid.*, pp.351-2.
19. *Ibid.*, p. 356.
20. Buckle, *The Letters of Queen Victoria: Series Three 1886-1901*, vol. 3, p.583.
21. *Ibid.*
22. RA VIC/MAIN/QVJ (W) 25 June 1900 (Princess Beatrice's copies). Retrieved 7 November 2021.
23. Buckle, *The Letters of Queen Victoria: Series Three 1886-1901*, vol. 3, p.576.
24. St. Aubyn, p.578.
25. Hibbert, *QV in Her letters*, p.346.
26. Pakula, p.588.
27. Frederick Ponsonby, (ed.), *Letters of Empress Frederick*, p.46.
28. St. Aubyn, p.581.
29. Mallet, p.195.
30. Hubbard, p.347.

31. St. Aubyn, p.592.
32. RA VIC/MAIN/QVJ 25 December 1900 (Princess Beatrice's copies). Retrieved 7 November 2021.
33. Hibbert, 1 January 1901, *QV in Her Letters*, p.348.
34. Charlotte Zeepvat, 'The Death of a Queen, *Royalty Digest*, vol. 10, no. 7, p.213.
35. St. Aubyn, p.594.
36. Frederick Ponsonby, *Three Reigns*, p.128.
37. E.F. Benson, *The Kaiser and English Relations*, p.165.
38. Packard, *Farewell*, p. 158.
39. Bolitho, p.278.

Chapter Fourteen: '…a long, full and beautiful life.'…
1. *The Lancet* quoted in Packard, *Farewell*, p.160.
2. *New York Times*, 23 January 1901.
3. Hubbard, p.360.
4. VMH, p.129.
5. *New York Times*, 23 January 1901.
6. Packard, *Farewell*, p.152.
7. RA VIC/MAIN/ADDL. MSS. A/17.
8. Sophie Buxhoeveden, Alexandra Feodorovna to VMH, 28 January 1901, p.90.
9. VMH, p.125.
10. Arthur Ponsonby, p.70.
11. Ward, p.10.
12. Princess Alice, p.160.
13. *New York Times* 4 January 1981.

Bibliography

Abbreviations
VMH – Victoria Milford Haven, Princess Victoria of Hesse and by Rhine, Victoria Battenberg
QV – Queen Victoria

Archives
BA – Broadlands Archives
RA – Royal Archives

Books
Alexander, Grand Duke of Russia, *Once A Grand Duke*, (Cassell: London, 1932).
Alice, Prince, Countess of Athlone, *For My Grandchildren: Some Reminiscences of Her Royal Highness Princess Alice, Countess of Athlone*, (Evans Brothers Ltd.: London, 1966).
Arnstein, Walter L. *Queen Victoria*, (Palgrave Macmillan: New York, 2003).
Aronson, Theo, *The King in Love*, (Harper and Row Publishers: New York, 1988).
——, *Queen Victoria and the Bonapartes*, (The Bobbs-Merrill Company: Indianapolis/New York, 1972).
——, *Victoria and Disraeli: The Making of a Romantic Partnership*, (Macmillan Publishing Company Inc.: New York, 1977).
Auchincloss, Louis, *Persons of Consequence: Queen Victoria and Her Circle*, (Random House: New York, 1979).
Baird, Julia, *Victoria the Queen*, (Random House: New York, 2016).
Balsan, Consuelo Vanderbilt, *The Glitter & the Gold*, (George Mann: Maidstone, 1973).
Basu, Shrabani, *Victoria & Abdul: The True Story of the Queen's Closest Confident*, (Vintage Books: New York, 2017).
Battiscombe, Georgina, *Queen Alexandra*, (Houghton Mifflin Company: Boston, 1969).
Beéche, Arturo, *The Coburgs of Europe: The Rise and Fall of Queen Victoria and Prince Albert's European Family*, (Eurohistory.com: Richmond, California, 2013).
Benson, E.F., *The Kaiser and English Relations*, (Longmans, Green and Co.: London, 1936).
—— *Queen Victoria's Daughters*, (D. Appleton-Century Company: New York, 1938).
Black, Eugene C. (ed.), *British Politics in the Nineteenth Century*, (Walker and Company: New York, 1969).
Bolitho, Hector *Further Letters of Queen Victoria*, (Thornton Butterworth Ltd: London, 1938).
Brook-Shepherd, Gordon, *Uncle of Europe*, (Collins: London, 1975).
Buchanan, Meriel *Queen Victoria's Relations*, (Cassel & Co. Ltd.: London, 1954).
Buckle, George Earle (ed.), *The Letters of Queen Victoria: Second Series 1862-1878*, vol.1 (Longmans, Green & Co.: New York, 1926).
——, *The Letters of Queen Victoria: Second Series 1862-1878*, vol.2 (Longmans, Green & Co.: New York, 1926).
——, *The Letters of Queen Victoria: Second Series 1862-1878*, vol.3 (Longmans, Green & Co.: New York, 1928).

—— *Letters of Queen Victoria Third Series: A Selection From Her Majesty's Correspondence and Journal Between the Years 1886 and 1901*, vol.1 (Longmans, Green & Company: New York, 1930).

—— *Letters of Queen Victoria Third Series: A Selection From Her Majesty's Correspondence and Journal Between the Years 1886 and 1901*, vol.2 (Longmans, Green & Company: New York, 1931).

—— *Letters of Queen Victoria Third Series: A Selection From Her Majesty's Correspondence and Journal Between the Years 1886 and 1901*, vol.3 (Longmans, Green & Company: New York, 1932).

Buxhoeveden, Baroness Sophie, *The Life and Tragedy of Alexandra Feodorovna Empress of Russia*, (Longmans, Green and Co.: London, 1930. Reprinted by Royal Digest: Ticehurst 1996).

Cadbury, Deborah, *Queen Victoria's Matchmaking*, (PublicAffairs: New York, 2017).

Cecil, David, *Melbourne*, (The Bobbs-Merrill Company, Inc.: New York, 1954).

Chomet, Selwyn *Helena: A Princess Reclaimed*, (Begell House Inc.: New York, 1999).

Clarke, John and Jasper Ridley, Fraser, Antonia (ed.), *The Houses of Hanover and Saxe-Coburg-Gotha*, (University of California Press: Berkeley, Los Angeles, 2000).

Dennison, Matthew, *The Last Princess: The Devoted Life of Queen Victoria's Youngest Daughter*, (Weidenfeld & Nicolson: London, 2007).

——, *Queen Victoria: A Life of Contradictions*, (St. Martin's Press: New York, 2012).

Dimond, Frances, *Queen Alexandra: Loyalty and Love*, (History & Heritage Publishing: United Kingdom, 2022).

Duff, David, *The Shy Princess*, (Frederick Muller, Ltd.: London, 1974).

——, *Victoria Travels*, (Taplinger Publishing Company: New York, 1970).

Erbach-Schönberg, Marie (Princess of Battenberg) *Reminiscences*, (George Allen & Unwin Ltd.: London, 1925).

Esher, Viscount (ed.), *The Girlhood of Queen Victoria: A Selection from Her Majesty's Diaries Between the Years 1832 and 1840*, In two volumes, (Longmans, Green & Co.: New York, 1912).

Fraser, Antonia (ed.), *The Lives of the Kings & Queens of England*, (Weidenfeld & Nicholson: London, 1975).

Fulford, Roger, (ed.), *Beloved Mama: Private Correspondence of Queen Victoria and the German Crown Princess 1878-1885*, (Evans Brothers Ltd.: London, 1981).

——, *The Wicked Uncles*, (G.P. Putnam's Sons: New York, 1933).

——, (ed.), *Your Dear Letter: Private Correspondence of Queen Victoria and the Crown Princess of Prussia 1865-1871*, (Charles Scribner's Sons: New York, 1971).

Golden, Robert and Arturo Beéche, *Albany: One Dynasty, Two Destinies*, (Eurohistory.com: Richmond, California, 2016).

Guedalla, Philip, *The Queen and Mr Gladstone*, (Doubleday, Doran & Company, Inc.: New York, 1934).

Hawklsey, Lucinda, *Queen Victoria's Mysterious Daughter*, (Thomas Dunne Books, St. Martin's Press: New York, 2013).

Helena, Princess *Alice Grand Duchess of Hesse: Biographical Sketch and Letters*, (G.P. Putnam's Sons: New York, 1884).

Hibbert, Christopher, *Queen Victoria: a Personal History*, (DaCapo Press: Cambridge, 2000).

—— *Queen Victoria in her Letters and Journals*, (Sutton Publishing: Stroud, 2001).

Hough, Richard, (ed.) *Advice to My Granddaughter: Letters from Queen Victoria to Princess Victoria of Hesse*, (Simon and Schuster: New York, 1975).

——, *Louis and Victoria: The First Mountbattens*, (Hutchison of London: London, 1974).

——, *Victoria and Albert*, (St. Martin's Press: New York, 1996).

Hubbard, Kate, *Serving Victoria*, (Harper Collins: New York, 2012).
Jerrold, Clare, *The Widowhood of Queen Victoria*, (G.P. Putnam's Sons: New York, 1916).
King, Greg, *Twilight of Splendor*, (John Wiley & Sons, Inc.: New York, 2007).
Kinloch-Cooke, Clement, Sir, (2 vols.) *A Memoir of Her Royal Highness Princess Mary Adelaide Duchess of Teck*, (Charles Scribner's Sons: New York, 1900).
Koenig, Marlene A. Eilers, *Queen Victoria's Descendants*, (Rosvall Royal Books: Falköping, Sweden, 1997).
Kuhn, William M., *Henry & Mary Ponsonby: Life at the Court of Queen Victoria*, (Duckworth: London, 2002).
Lee, Sidney, *Queen Victoria: A Biography*, (John Murray: London, 1904).
Lennon, Florence Becker, *The Life of Lewis Carroll*, (Simon and Shuster: New York, 1962).
Longford, Elizabeth, *Born to Succeed*, (Harper & Row: New York, 1964).
Longford, Elizabeth (ed.), *The Oxford Book of Royal Anecdotes*, (Oxford University Press: Oxford, 1984).
Mallet, Marie, *Life with Queen Victoria: Marie Mallet's Letters from Court 1887-1901*, (John Murray: London, 1968).
Mandache, Diana, *Dearest Missy*, (Rosvall Royal Books: Falkoping, 2011).
Marie, Queen of Roumania, *The Story of My Life*, (in 3 vols.) (Cassell and Company, Ltd.: London, 1934).
Marie Louise, Princess, *My Memories of Six Reigns*, (Evans Brothers Ltd.: London, 1956).
Millar, Lubov, *Grand Duchess Elizabeth of Russia: New Martyr of the Communist Yoke*, (Nikodemos Orthodox Publication Society: Richfield Springs, New York, 1991).
Miller, Ilana D. *The Four Graces: Queen Victoria's Hessian Granddaughters*, (Kensington House Books: East Richmond Heights, 2011).
—— Reports *from America: William Howard Russell and the Civil War*, (Sutton Publishing: Stroud, 2001).
Murray, Jane, *The Kings and Queens of England: A Tourist Guide*, (Charles Scribner's Sons: New York, 1974).
Nevill, Barry St. John (ed. w/additional material by) *Life at the Court of Queen Victoria: With Selections from the Journals of Queen Victoria*, (Sutton: Stroud, 1997).
Noel, Gerard *Princess Alice: Queen Victoria's Forgotten Daughter*, (Michael Russell Ltd: Norwich, 1974).
Packard, Jerrold M., *Farewell in Splendor*, (Dutton: New York, 1995).
——, *Victoria's Daughters*, (St. Martin's Press: New York, 1998).
Pakula, Hannah, *An Uncommon Woman*, (Simon & Schuster: New York, 1995).
Pearson, Hesketh *Dizzy; the life and personality of Benjamin Disraeli, Earl of Beaconsfield*, (Harper: New York, 1951).
Ponsonby, Arthur *Henry Ponsonby: Queen Victoria's Private Secretary*, (The Macmillan Company: New York, 1943).
Ponsonby, Frederick, (ed.) *Letters of the Empress Frederick*, (Macmillan and Co., Limited: London, 1929).
——, *Sidelights on Queen Victoria*, (Sears Publishing Co., Inc.: New York, 1930).
——, *Recollections of Three Reigns*, (E.P. Dutton & Co., Inc: New York, 1952).
Pope-Hennessy, James, *Queen Mary*, (George Allen and Unwin Limited: London, 1959).
Potts, D.M. and W.T.W. Potts *Queen Victoria's Gene: Haemophilia and the Royal Family*, (Alan Sutton: Stroud, 1995).
Ramm, Agatha (ed.), *Beloved and Darling Child: Last Letters Between Queen Victoria and Her Eldest Daughter 1886-1901*, (Alan Sutton: Stroud, 1990).
Rappaport, Helen, *Four Sisters*, (Macmillan: London, 2014).
——, *A Magnificent Obsession: Victoria, Albert, and The Death That Changed the British Monarchy*, (St. Martins Griffin: New York, 2013).

Reid, Michaela, *Ask Sir James*, (Penguin Books: New York, 1987).
Roff-Lawrence, Kori, *Becoming Queen Mary*, vol. (published by the author, 2020).
Salway, Lance *Queen Victoria's Grandchildren*, (Collins & Brown Ltd.: London, 1991).
Sara, M.E. *The Life and Times of H.R.H. Princess Beatrice*, (Stanley Paul & Co., Ltd.: London, 1945).
Sitwell, Edith, *Victoria of England*, (The Riverside Press: Cambridge, 1936).
St. Aubyn, Giles, *Queen Victoria: A Portrait*, (Atheneum: New York, 1992).
Strachey, Lytton (intro. by Michael Holroyd), *Queen Victoria*, (Weidenfeld & Nicholson: New York, 1987).
Synge, M.B. *The Reign of Queen Victoria*, (Oxford University Press: London, 1919).
Taylor, Miles, *Empress: Queen Victoria and India*, (Yale University Press: New Haven and London, 2018).
Tisdall, E.E.P. *Queen Victoria's Mr Brown*, (Frederick A. Stokes Company: New York, 1938).
Vallone, Lynne, *Becoming Victoria*, (Yale University Press: New Haven and London, 2001).
Van der Kiste, John, *Childhood in Court 1819-1914*, (Alan Sutton: Stroud, 1995).
——, *Dearest Vicky, Darling Fritz*, (Sutton Publishing Lmtd.: Stroud, 2001).
——, *Edward VII's Children*, (Alan Sutton: Stroud, 1989).
——, *George III's Children*, (Alan Sutton: Stroud, 1995).
——, *Kings of the Hellenes: The Greek Kings 1863-1974*, (Alan Sutton: Stroud, 1999).
—— and Bee Jordaan, *Dearest Affie...*, (Alan Sutton: Stroud, 1984).
Victoria, Marchioness of Milford Haven, (ed. and annotated by Beéche, Arturo and Ilana D. Miller) *Recollections*, (Eurohistory & Kensington House Books: Richmond, California, 2020).
Victoria, Princess of Prussia, *My Memoirs*, (Eveleigh Nash and Grayson Limited: London, 1929).
Victoria, Queen, *More Leaves From the Journal of A Life in the Highlands: From 1862 to 1882*, (Smith, Elder, & Co.: London, 1884).
Ward, Yvonne M. *Censoring Queen Victoria: How Two Gentleman Edited a Queen and Created an Icon*, (Oneworld: London, 2014).
Warwick, Christopher, *Ella: Princess, Saint & Martyr*, (Wiley: West Sussex, 2006).
Weintraub, Stanley, *Edward the Caresser: The Playboy Prince who became Edward VII*, (The Free Press: New York, 2001).
——, *Uncrowned King: The Life of Prince Albert*, (The Free Press: New York, 1997).
——, *Victoria: An Intimate Biography*, (Truman Talley Books/E.P. Dutton, New York, 1987).
William II, Ex-Emperor of Germany, *My Early Life*, (Metheun & Co. Ltd.: London, 1926).
Wilson, A.N. *Victoria: A Life*, (Penguin Press: New York, 2014).
Woodham-Smith, Cecil, *Queen Victoria: From her birth to the death of the Prince Consort*, (Alfred A. Knopf: New York, 1973).
Zeepvat, Charlotte, *Prince Leopold: The Untold Story of Queen Victoria's Youngest Son*, (Sutton Publishing Ltd.: Stroud, 1998).
——, *Queen Victoria's Family: A Century of Photographs*, (Sutton: Stroud, 2001).

Magazines and Newspapers
Daily Mail
European Royal History Journal
New York Times
Royalty Digest

Articles
Arildsen, Emilie, 'Challenging or Conforming to the Norms of Victorian Society.', *Leviathan*, no. 3 (2018-08-30) pp.18-29

Mosse, W.E., 'The Austro-Prussian Conflict, March-May 1866.' *The Cambridge Historical Journal*, vol.10, no.2 (1951), pp.205-223.

Websites
https://artsandculture.google.com/exhibit/empress-of-india-the-durbar-room-english-heritage/gwKi8uM3CkhkIQ?hl=en

www.biographi.ca/en/bio/campbell_john_george_edward_henry_douglas_sutherland_14E.html

www.codyyellowstone.org/blog/that-time-buffalo-bill-rode-for-royalty/

www.dailymail.co.uk/news/article-10018695/Queen-Victoria-nagging-wife-Prince-Alberts-revealing-letters-tell-selfish-Queen.htmlhttps://www.dailymail.co.uk/news/article-10018695/Queen-Victoria-nagging-wife-Prince-Alberts-revealing-letters-tell-selfish-Queen.html

https://en.wikipedia.org/wiki/Albert,_Prince_Consort#Consort_of_the_Queen

https://en.wikisource.org/wiki/Dictionary_of_National_Biography,_1885-1900/Ponsonby,_Frederic_Cavendish

https://en.wikipedia.org/wiki/Schleswig-Holstein_Question

https://en.wikipedia.org/wiki/Suez_Canal#cite_note-1

https://en.wikipedia.org/wiki/William_Ewart_Gladstone#cite_note-173

www.english-heritage.org.uk/visit/places/osborne/history-and-stories/description/

www.historyofroyalwomen.com/the-year-of-queen-victoria-2019/the-year-of-queen-victoria-queen-victorias-half-brother-charles-3rd-prince-of-leiningen/?fbclid=IwAR0LigoKZslMeI3zc-ALkIQcj3DdIAGAWyGRGCgUmO9iAZEuS5Ku8Jv95bY

Oxford Dictionary of Biography Online

The Royal Archives/Bodleian Library/Proquest website Queen Victoria's Journals (qvj.chadwyck.com)

Royalty Digest Online

www.tshaonline.org/handbook/entries/leiningen-carl-friedrich-wilhelm-emich-iii-prince-

Unofficial Royalty

Videos
www.c-span.org/video/?54339-1/disraeli-biography. Interview with Stanley Weintraub on the publication of his biography of Disraeli.

https://youtu.be/E10c50DNhHY

Index

Abbreviations:
PM, prime minister
QV, Queen Victoria

Act of Settlement, 3, 5
Adelaide of Saxe-Meiningen, 7, 8
Adolph, Prince of Schaumburg-Lippe
  129, 130, 157
Adolphus, Prince Duke of Cambridge,
  189, 210
Ahmed, Rafiuddin, 173, 177
Albert of Saxe-Coburg and Gotha, Prince
  Consort, 9, 14, 28, 30-44, 59, 60, 62, 64,
  65, 66, 67, 69, 72, 73, 77, 82, 84, 88, 99,
  103, 104, 105, 144, 145, 146, 147, 149,
  151, 166, 178, 187, 194, 194, 202, 205
  Balmoral, 35
  birth, 26
  character, 27, 30
  Crystal Palace, 37
  marriage to QV, 23
  death, 44
  funeral and aftermath, 48-54
  Osborne House, 35
  political views and goals, 36, 40
  relationship with 'Bertie', 33, 40-1, 42, 89
  Trent Affair, 42-3
Albert, Prince of Schleswig-Holstein, 74,
  159
Albert Victor, Prince (Eddy), 55, 143, 152,
  166, 167, 168
  character, 160, 162
  death, 162
  marriage Prospects, 161
Albert Wilhelm Heinrich of Prussia *see*
  Prince Henry of Prussia
Alexander II of Russia, Tsarevich
  Alexander Nikolaievich, 25, 89, 117,
  119, 122, 128
  assassination, 116

Alexander III of Russia
  death, 275
Alexander, Prince of Battenberg, later
  Prince of Bulgaria, Count von
  Hartenau ('Sandro'), 119, 124, 126, 128,
  129, 130, 132, 151
  engagement to Princess Viktoria of
    Prussia (Moretta) 128, 129, 149
  marriage to Johanna Loisinger, 130
  Prince of Bulgaria, 128
Alexander, Prince of Battenberg,
  Marquess of Carisbrook ('Drino'), 151
Alexander, Prince of Orange-Nassau, 24
Alexander, Prince of Teck, Alexander
  Cambridge, 1st Earl of Athlone, 207
Alexander of Württemberg, 24
Alexandra, Princess of Denmark, Princess
  of Wales *later* Queen Alexandra ('Alix'),
  43, 55, 59, 61, 62, 74, 80, 83, 84, 89, 95,
  145, 146, 159, 162, 163, 164, 177, 180,
  183, 205
  Diamond Jubilee, 187, 188
  'Fashion Icon', 156
  health and temperament 75, 76
  marriage prospect for Bertie, 43, 53, 54
Alexandra, Princess of Edinburgh and
  Saxe-Coburg and Gotha, *later* Princess
  of Hohenlohe-Langenburg ('Sandra')
  133, 165
  birth, 91
Alexandrina of Prussia, 43
Alexandrine, Princess of Baden, 166
Alexandrovich, Grand Duke Serge, 118,
  119
  marriage to Ella, 122
  temperament, 123
Alfred, Prince, Duke of Edinburgh, Duke
  of Saxe-Coburg and Gotha ('Affie') 32,
  58, 59, 89, 165, 173, 175, 180, 191

birth, 32
death 197-8
dislike of John Brown, 55
heir and accession to Duchy of Saxe-Coburg and Gotha, 166-67
Golden Jubilee, 147
marriage, 88
naval career, 88, 92, 163
temperament, 88-9, 91, 101
Alfred Jr., Prince of Edinburgh, Hereditary Prince of Saxe-Coburg and Gotha, 191
birth, 91
death, 191-2
Alice, Princess, Grand Duchess of Hesse and by Rhine, 44, 50, 51, 52, 54, 59, 73, 74, 77, 79, 83, 86, 91, 107, 108, 119, 202
birth, 32
carrier of Haemophilia, 38
clash with QV over Helena's engagement, 61, 62
death, 98-99
engagement, 41
nursing and social welfare, 99
temperament, 41, 50, 99
marriage to Ludwig of Hesse and by Rhine, 49
Alice, Princess of Albany, *later* Countess of Athlone, 206, 207
birth, 109
death, 207
Alice, Princess of Battenberg, *later* Princess Andrew of Greece, 131, 165,
birth, 130
marriage, 206
Alix, Princess of Hesse and by Rhine, later Tsarina Alexandra Feodorovna of Russia (Alicky) 86, 118, 121, 123, 126, 133, 158, 167, 174-5, 183-4
birth, 98
coronation, 180-1
death of QV, 204
engagement, 169
marriage prospects, 143, 161, 168
temperament, 183
American Civil War, 69
Anglo-Egyptian War of 1882, 127
Anna Pavlovna of Russia, 24

Anna, Princess of Montenegro, Princess of Battenberg
engagement, 185
Anne, Queen, 3, 4
Aribert, Prince of Anhalt-Dessau, 158
marriage and divorce, 159
Arthur, Duke of Connaught, 44, 58, 63, 82, 85,105, 109, 113, 114, 141, 179, 188, 192, 200, 202, 205
birth, 32
marriage, 101-102
Arthur, Prince of Connaught, 113, 114, 154, 192, 202
Augusta of Hesse-Kassel, 24
Augusta, Dowager Duchess of Saxe-Coburg and Gotha, 9
Augusta of Saxe-Gotha-Altenburg, 5
Augusta of Saxe-Weimar-Eisenach, 39
Augusta Viktoria, Princess of Schleswig-Holstein, Kaiserin Augusta Viktoria of Germany ('Dona'), 116, 142, 158
marriage, 115
Augustus, Grand Duke of Oldenburg, 60
Augustus of Saxe-Coburg-Koháry, 24
Augustus Frederick, Duke of Sussex, 28
Austen, Jane, 131
Austro-Prussian War of 1866 (*see:* Schleswig-Holstein War of !866)

Baden-Powell, Robert, 194
Balfour, Arthur, 194, 195
Baring, Mary, 107
Baring, Susan *later* Lady Reid, 190
Beatrice, Princess, Princess Henry of Battenberg ('Baby'), 50, 52, 53, 55, 77, 80, 85, 91, 100, 107, 114, 118, 119, 120, 129, 135, 145, 150, 151, 160, 169, 177, 178, 179, 180, 184, 188, 195, 198, 199, 200, 201
birth, 32
carrier of haemophilia, 38
Diamond Jubilee, 185-6
editor of QV's Journals, 189, 206
engaged, 125
marriage, 132-34
Beatrice, Princess of Edinburgh and Saxe-Coburg and Gotha, *later* Infanta

of Spain and 5th Duchess of Galliera
  ('Baby Bee'), 92
Bedchamber Question, 19, 23
Benz, Karl, 153
Berlin, Congress of, 97, 136
Biddulph, Sir Thomas, 69
Bigge, Sir Arthur, 1st Lord Stamfordham
  possible affair with Princess Louise,
    180
Bismarck, Chancellor Otto von, 51, 61,
  76, 97, 115, 117, 121, 128, 129, 190
Boehm, Joseph Edgar, 80, 110
  possible affair with Princess Louise,
    180
Brown, Archie, 111
Brown, Hugh, 111
Brown, John, 56, 57, 63, 66, 71,76, 85, 93,
  97, 98, 103, 105, 110, 112, 157, 173,
  174, 178, 202
  background, 55
  death, 111
Bruce, Colonel Robert, 40
Buffalo Bill and his Wild West Show, 143
Buksh, Mohamed, 147, 148
Bulteel, Mary Elizabeth, 69

Campbell, John Marquess of Lorne, 9th
  Duke of Argyll, 72, 107, 180, 206
  background, 81
  Governor-General of Canada, 106
Canning, Lady Charlotte, 56
Carl, Prince of Denmark, later King
  Haakon VII of Norway
  marriage to Princess Maud of Wales,
    182
Carnegie, Andrew, 37
Carnegie, Lord *later* the 11th Earl of
  Southesk, 154
Carol I, King of Romania *formerly*, Prince
  Karl of Hohenzollern-Sigmaringen,
  158
Caroline of Ansbach, 4
Caroline of Brunswick, 5, 9
Casals, Pablo, 189
Catherine of Aragon, 3
Cecilia of Sweden, 60
Chamberlain, Joseph, 186
Charles I, King of England, 3

Charles II, King of England, 3
Charles II, Duke of Brunswick, 25
Charles Edward, Duke of Albany, later
  Karl Eduard Duke of Saxe-Coburg and
  Gotha, 109, 113, 192, 207
Charlotte, Empress Carlotta of Mexico,
  14
Charlotte of Mecklenburg-Strelitz, 5
Charlotte, Princess of Prussia, *later*
  Duchess of Saxe-Meiningen
  ('Charley'), 102, 149
  birth, 73
  temperament, 114-15
Charlotte, Princess of Wales, 5, 8, 9, 28,
  31, 61
  childhood, 6
  death, 6
  marriage, 6
Christian IX of Denmark, 54, 146, 164
Christian, Prince of Schleswig-Holstein,
  61, 62, 74, 205
  engaged, 60
Christian Victor, Prince of Schleswig-
  Holstein, 74, 159, 198
Churchill, Sarah, Duchess of
  Marlborough, 4
Churchill, Winston, 114, 193
Clark, Sir James, 20, 32, 40, 77
Clarke, Sir Charles, 20
Clifden, Nellie, 42
Conroy, John, 10-12, 13, 14, 15, 19, 27, 28,
  31, 41, 73
  background, 10
  banished, 17
  and Lady Flora Hastings, 20-1, 23
Constantine, Crown Prince of Greece,
  later King of the Hellenes ('Tino')
  engaged, 157
Crimean War, 38, 69, 71, 90
Crystal Palace, 37, 88
Cubitt, Thomas, 35
Cult of True Womanhood *or* Domesticity,
  36

Dagmar, Princess of Denmark,
  (*see:* Tsarina Marie Feodorovna)
Davis, Jefferson, 42
Dennison, Lady Irene, 151

Diamond Jubilee 1897, 156, 181, 186-88, 189, 207
Din, Nasr-Ed, Shah of Persia, 87
Disraeli, Benjamin, Viscount Beaconsfield (PM), 49, 69, 70, 71, 87, 92, 94, 95, 96, 97, 100, 101, 106, 114, 136, 148, 149, 157, 174
  birth and background, 66-7
  death, 103
  relationship with QV, 68, 72, 93, 104
Disraeli, Mary Ann Lewis, Viscountess Beaconsfield, 67, 87, 103
'Drina' (see: Victoria R. & I. Queen-Empress of Great Britain and Ireland)
Duff, Alexander, 6th Earl and later 1st Duke of Fife, 154

East India Company, 95
Eastern Question, 96
Edward VI, 3
Edward VII, formerly Prince Albert Edward of Wales ('Bertie'), 38, 41, 42, 44, 48, 53, 58, 59, 60, 61, 62, 69, 74, 76, 81, 82, 88, 91, 92, 93, 97, 101, 102, 108, 109, 112, 121, 124, 125, 156, 159, 165, 168, 175, 177, 180, 183, 188, 195, 198, 201, 202
  becomes king, 205
  birth, 32, 33
  death, 205
  death of 'Eddy', 162-3
  engaged and married, 54
  and John Brown, 55, 110
  relationship with Kaiser Wilhelm II ('Willy'), 193
  relationship with QV improves, 194
  marriage prospects, 43
  temperament, 33, 40, 75, 85
  Tranby Croft, 155
  trip to India, 95
  typhoid, 83-84
Edward VIII, formerly Prince of Wales, Duke of Windsor ('David'), 166, 184, 208
Edward, Duke of Kent, 10
  temperament, 7
Elimar, Prince of Oldenberg, 60
Elisabeth, Princess of Hesse and by Rhine (Ernst Ludwig's daughter), 170

Elisabeth, Princess of Hesse and by Rhine, Grand Duchess Elisabeth Feodorovna ('Ella'), 74, 98, 99, 118, 123, 141, 168, 169, 175, 181
  birth, 59
  engaged, 119
  marriage, 122
  rejects 'Willy', 115
Elizabeth I, 3, 136
Elizabeth II, 193, 207
Elizabeth of Wied, Queen of Romania ('Carmen Sylva'), 43
Ely, Lady, 51, 96, 121
  background and temperament, 52
  departure from QV, 154
Emich Karl, 2nd Prince of Leiningen, 8
Ems Dispatch, 76
Ernst I of Hohenlohe-Langenburg, 10
Ernst I of Saxe-Coburg and Gotha, 26
Ernst II of Saxe-Coburg and Gotha, 14, 24, 25, 26, 27, 30, 44, 82, 88, 147
  death, 166
Ernst of Württemberg, 24
Ernst Ludwig, Hereditary Prince of Hesse and by Rhine, Grand Duke of Hesse and by Rhine ('Ernie'), 91, 167
  birth, 73
Eugenie, Empress of the French, 52, 64, 77, 84, 87

Feodora of Leiningen, Princess of Hohenlohe-Langenburg, 12, 25, 62, 115
  death, 86
  marriage, 10
  relationship with QV, 10
Feodora of Saxe-Meiningen, Princess Heinrich XXX Reuss of Köstritz, 102
Ferdinand, Crown Prince of Romania, later King of Romania ('Nando'), 158, 163
  engagement, 167
Ferdinand of Saxe-Coburg-Koháry, later Ferdinand II of Portugal, 24
Ferdinand of Saxe-Coburg-Koháry, later Tsar Ferdinand of the Bulgarians, 129
Fitzherbert, Maria, 5
Florschütz, Christoph, 26

Francis, Duke of Teck, 162
Franco-Prussia War of 1870, 76, 99
Franz Ferdinand, Archduke of Austria, 186
Franz Friedrich Anton, Duke of Saxe-Coburg-Saalfeld, 6
Franz Joseph I, 186
Franz Joseph, Prince of Battenberg ('Franzjos'), 117, 185
Frederick, Prince of Denmark, Frederick VIII of Denmark, 182
Frederick, Prince of Wales, 4
Frederick Augustus, Duke of York, and Albany, 7
Frederica, Princess of Hanover, 107
Frederika Charlotte of Prussia, 7
Friedrich, Hereditary Prince of Baden, Grand Duke of Baden, 119
Friedrich, Prince of Hesse and by Rhine ('Frittie'), 98
Friedrich Wilhelm, Prince of Prussia, Kaiser Friedrich III of Germany ('Fritz'), 39, 61, 101, 102, 116, 144, 145, 152
   death, 150
   illness, 148-9
   marriage, 40

Gascoyne-Cecil, Robert 3rd Marquess of Salisbury (*see:* Lord Salisbury) 132, 149, 150, 152, 155, 174, 177
   prime minister, 135, 172
   relationship with QV, 136
   temperament, 136
George I, 4
George II, 4
George III, 5, 6, 7, 8, 9, 24, 189, 193
   death, 10
George IV, 'Prince Regent', 7, 10, 14
   death, 14
George V ('Georgie') 143, 176, 206, 208
George VI ('Bertie') 208
George, Prince of Cambridge, 24
George Victor, Prince of Waldeck and Pyrmont, 108
Gladstone, Sir William Ewart (PM), 67, 69, 70, 71, 76, 82, 85, 87, 96, 103, 105, 109, 126, 131, 132, 135, 136, 137, 149, 155, 176
   birth and background, 71
   contrasted with Disraeli, 93-4, 95
   death, 171, 190
   relationship with QV, 72-3, 92, 127
Glynne, Catherine, 71, 171
Golden Jubilee 1887, 49, 144, 156, 181, 186
Gordon, General Charles George, 135
   death, 127
Gospel of Wealth, 37
Grancy, August von Senarclens, 117
Granville, Lord, 126
Great Exhibition, 37, 39
Greville, Lord, 34
Grey, Charles, 40, 69
Gustaf Adolf, Crown Prince of Sweden, *later* King Gustaf VI Adolf, 152, 160

Hanstein, Baron Alexander von, 26
Hastings, Lady Flora, 19-23, 117
Hauke, Countess Julia von, Princess of Battenberg
Helen, Princess of Waldeck and Pyrmont, Duchess of Albany, 112-13
   engaged to Prince Leopold, 108
Helena, Princess of Nassau, 108
Helena, Princess, Princess Christian of Schleswig-Holstein ('Lenchen') 44, 50, 58, 59, 74, 79, 80, 81, 83, 86, 147, 159, 160, 162, 186, 187, 195, 198, 199, 200, 201
   birth, 32
   death, 205
   engagement and controversy, 60-1
   laudanum addiction, 63
   marriage, 62
Helena Victoria, Princess of Schleswig-Holstein ('Thora'), 62, 86, 126, 158, 159, 160, 165, 184, 185, 199
Hélène, Princess of Orléans, 161
Hamilton, Lord George, 173, 174
Henry IV, 75
Henry VIII, 3
Henry, Prince of Battenberg ('Liko') 117, 118, 120
   background, 124
Henry, Prince of Hesse, 60

Henry, Prince of Prussia ('Harry'), 73, 102, 114, 141, 142-3, 144, 149
Hilda, Princess of Dessau, 43

Irène, Princess of Hesse and by Rhine, Princess Henry of Prussia, 118, 121, 126, 133, 141, 142, 143, 204
  birth, 74
  marriage, 149
Irish Home Bill of 1893, 135, 171, 172

Jack the Ripper, 152, 160
James VI aka James I, 3
Jenner, Sir William, 44, 55, 56, 83, 84, 98, 110, 167, 174
Jordan, Dorothea, 7

Kapeolani, Queen of Hawaii, 145
Karim, Abdul (*see:* Munshi)
Karl of Leiningen, 11
Kennedy, John F., 189
Kensington System, The, 11, 17, 20
Khodynka Field, 181, 186
Kielmansegg, Sophia von 4
Kipling, John Lockwood, 156
Kolemine, Alexandrine de 120, 121, 124
Kruger, Paul, 193

Lamb, Lady Caroline, *formerly* Lady Caroline Ponsonby, 17, 18
Landlord and Tenant Act 1870, 72
Leaves from the Journal of Our Life in the Highlands 1848-1861, 65, 68, 88, 112
Lehzen, Baroness Louise, 11, 19, 28, 31, 32, 34, 41, 47
  death, 77
  departure from QV, 33
  education of QV, 12-13
Leopold I, King of the Belgians, 6, 8, 13, 15, 17, 24, 25, 26, 28, 40, 41, 47, 49, 53, 56, 60
  becomes King of Belgium, 13
  death, 61
  temperament, 6
Leopold II, King of the Belgians, 14
Leopold, Prince, Duke of Albany ('Leo'), 55, 96, 106-109, 111, 113, 118, 192, 206
  birth, 32

  death, 112
  haemophilia, 38
  marriage, 108
Leopold, Prince of Battenberg, *later* Lord Leopold Mountbatten, 151
Leopold, Prince of Hohenzollern-Sigmaringen, 76, 158
Leopold of Saxe-Coburg-Saalfeld, (*see:* Leopold I, King of the Belgians)
Leslie, Lady Leona, 114
Lesseps, Ferdinand de, 94
Liddell, Alice, 107, 108
Liliuokalani, Princess of Hawaii, Queen of Hawaii, 145
Lincoln, Abraham, 43
Lincoln, Mary Todd, 63
Lister, Joseph, Baron Lister of Lyme Regis, 83
Locock, Dr Charles, 32
Loftus, Jane, Baroness Ely (*see:* Lady Ely)
Loisinger, Johanna, 129, 130
London Protocol of 1830, 13
Louis, Prince of Battenberg, *later* Lord Louis Mountbatten, Earl Mountbatten of Burma ('Dickie'), 197, 206
  birth, 196
Louis, Prince of Battenberg, *later* 1st Marquess of Milford Haven, 118, 206
Louis Napoléon, Prince Imperial, 77
  death, 100
Louise, Princess, Duchess of Argyll, 38, 44, 50, 58, 59, 83, 106, 107, 124, 200, 201
  birth, 32
  death, 206
  marriage, 81-2
  temperament, 80, 180
Louise, Princess of Battenberg, *later* Queen Louise of Sweden, 152, 160
Louise of Hesse-Kassel, Queen of Denmark, 164
Louise of Orléans, Queen of the Belgians, 14
Louise, Princess of Wales, Princess Royal, Duchess of Fife, 75, 126, 133
  birth, 74
  death, 155
  marriage, 154

Louise of Saxe-Gotha-Altenburg (Prince Albert's mother), 26
Louise Margaret, Princess of Prussia, Duchess of Connaught ('Louischen'), 102, 113, 114, 141, 199
　marriage, 101
Ludwig, Hereditary Prince, Grand Duke Ludwig IV of Hesse and by Rhine, 41, 50, 107, 108, 115, 117,119, 121, 124, 125, 134, 147
　death, 167
　marriage, 49
　marriage to Madame de Kolemine, 120

Mackenzie, Dr Morell, 148, 149
Mahdi, The, 127, 128
Mallet, Marie, 166, 177, 180
Mascagni, Pietro, 189
Margaret, Princess of Connaught, *later* Crown Princess Margarethe of Sweden ('Daisy'), 113, 160, 165
Margaret, Princess of Prussia ('Mossy'), 86, 150, 161
Maria Anna, Princess of Anhalt-Dessau, 101
Marie Alexandrovna, Grand Duchess of Russia, *later* Duchess of Edinburgh, Duchess of Saxe-Coburg and Gotha 89-90, 92, 116, 163, 165, 167, 180, 191, 192
　death, 197
　precedence Issue, 90
　marriage to Affie, 90-1
Marie Feodorovna, Tsarina of Russia, 89, 146
Marie of the Netherlands, 43
Marie, Princess of Edinburgh and Saxe-Coburg and Gotha, *later* Queen Marie of Romania ('Missy'), 115, 122, 126, 163, 192
Marie, Princess of Hesse and by Rhine ('May'), 98
Marie of Württemberg, 27
Marie Louise, Princess of Schleswig-Holstein, 98, 126, 133, 158, 160
　birth, 86
　marriage, 159
Martin, Sir Theodore, 66
Mary I, Stuart, 3

Mary Tudor 'Bloody Mary', 3
Mary Adelaide, Princess, Duchess of Teck, 162, 188
Maud, Princess of Wales, Queen of Norway, 74, 126, 133, 165
　becomes Queen of Norway, 182
　engaged, 182
Maurice, Prince of Battenberg, 151
May, Princess of Teck, *later* Duchess of York, *later* Queen Mary
Maynard, Daisy Greville, Countess of Warwick, 107
McKinley, William, 203
Melbourne, Lord, Charles Lamb, 2nd Viscount Melbourne ('Lord M'), 17, 18, 22, 27, 28, 32, 67, 68, 104, 148, 149, 174
　death, 65
　and Flora Hastings Scandal, 20, 21, 23
　relationship with QV, 18-9
Mordaunt, Sir Charles, 74
Mordaunt, Lady Harriet Moncreiffe, 74
More Leaves from the Journal of Our Life in the Highlands, 112
Mountbatten, Lady Iris, 151
Munshi, The, 152, 172, 174, 176, 185, 202
　background, 148
　death, 178
　and Moslem Patriotic League, 177
　relationship with QV, 156-7
　QV investigates, 173
My Life by Queen Marie of Romania, 164

Napoleon III, 64, 77, 87, 148
Nicholas II *formerly* Tsarevich Nicholas of Russia ('Nicky'), 123, 161, 165, 168, 182, 183, 184, 186
　becomes Tsar, 175
　coronation, 180-1
　engaged to Alix, 169
Nightingale, Florence, 39, 99

Olav, Prince of Norway *formerly* Prince Alexander of Denmark *later* King Olav V of Norway, 182
Olga Nicholaevna, Grand Duchess of Russia, 183, 184
Owen, Robert, 7
Oxford, Edward, 31

Paderewski, Ignaz, 189
Palmerston, Lord, Henry John Temple,
    3rd Viscount Palmerston, 43, 65
    and Trent Affair, 64
Pasha, Isma'il Khedive of Egypt, 94
Patricia, Princess of Connaught, Lady
    Patricia Ramsay ('Patsy'), 113, 141, 165
Peel, Sir Robert, 33, 34
    becomes PM and Bedchamber Crisis,
    21
Philip, Prince of Greece of Denmark, *later*
    Mountbatten RN, *later* Prince Philip,
    Duke of Edinburgh, 131, 160, 197, 207,
    208
Phipps, Harriet, 177, 199,
Ponsonby, Arthur, 204
Ponsonby, Frederick, 189
Ponsonby, Sir Henry, 110, 174, 175
    becomes QV's private secretary, 69
    death, 176
Ponsonby, Mary (*see:* Mary Bulteel)
Primrose, Archibald, (*see:* Lord Rosebery)
Proclamation Durbar 1877, 95
Public Worship Regulation Act 1874, 94

Reform Act of 1867, 65
Reform Bill of 1884, 126, 136
Reid, Sir James (doctor), 63, 110, 111,
    173, 174, 176, 197, 198, 199, 200
    background, 109
    created baronet, 190
    and death of QV, 201, 202
Roberts, Lord, 200
Roosevelt, Franklin, 203
Rosebery, Lord, 172
    becomes PM, 171
Rothchild, Hannah de, 172
Rothchild, Baron Lionel de, 94
Russell, Lord John (PM), 58, 65
Russell, William Howard, 38-39
Russo-Turkish War, 128

St. Laurent, Julie, 7, 8
Salisbury, Lord (PM), 135, 137, 149, 150,
    152, 155, 171, 172, 174, 177
    background, 136
    becomes PM, 132
    relationship with QV, 136

San Stefano, Treaty of, 97
Schleswig-Holstein, Valerie Marie zu,
    159
Schleswig-Holstein War 1866, 77
Schulenburg, Melusine von der, 4
Scott, Sir Walter, 35
Second Ashanti Expedition, 179
Second Boer War 1899, 193-5, 198
Siebold, Fräulein, 8
Siege and Battle of Khartoum, 126-8
Simpson, Wallis, 166, 208
Singh, Bhai Ram, 156
Sophia, Electress of Hanover and
    Duchess of Brunswick-Lüneburg, 3
Sophia Dorothea of Celle, 4
Sophie, Princess of Prussia *later* Queen of
    the Hellenes ('Sossie') 150, 158, 169
    birth, 86
    engaged, 157
    conversion, 157
Spencer, Lady Diana, 4
Spencer, Jane, Baroness Churchill, 52
    background, 51
    death, 199
Stockmar, Baron Christina Frederick, 8,
    11, 28, 31, 47
    as Albert's mentor, 33
Stanley, Lord, Earl of Derby (PM), 65

Tavistock, Lady, Anna Russell, Duchess of
    Bedford, 20
Tranby Croft Scandal, 155
Trent Affair, 42, 44, 64
Tudor, Margaret, 3
Tuxen, Laurits, 157
Twain, Mark, 9

Vanderbilt, Consuelo, 185
Victoire of Saxe-Coburg-Saalfeld,
    Duchess of Kent, 14
    birth of QV, 8
    and Conroy, 10
    marriage, 8
    temperament, 8
Victoria, Princess of Hesse and by Rhine,
    Princess Louis Battenberg, *later*
    Marchioness of Milford Haven, 68, 74,
    84, 98, 99, 117, 118, 119, 1212 122, 125,

126, 130, 134, 141, 144, 152, 160, 161, 163, 168, 175, 180, 196, 203, 204, 206
birth, 54
death, 207
Victoria, Princess Royal, Empress Frederick of Prussia (Vicky), 38, 43, 51, 53, 60, 61, 70, 73, 74, 77, 84, 86, 91, 99, 101, 102, 108, 111, 112, 114, 115, 116, 118, 119, 120, 124, 125, 128, 131, 141, 142, 143, 144, 145, 146, 147, 148, 149, 150, 157, 161, 165, 185, 187, 188, 190, 191, 192, 194, 197, 198, 204
birth, 32
death, 205
marriage, 40
temperament, 33, 39
Victoria, Princess of Wales (Toria), 126, 133, 165, 172
birth, 74
Victoria Eugenie, Princess of Battenberg, Queen of Spain (Ena), 151, 165
birth, 150
Victoria Mary, Princess of Teck (*see:* Princess May of Teck)
background, 161-2, 165-6, 178, 183, 188, 207
engaged to 'Eddy', 162
marriage to George, 164
marriage prospect for 'Eddy', 160, 161
Victoria Melita, Princess of Edinburgh and Saxe-Coburg and Gotha, *later* Grand Duchess of Hesse and by Rhine ('Ducky'), 126, 133, 165, 167
birth, 91
engaged, 186
temperament, 170
Victoria R. & I. ('Drina'), Queen-Empress of Great Britain and Ireland, appearance, 18
becomes empress of India, 95
becomes queen, 16
birth and names, 8-9
childhood, 10, 11
children, 32
Conroy, 10, 12
coronation, 19

death, 201
education, 12
funeral, 204-5
and haemophilia, 38
marriage, 23, 27, 28
marriage prospects, 24
opinion of Russia, 90, 96, 168, 180
relationships with: Brown, 56-7, 111, Disraeli, 67, 104, Feodora, 10, 86, Gladstone, 72-3, 92, Lord Melbourne, 17, Lord Salisbury, 135, 136, Victoire, 12, 34
temperament and beliefs, 30, 72, 79, 120, 131, 148
Viktoria, Princess of Prussia (Moretta), 119, 150
birth, 73
death, 130
marriage, 157
and Sandro, 128, 129, 132, 149

Waugh, Evelyn, 197
Wellington, 1st Duke of Arthur Wellesley, 5, 21, 101
Wellesley, Gerald, Dean of Windsor, 57
Wilhelm, Prince of Prussia, Kaiser Wilhelm I of Germany, 125, 128, 141, 145
becomes German Kaiser, 77
death, 149
Wilhelm, Prince of Prussia, Kaiser Wilhelm II of Germany ('Willy') 35, 50, 102, 114, 128, 141-3, 1445, 149, 155, 157, 158, 169, 193, 200, 201, 202, 205
birth, 40
relationship with QV, 129, 150, 194
Wilkes, Captain Charles, 42
William I, of Orange), 6
William II (Hereditary Prince of Orange), 24
William IV, 24
becomes king, 7
death, 16
Zoubkoff, Alexander, 130